BECOMING AN EFFECTIVE COUNSELOR

Becoming an Effective Counselor is a textbook for advanced clinical courses that guides counselors in training through the most challenging phases of their academic preparation. Chapters blend skills-based content, real-world student examples, and opportunities for personal reflection to help students navigate some of the most difficult aspects of clinical counseling. Written by authors with over 50 years of combined counseling experience, this volume prepares aspiring counselors to assess their progress, remediate deficiencies, and deepen their existing skills in a way that is attentive to both core counseling skills and counselors' internal processes.

Justin E. Levitov, PhD, is professor emeritus in the Department of Counseling at Loyola University New Orleans.

Kevin A. Fall, PhD, is a professor and chair of the Department of Counseling, Leadership, Adult Education, and School Psychology at Texas State University.

BECOMING AN EFFECTIVE COUNSELOR

A Guide for Advanced Clinical Courses

Justin E. Levitov
Kevin A. Fall

Routledge
Taylor & Francis Group

NEW YORK AND LONDON

First published 2019
by Routledge
52 Vanderbilt Avenue, New York, NY 10017

and by Routledge
2 Park Square, Milton Park, Abingdon, Oxon, OX14 4RN

Routledge is an imprint of the Taylor & Francis Group, an informa business

Library of Congress Cataloging-in-Publication Data
Names: Levitov, Justin E., author. | Fall, Kevin A., author.
Title: Becoming an effective counselor : a guide for advanced clinical
    courses / Justin E. Levitov, Kevin A. Fall.
Description: New York : Routledge, 2019. | Includes bibliographical
    references and index.
Identifiers: LCCN 2018058256 (print) | LCCN 2019002102 (ebook) |
    ISBN 9781351133593 (eBook) | ISBN 9780815395119 (hardback) |
    ISBN 9780815395126 (pbk.) | ISBN 9781351133593 (ebk)
Subjects: LCSH: Counseling.
Classification: LCC BF636.6 (ebook) | LCC BF636.6 .L48 2019 (print) |
    DDC 158.3—dc23
LC record available at https://lccn.loc.gov/2018058256

ISBN: 978-0-8153-9511-9 (hbk)
ISBN: 978-0-8153-9512-6 (pbk)
ISBN: 978-1-351-13359-3 (ebk)

Typeset in Joanna
by Apex CoVantage, LLC

To the memory of Kathi Levitov. She was an amazing friend, wife, mother, grandmother, and muse.

CONTENTS

PREFACE

As we prepared this book, we were again reminded that: At one time or another, each of us has been asked questions about how we accomplished something that someone else was about to attempt. The mundane requests are not too difficult but if we are passionate about what the questioner is trying to learn, we not only answer their questions but flood them with information because our enthusiasm for the topic drives us to be as "helpful" and complete as possible. The result is often an endless list of suggestions, comments, cautions, and encouragements. "Oh, by the way, be sure and take . . ."; "Once you get there you have to try. . . ."; "Make sure that you talk to. . . ."; "Did I mention that . . ." or "You have got to get back to me once you finish so we can compare notes."

Since we remain counselor educators and practicing mental health counselors with a passion for counseling and teaching, we again realize that we needed limits on the information we would ultimately include in this text. We know that much of what you will learn from advanced clinical courses will come through the unique experiences these courses offer. Your readings should not interfere with or replace those rich clinical opportunities. We struggled with identifying the point where the information sharing needed to end and your personal experiences needed to begin. That said, we apologize in advance for those places where we might interfere with your experiential learning by being too detailed or too prescriptive. Our overarching goal was to offer a revised text that would help prepare you for the challenge of clinical training and improve your ability to learn from the personal and professional training experiences you will soon encounter.

We still believe that having the time to write a book is a gift given by a family to a writer. We are grateful to our families for their support, understanding, and encouragement. Finally, we again acknowledge that without clients we cannot be counselors and without students we cannot be professors. That said, we offer our appreciation to countless clients and students who have enlightened us, taught us, and earned our respect. It will not be possible for you to identify exactly where these students and clients directly contributed to this text but it is important for you to know that their influence, wisdom, and insights exist throughout. We deeply appreciate their confidence in us, their willingness to bring us along on their journeys and to share their lives with us in such intimate and at times painful detail. To each and to all, we are most grateful.

1

THE CHALLENGE OF BECOMING AN EFFECTIVE COUNSELOR

During his first semester of college, Chris decided that as soon as he finished his bachelor's degree, he would directly enter a graduate counseling program. He had always wanted to be a counselor, and already was looking forward to greeting, evaluating, and treating his first "real client." So strong was his interest that at some level he felt that the counseling profession selected him, not the other way around. After all, his friends had always sought him out when they were troubled or concerned about their problems with school, parents, or other friends. He was a great listener, and his concern for them was real. In addition, the personal trait that others found most remarkable was his uncanny insight. He could define a problem, explain why it was happening, and identify realistic solutions better than anyone else could. He finished his undergraduate program in record time and was immediately accepted into the school's graduate counseling program.

While Chris enjoyed the counseling theory and practice courses as well as the counseling electives, he found them useful only to a point. Early in his graduate training, Chris predicted that practicum and internship would be mostly a matter of continuing to do what he had always done so well with his friends. He would just listen carefully, determine what they needed to do, and then advise them to do it.

As the time for practicum approached, Chris, unlike his peers, seemed unconcerned about the choice of a field site. He was confident that wherever he went, he would succeed. He continued as he had through most of his training, spending more of his time assisting other students with their myriad concerns rather than focusing on his own. Since he and his classmates were now in the process of selecting field sites, he would carefully question others about where they wanted to work, what types of clients they would most prefer, and what they planned to do when they graduated. Once again, his insights proved invaluable to his cohorts as they refined their site choices and began to face this important element of their training.

As the course began, weekly group supervision meetings were filled with the questions with which all counseling novices struggle. Chris reflected on each one and rarely missed an opportunity to share his insights with other members of the group. Yet although he was sure that his advice was accurate and useful, he grew increasingly frustrated as one student after another seemed to become less interested in what he had to say. By the third week of supervision, Chris had become unhappy; at times he secretly dreaded having to attend the weekly group meetings. What's more, he sensed a struggle building with his site supervisor. Chris felt insulted when his site supervisor questioned him about why he rarely brought up questions about his own clients during group supervision meetings, preferring to discuss problems that other students were having at their field sites rather than addressing his own concerns. Unfortunately, Chris misread the supervisor's intent when he incorrectly concluded that the supervisor was intimidated by him, a student with many natural skills needing very little direction.

It was not until the sixth week that Chris began to wonder about his progress in a more thoughtful and reflective way. He had completed intake evaluations on four clients. Two had not shown up for the next scheduled counseling session, and one had asked for a transfer to another counselor. Chris was now becoming worried, confused, and at times angry about these developments. He knew that his advice was good and that the clients should be listening, but they were not. He found them frustrating. He wondered why these people weren't more enthusiastic about returning to meet with him and more willing to do what he recommended. His certainty about the clients' needs and the clarity of his expectations of them made the fact that they would not engage with him in the process of counseling all the more baffling. He knew things were not going well, but he was at a loss to explain why.

Chris' supervisor sensed his level of frustration and suggested that Chris come to his office for an individual meeting. The supervisor recognized Chris' strengths and abilities, but he also knew that the way Chris was conceptualizing the process was interfering with his ability to properly manage the important relationships that form the basis of clinical training. Though brief, the individual meeting seemed to help. Soon after, Chris began to move away from advice- giving and directing clients and toward developing his relationships with not only clients but supervisors, peers, and even himself. This redirection produced results. Within weeks Chris was experiencing *a redefined sense of purpose, greater comfort with the process, and a decrease in frustration levels. He actively participated in supervision by raising questions about his assigned cases, encouraging comments from others, and becoming more open to suggestions. He looked forward to counseling sessions, supervision meetings, and peer meetings. Most of all he was relieved that his caseload was growing and clients were returning for regular sessions.*

Introduction

Chris' transition into supervised clinical work contains many useful lessons for you as you make the same shift in your training. We realize that Chris' transition will be most valuable to you when it becomes a platform for discussion with your classmates and instructors. At the same time, Chris' experiences usefully illustrate how at least one intern faced the challenge of simultaneously managing knowledge of theoretical information and key elements of his own personality as he tried to constructively relate to clinical supervisors, peers, faculty, clients, and himself. According to Kiser (2015), "[p]erhaps the greatest challenge for students in a human service field experience is not one of 'possessing knowledge' but one of 'making use of' that knowledge in practical ways" (p. xv). Though a complicated and demanding process, developing effective clinical competencies is also intensely rewarding. You can expect this process to produce a wealth of new insights about yourself and a greater appreciation for the forces that will help you develop into a competent, trained professional. As you enter this phase of your training, you should derive some comfort from the knowledge that you are about to negotiate the same path that every mental health professional before you followed as he or she underwent the critical professional transformations that advanced clinical courses produce.

Careful planning and personal preparation for advanced clinical experiences dramatically improve outcomes. Historically, counselor training programs exhibited a wide distribution of positions regarding clinical training. Stances ranged from sending students "off on their own" to find and complete fieldwork to providing carefully planned and highly organized courses with articulated agreements between the university, the field site, and the field supervisors. Ethical guidelines for the training of counselors have aspired to ensure that the appropriate amount of time and attention is paid to this critical aspect of training. While these improvements have helped, you can also contribute by becoming thoroughly familiar with ethical codes, developing a willingness to learn more about yourself, exploring methods of enhancing the effects of supervision, and being prepared to identify the types of clients and agencies you would find most valuable.

Because the counseling process relies so heavily upon the counselor–client relationship, each counselor must develop a clinical style that not only honors the counselor's individual character but also meets the multiple requirements of a healthy and effective clinical relationship. This reality, coupled with what we have gleaned from our teaching and supervision experiences, suggests that while you are obligated to make this transition from theory to practice, *you must do so in your own way*. This text focuses on helping you make this transformation while honoring the unique elements of your personality and character.

Mixed feelings about this portion of your training are common. If you are eager to begin seeing clients but worried about how you will balance all of the elements that combine to form a successful clinical experience, you are not alone. Taking an academic course for credit and completing a clinical course place very different demands upon you. It is one thing to study theory and quite another to apply theory in combination with key elements of your own personality so that you can craft an approach that allows you to ethically and effectively help others. The complexity of the task becomes clearer when you recognize that (a) each counselor is a unique individual, (b) each client is a unique individual, and (c) there are a number of different theories from which to choose. Any practical study of how these three highly variable components interact would be challenging. Fortunately, insights about yourself combined with your personal relationship to counseling theory, other professionals, supervisors, agencies, and, ultimately, clients follow predictable patterns. These patterns define and explain the forces that govern relationships, and these forces can be refined to improve your efforts to be helpful to others.

As noted earlier, unlike content courses, clinical courses produce a constellation of personal and professional responsibilities for which students must carefully prepare. Fortunately, supervisors and professors can help you because of their training and experience and because they traveled the path that you are about to embark upon. Their wisdom is available and useful. Most skilled clinicians are happy to answer questions about their clinical training experiences and many will offer useful suggestions. This book explores these relationships and offers suggestions on how you can translate theory into effective clinical practice. It is important to be thoughtful about these ideas because habits and patterns formed at this early stage are likely to endure throughout the course of your professional life.

Relationships

You will encounter various types of relationships during your clinical training. Each one is critical to your professional development; in the aggregate, they will combine to help form you into a skilled clinician. While the counselor–client relationship may be the most obvious, a number of other equally critical relationships exist. By carefully addressing each of these, you will discover valuable sources of information, support, guidance, and understanding. Ultimately, what you learn as you negotiate these relationships will greatly benefit your counselor–client relationships.

The following relationships and the term used to describe each, offered in no specific order, compose the types of interaction you can expect during your clinical work:

Student–Professor	Faculty Supervision
Student–Site Supervisor	Site Supervision
Student–Student	Peer Consultation/Peer Relationships
Student–Agency Staff	Work Relationships (Other Professionals and Support Staff)
Student–Client	Counseling Relationship

Just as a majority of mental health professionals subscribe to the notion that within the counselor–client dyad, it is the relationship that heals, (Baldwin & Imed, 2015; Norcross & Lambert, 2011), counselor educators would likely agree that the five basic professional relationships listed above form students into trained counselors. These relationships, along with the lines of communication, are illustrated in Figure 1.1.

The network of interaction depicted in the figure reveals a range of opportunities for you to learn about self, others, and the mental health profession. Some of these encounters can produce personal reactions that are worrisome or disquieting while others may be positive and easy to embrace. Because of the potential for such a wide range of personal

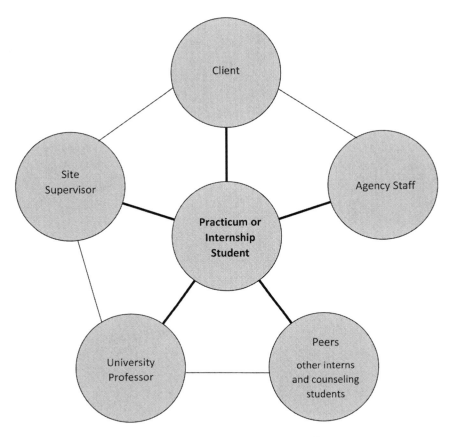

Figure 1.1 Important Relationships for the Developing Professional

reactions, it is essential that professional relationships and mentorships be constructed upon a solid foundation formed from honesty, trust, respect, understanding, knowledge, and a shared commitment to personal and professional development. Reliance on such a foundation ensures that clinical training experiences can be used consistently to improve yourself, regardless of how personally difficult they may be. Learning new things about yourself, managing anxiety and uncertainty with greater skill, and developing better methods to communicate and work with people are as valuable to you as a counseling student as they are to the clients with whom you work. Improving your ability to interact in all five relationship areas ultimately ensures greater levels of success in the counselor–client relationship.

Counselor Formation

Because we believe that the effects produced by these five core relationships are so central to the process that transforms students into clinicians, we prefer the term *counselor formation* to *counselor training* when describing the process. The term *formation* implies that necessary ingredients for effective counseling (as well as those that may obstruct efforts) coexist within you. As a trainee, you will encounter professional relationships that will help evoke these qualities. This perspective is both realistic and optimistic. The idea that counselors are formed instead of trained beckons supervisors and faculty to develop modes of interaction that honor your uniqueness, help you draw upon those characteristics of yourself that enhance your skills, and simultaneously manage those aspects of self that may interfere with your efforts to be helpful to others. Such relationships with supervisors and colleagues can motivate and guide you toward a process of continuous self-improvement, a goal shared by most skilled mental health professionals. What makes you unique is as important to the development and maintenance of the critical relationships that form the basis for counseling as any theory or collection of clinical skills. As Auxier, Hughes, and Kline (2003 point out,

> [c]ounselors' identities differ from identities formed in many other professions because, in addition to forming attitudes about their professional selves, counselors develop a 'therapeutic self that consists of a unique personal blend of the developed professional and personal selves [Skovholt & Ronnestad, 1992, p. 507]'.

> (p. 25)

Counseling: Art and Science

Counseling is both an art and a science. As a science it relies heavily upon a growing body of research and theory to guide decision-making and to encourage the proper use of counseling strategies. Advances in psychopharmacology, discoveries of more effective treatment protocols for specific types of psychological problems, and refined diagnostic criteria emphasize the importance of recognizing the more-scientific elements found in effective counseling. At the same time, "the practice of professional counseling is certainly not an objective science" (Osborn, 2004,

p. 325) and because of its subjectivity, the counseling process calls for more-ambiguous yet equally useful skills of interpretation, expression, and relationship building, all of which are important to counseling outcomes. Research findings are useful, but findings alone rarely influence individuals enough to make the difficult changes that are necessary to improve the quality of their lives. Thus, if we accept that counseling is both an art and a science, then it follows that counselor formation, a process of evoking effective ways of balancing what you know with unique, useful, and often creative ways of delivering this information to clients, would be the learning model of choice.

By way of example, consider the problem of making an appropriate diagnosis, conveying that information to the client, and then providing counseling services. A purely scientific approach could produce a plausible diagnosis. The client could be notified of the diagnosis in a variety of ways, and a recommendation for treatment could be included in the diagnostic report. All of us know someone who had such information delivered in this way by some well-meaning professional of one sort or another. Interestingly enough, this model works, especially when the science is refined enough to produce consistently accurate diagnoses and consistently effective interventions. The professional in this scenario defines what is wrong and does something to correct it. Whether mental health will evolve to this level of science, or even should evolve to this level of science, forms the basis for a very interesting debate about personal rights and responsibilities. Suffice to say, the discipline, for better or worse, remains as much an art as a science. In counseling, what we *do to* clients is important, but *who* we are and *how* we are in our relationship with them ultimately determines the success of our efforts.

Counseling Theory

Counseling theory offers a guide or framework from which counselors work to help others. Theories present serviceable explanations of human behavior and models for intervention. Working without benefit of a theory or theories presents a range of hazards. Counselors rely upon theory to guide them as they determine the nature of psychological problems, assess the level of seriousness, identify potential hazards, predict which efforts will be more successful and which will worsen symptoms, assess progress, identify treatment alternatives, and determine when counseling efforts have achieved maximum benefit.

As a graduate student who has taken at least one or two courses in counseling theory, you can easily recognize the importance of theory. The problem that most students at this level of training experience has more to do with selecting a theory that makes sense to them and then learning the theory well enough to rely upon it in counseling sessions. Surveys and anecdotal evidence consistently illustrate the difficulties that students encounter as they (a) select a theory and (b) attempt to translate it into effective clinical initiatives.

While research studies identifying which theories are better suited to particular problem types are becoming more widely available, at this stage of your training it would be better to select a theory because it matches your personality and worldview. A number of useful texts exist to ease the process of selecting a theory (see, e.g., Fall, Holden, & Marquis, 2017). During your initial clinical work, review one or more of the theory texts you read in your Counseling Theories course as you search for a theory that makes sense to you. You can and should expect site supervisors and teachers to question you about your theoretical orientation. While you may find this line of questioning unsettling, it is important. Your ability to espouse a theory, defend it, and effectively implement it will be a general expectation of anyone responsible for your supervision. You need to be thoroughly familiar with at least one theory. Consider such knowledge an essential requirement for this phase of counselor preparation. The following questions may be useful to ponder as you select a particular theory:

1. Are people influenced most by their emotions, thoughts, environment, or spiritual experiences?
2. What role does genetics play in behavior?
3. What role does pharmacotherapy play in behavior?
4. What role does family influence play in behavior?
5. Why do people persist in behaving in ways that continue to produce problems and distress?
6. What motivates or causes people to change their behavior?
7. What constitutes success in counseling?
8. Why does counseling work?

9. What is the role of the counselor?
10. What is the role of the client?

Answers to the preceding questions coupled with basic information about various theories and discussions with others will go a long way toward helping you find a theory that matches your personal assumptions about the nature of behavior and human experience.

Finally, we advise against adopting an eclectic approach at this stage in your education. While eclectic models can be very useful, we believe that they are best left to highly experienced counselors who are in a position to choose elements of varied theories based upon their experience employing different theories over an extended period of time. For novices, eclectic approaches are problematic because choices about what to take from different theories may be more a function of chance or sheer panic rather than carefully thought-out decisions regarding what works best where. Enough theories exist for you to find at least one that makes sense to you without having to pursue an eclectic approach or, even worse, developing your own approach. The latter option has fallen from favor, but in the 1960s and 70s it was common for counseling faculty to require students to develop their own approaches to counseling. We were never sure why this alternative became so popular, but it is clear that the same forces that advanced counseling as a profession simultaneously suppressed practices like developing and relying upon your own theory of counseling.

The process of identifying, developing, and integrating a guiding theory can, at first, seem daunting. Keep in mind that your primary task is not to choose a theory, like you would choose food off a menu. Instead, it is a process of identification (Fall et al., 2017). The term identification refers to the idea that certain theories will feel more congruent to your values, your way of seeing the world. It is your task to know yourself enough to be able to identify which theories most closely connect with your own natural way of working toward change. We want you to connect and be congruent with the theory you choose on a philosophical level. This commitment to introspection and theory exploration is not a one-time event that occurs in your theory course, but is instead a process of evolution and learning that may continue until you retire. To help you structure this process, we outline the following developmental framework.

Watts (1993) developed a four-stage developmental model that succinctly provides scaffolding to the complex process of theory integration. The first stage is "exploration." This is the stage of deep introspection and reflection on your own beliefs about:

1. How do people develop? How did I develop? What factors shaped me?
2. How do people become maladjusted? When I have encountered problems in my life, what was my explanation of those issues?
3. How do people change? When I have made changes in my life, how did that happen?

Wherever you are in your coursework, you can create a personal inventory of your values and beliefs. Out of this sense of self-awareness, you will have a foundation on which to compare and contrast the available theories of counseling. Mastery of the exploration stage means having a process by which you are able to assess your own beliefs and then use that personal insight in your exploration of literature on theory.

After the self-exploration phase of exploration, you move to the second stage of "examination," where you are tasked with trying to find the theory that most resonates with your own values and beliefs. You can create a working document that lists the points on divergence and convergence based on knowledge gleaned from your survey course. From that list, you should have a shorter collection on theories that match your worldview. From that shorter list, you can begin to immerse yourself in primary resources (those resources produced by proponents, researchers, and practitioners of the theory). As you examine each theory for content, be aware of how your connection to the theory ebbs and flows. If you get stuck or feel a lack of fit, then return to the exploration stage to revisit your personal values.

Hopefully, as you explore you will feel a deepening congruence between personal beliefs and one of the theories you are examining. If so, you can begin to apply your theory with clients under supervision in your advanced clinical course. At first, this will be awkward and anxiety-producing, which is completely normal. Anytime a person learns a new skill, there is a learning curve. Fall et al. (2017) provided this metaphor of the experience:

Remember when you were first learning to drive? You may have sincerely believed in the appropriateness of all the skills your instructor was helping you learn, but doing them all simultaneously and well was another thing altogether! You probably felt somewhat overwhelmed, whereas by now you have probably had the experience of driving from point A to point B without even thinking consciously of what you were doing! In driving, as in counseling, it is important to persevere in practicing skills that you believe in but that might feel initially quite foreign until those skills become second nature.

(p. 12)

As you begin to work with clients, you have several resources at your disposal to help with theory development. First, you have a real person to work with and push you to conceptualize and facilitate the change process in a concrete, here-and-now way, which is distinctly different from dealing with abstract case studies. The pressure will be real and that anxiety can motivate you to think more deeply about the art of theory integration. It's no longer a class exercise, it's an actual person sitting across from you and expecting that you know how to synthesize information in a cohesive manner. If you are seeing more than one client, compare and contrast your activity among your various clients. What consistency exists in the way you develop rapport, establish goals, and work toward meeting those goals? What differences occur and why? All this information can help you see where you are integrating the theory and what is still unanswered. You should also avail yourself of peer and supervisor feedback. Ask these parties specific questions related to theory and your work in order to get the most out of these interactions.

Using your time with clients as a catalyst for theory development should produce greater confidence in your conceptualization skills and your overall sense of purpose within the session. If you continue to struggle putting the theory into practice, you can always move back to the exploration stage and invest more time in personal clarity

If personal exploration, literature examination, and supervised practice produces a growing sense of comfort with your theory, you transition into the third and fourth stages of the developmental model: integration and personalization. The goal of the integration stage is to create a growing cohesion between personal beliefs and theoretical concepts. This is not a static process, in that, as you discover more about yourself and the theory, these changes are folded into your consistent worldview. As you encounter new client issues, you use your theory as a seamless way to understand

these new dynamics. You may begin to experiment with technical eclecticism; pulling techniques from other theories that are congruent with your
approach at a philosophical level.

The last stage, personalization, reflects a career-long process of refining
and deepening all of the other steps. Whereas the first two of Watts' stages
are achievable within the structure of your graduate program, the stages
of integration and personalization require a level of commitment that will
probably span your entire career. In this sense, theory development is not
stagnating and limiting, but instead, encourages practitioners to consistently strive toward greater levels of self-awareness and motivates them to
stay current with developments in the field.

Personal Risk

During admission interviews for our university's counseling program,
we inform all applicants of this caveat to beginning a course of study in
counseling:

> What you are asking to undertake is a serious and, in some cases, dan-
> gerous, process. Studying counseling is different from other professions.
> We are not in the business of studying fish or dirt. We do not run num-
> bers or examine molecules. Most other professionals have the luxury of
> studying external phenomena. We don't have that buffer zone. We study
> the internal workings of humanity, and as you study counseling, you will
> be studying your family, your children, and yourself.

When we discuss this issue with applicants, we sometimes get a vision of
that sign at the entrance to hell in Dante's *Inferno*, "Abandon hope, all ye
who enter here." Very ominous indeed! The purpose of the speech is not to
encourage students to abandon hope, however, simply to understand that
counseling is a serious proposition. It is the intersection of two lives: one in
emotional pain and the other presumably healthy enough to help. It is only
when counselors do not take care of themselves that the pain of the client
can overwhelm or resonate so deeply with our own pain that we lose objectivity. It is in those two dynamics that *empathy poisoning* takes place.

Strange as it may seem, Freud had an excellent explanation of the process of empathy poisoning in his conceptualization of transference and

countertransference. The Freudian version of an empathic connection or understanding of a client's world came in the process known as *transference*. The idea here is that the client would connect (in Freudian terms, "cathect") with the counselor and the issues would flow into the counselor whereas the counselor, ideally, would be a safe holding environment for the processing of those issues (Freudians, bear with us here and give us some latitude). Counselors create a safe holding environment by being "empty buckets" for the client's "stuff" (this is why psychoanalysts undergo years of psychoanalysis—to empty their buckets). If the connection goes as planned, the client gains insight and the transference is complete.

However, the process does not always go so smoothly. If the counselor's bucket is not empty, then it may not have enough space for the client's stuff. As the client transfers issues, they get all mixed up with the counselor's issues, and spillage occurs. This process is known as countertransference. Freudian material aside, empathy poisoning occurs when your bucket is too full and your issues get tangled up with the client's issues. Now that we have the bucket metaphor firmly implanted in your mind, we can explore specific examples and how to empty your bucket.

One example of empathy poisoning comes from being overwhelmed by client material. It is indicative of poor processing and compartmentalizing of client material so that as the counselor moves from session to session, remnants of the last client's material are left in the bucket. By the end of the day, the counselor is left with a conglomeration of emotional pain; the leftovers from a day of helping. One counselor summed up the effects of this form of empathy poisoning:

> Every day I would go home and feel like the weight of the world was on my shoulders. So much pain. In one particularly difficult day I saw two kids who had been abused by parents, a woman who lost her son in a traffic accident, and a couple going through a divorce. That's four "working" hours in an eight-hour workday, and I felt demolished. I couldn't even talk to my family. I went straight to bed and cried myself to sleep. That night I dreamed about them, almost playing the sessions over and over again in my mind. I felt haunted.

With this type of empathy poisoning, the counselor must learn appropriate ways to process the client material and distance the self from the process. Empathy is about temporarily entering the client's world, not living there.

You are a visitor. It is also about entering the client's world without losing a sense of your own world and how you are separate from the client's life. One practical suggestion is to monitor the types of clients you see and arrange them so you do not see back-to-back clients you experience as challenging. In our clinical work, we try to arrange for diverse groups of clients so that issues do not have a multiplying effect. Counselors often develop rituals to help themselves delineate between sessions and between work and home. For example, one supervisee used the sound of the front door closing and locking as a symbolic way to keep work material at work. One counselor remarked, "You just have to develop a mechanism that works for you. You are training your brain to compartmentalize."

Another type of empathy poisoning occurs when you have unresolved issues in your bucket. As clients dump their issues into you, your bucket overflows. Counselors are people too. In your professional lifetime you will have all sorts of life changes occurring in the same time period as you are seeing clients. Relationship issues, trauma, illness, bad moods, parenting struggles, and work stress are all examples of issues counselors must deal with on a regular basis in their personal lives. The difficult thing is that there is no hard-and-fast rule about how to manage the issues. For example, no one says, "Well, if you are having a fight with your spouse, you shouldn't do couples counseling that day," or "If you were just in a car accident, you must cancel your clients for a week." Absent objective rules, the counselor must be self-aware and self-disciplined to effectively handle both the personal issues and the client.

Box 1.1 Beginning Clinician Concerns

I (KAF) have taught an advanced clinical course every semester for the past 21 years. As a part of the first class, I usually ask my students to reflect on their greatest hopes and fears associated with their work as a counselor. I have kept a running list of their responses over the two decades and found some universality in their responses. I find it interesting that with every common hope, there was usually a co-existing fear; like two sides of the same counseling career coin. Below find the most common hopes and fears of my beginning clinicians.

HOPES	FEARS
I want my client to change.	My clients won't change.
I want to earn a living to support my family.	I won't make any money doing this and I'll have to find another line of work.
I want to enjoy my work.	I am afraid I'll be bored or that it will be too overwhelming for me.
I want to be good at what I do. I want to feel like I am good at what I do. I want my family and colleagues to respect me.	I will never feel like I am good enough. I will feel like an imposter in the room and with my colleagues.
I want to have good boundaries and not let my client's life impact my own.	I will take my work home with me and it will impact my relationships and my sleep.

From the outset we encourage students to obtain counseling from our professionally staffed counseling and career services center whenever they encounter such reactions to course material or their clients. We offer the same cautions and recommendations to you because:

(1) Your psychological health is important.
(2) Your personal issues can adversely affect your efforts to learn the material and help your clients.
(3) Experiencing the counseling process as a client improves your understanding of it.

Although not all counselor preparation programs require students to participate in personal counseling sessions, the need for students to obtain such support during the course of their training is quite common. Being open to the possibility of receiving counseling services is an excellent idea regardless of whether you are a beginner or an experienced counselor.

Professional Community

Counseling can be personally challenging because it is a solitary and often uncertain endeavor. Hours of individual therapy interspersed with brief periods of administrative activities like note-taking and report-writing can leave counselors with a seriously limited interpersonal sphere of interaction. As we have stressed, to be effective and healthy, counselors need a range of relationships. Counselors who believe that they are able to obtain all that they need interpersonally from the clients with whom they work seriously risk producing unproductive and unethical relationships with the very people they are trying to help.

In addition to isolation, counselors face a certain amount of ambiguity and uncertainty. According to Osborn (2004), "[t]o a great extent, the focus or nature of counseling is subjective and often ambiguous. 'Absolutes' are elusive, 'exact personality profiles' cannot be captured, 'correct diagnoses' are ephemeral" (p. 325). This ambiguity has the effect of creating an uncomfortable vacuum for novices. Under this type of pressure, students may leap to roles or models that they have observed rather than managing the anxiety in such a way as to propel them toward developing their own approach. "Playing the role of counselor," acting like their clinical supervisor, and imitating someone they have seen are all problematic examples of how the ambiguity can lead students to ineffective solutions.

Given that effective counselors rely almost exclusively upon what they know and who they are, the only way that they can gain some comfort with the process and simultaneously assure themselves that they are performing effectively is through regular interaction with other respected mental health professionals. While experienced counselors obtain this support through forms of supervision and consultation, we believe that practicum and internship students need to feel that they are participating in something that is psychologically larger. We encourage you to see yourself as a participant in a community of mental health professionals that includes faculty, peers, site supervisors, and various consultants. You are also expected to assume a level of responsibility to one another as each member of the community seeks to improve personally and professionally. With appropriate levels of trust, students quickly come to rely upon the members of their professional community for support and direction as they make clinical decisions, examine ethical concerns, explore counseling relationships, and form their unique professional identities. While all counselors, regardless of their level of training, benefit from contact with other professionals, novices find this type of support and professional interaction especially important to their development.

Issues of Burnout

If you are reading this text as a part of your clinical coursework, we hope boredom and burnout have not yet appeared on your radar of concerns. If you are like most students, you are slightly overwhelmed with the myriad unique situations that occur in the field on a day-to-day basis. When everything is new, it is probably difficult to imagine that you would ever feel bored, and most likely you are so enthusiastic about the work that burnout seems hardly possible as well. Unfortunately, for many mental health professionals, the newness erodes and disillusionment sets in.

As Kessler (1990) described burnout,

> Where once there was enthusiasm, conviction, and compassion for helping others, only frustration, apathy, and terrible loneliness remain. Paradoxically, the need to reach out and help is still there, but it is mired in a personal sense of reduced motivation, low energy, and an overwhelming sense of futility and fraud.
>
> (p. 301)

Edelwich and Brodsky (1980) identified four stages of burnout:

1. <u>Enthusiasm:</u> Hopefully every new member of the profession possesses a sense of excitement about the profession and work of counseling. Counselors prone to burnout tend to use the enthusiasm to dump themselves into their work, thus creating a fusing of identity between self and work. This overidentification can manifest in several behavior patterns noted by Gibson and Mitchell (2008): getting to work early and leaving late, working through lunch, taking work home evenings and weekends, rarely taking vacations, and being unable to say no to extra cases or work around the office. This misuse of enthusiasm can also lead to overidentification for clients [see section on empathy poisoning].

2. Stagnation: This stage comes after the counselor can no longer keep up the pace of the enthusiasm stage and a settling occurs. If your professional life is a marathon race, then the enthusiasm stage is like sprinting the first mile, then realizing that you are exhausted and you have 25 miles remaining. The slowing of the work pace can lead the counselor to begin to resent the colleagues for "not working as hard" or "not respecting what I do around here."

3. Frustration: As the discontent builds, the frustration stage is characterized by growing boredom and resentment. The counselor in this stage may find difficulty in motivating oneself to get work done. Non-counseling duties are usually the first to fall, such as note taking and insurance forms. Soon, others will begin to notice the lack of attention to basic duties and will often comment of the counselor's lack of professionalism. Feedback from others will be interpreted by the counselor as "one more reason this works stinks." It is also at this stage that counselors start secretly wishing their clients would not show up, not because of anxiety, but because they would rather have nothing to do. It is a sinking down into the boredom. Each work task that gets avoided and each client that does not show adds to the avalanche of boredom and restlessness of the counselor.

4. Apathy: In the final stage, the counselor may experience hopelessness and helplessness, perhaps even deep depression and anxiety. The counselor at this stage will often exhibit behaviors ranging from unethical (missing appointments, refusing to consult) to unprofessional and lazy (refusing to finish reports and instead spends non-counseling time sleeping or playing on the computer). By this time, the counselor has severed support ties with colleagues and views them as people who "don't understand me." Isolated and hopeless, a counselor at this stage poses serious risk to self and the clients seen.

Due to the serious nature of burnout, counselors must be vigilant and responsible for managing their own professional development. Boy and Pine (1980) propose some excellent suggestions for mental health professionals to use as they manage issues of boredom and burnout. We will use their suggestions as a four-part model for you to consider as you move forward in your career.

The first suggestion is to, when possible, try to spend the major portion of the day actually counseling clients. Boy and Pine noticed back in 1980 that counselors spend a lot of time doing non-counseling tasks. Unfortunately, it is as true today as it was in 1980. The counseling laws and accrediting agencies seem to recognize the reality that being a counselor requires more than counseling skills, as evidenced by the fact that indirect-hour requirements are always more than direct counseling-hour requirements. For example, in programs accredited by the Council for Accreditation of Counseling and Related Educational Programs (CACREP), the guidelines of a 600-hour internship include 240 direct client hours and 360 indirect hours. Students report early in their experience that seeing clients is "exciting" whereas the indirect duties such as doing paperwork, writing case notes, and attending meetings are less than invigorating.

Much like the experience of interns, most professionals would not say they entered the counseling field for the love of doing office work or administration. Instead, they would say they pursued their license so they could see clients. Counselors tend to get bored and burn out the more they participate in non-counseling activities. The key is finding a balance that works for you. We understand that your job may necessitate non-counseling activities, but you can be assertive about how you spend your time, especially when it comes to client services. The main idea here is: The more time you spend as a counselor, the more likely you will feel you are doing what you were trained to do, and satisfaction increases. The less time you spend doing counseling, the greater the chance of boredom and burnout. Consider this story from a professional, Pat, who was faced with the dilemma of non-counseling duties encroaching on counseling clients.

I thought I had really hit the big time when I was promoted to clinical director of the outpatient treatment program. I had worked so hard to create the type of program that I could be proud of and the administration was rewarding me with the directorship. I soon found that the administrative title meant more time spent doing reports, writing grants, evaluating staff, and attending meetings. Week by week, I found myself handing over my groups and individual clients to other staff. As that happened, I found myself dreading coming to work. This was a feeling I hadn't experienced at work before, so it worried me. I was faced with the realization that promotion was not going to work for me if it meant I had to sacrifice doing counseling for attending meetings. Luckily for me, I was the director, so I set aside a portion of every day to do counseling, and I treated that time as sacred. I also talked with my supervisor to explain that my passion was for counseling and that I could be a more effective director if I kept consistent with my client contact. My supervisor agreed, and I have loved my work even more.

The second strategy for fighting burnout is to stay connected with committed and caring colleagues. Once you have graduated, you realize that the world of graduate school was unlike the world of professional clinical practice. Although it does not have to be so isolating, many graduates find that they had no idea they would feel so alone. Graduate school had classes where you met with colleagues to discuss counseling topics. In your clinical courses, you routinely gathered together in group supervision and met with supervisors to discuss cases. In graduate school, you probably felt more connected and supported.

After graduation, you will begin to work on your licensure hours. You will feel some level of support from your supervisor, with whom you will have a close working relationship. However, from your colleagues, you may begin to notice the "I'm tired, I'm busy" attitude that clouds collegial relationships in the "real world." Everybody is trying to get hours and maintain a semblance of a personal life. This is a prime time to work on balancing your work life and personal life, but many professionals put their head down and try to plow through their experience, using their supervision as a professional lifeline. When they are finally finished with their hours, license obtained, many professionals find themselves isolated from any sense of professional community.

Within this dynamic of isolation, two primary activities can help you avoid this pitfall. First, find a good support network within your professional circle. The easiest place to start is with your group from graduate school. Your cohorts may be in different jobs, but you all are facing that same sense of isolation. Having a preexisting connection makes the process more natural even if the structure has changed due to graduation. The next place to look is at your job site. Developing a support network on-site is a great way to alleviate stress as it develops throughout the day. Once you have a group, what do you do with them? Well, whatever helps you feel more connected and less isolated. You can meet as an informal supervision group to discuss cases or you can meet for dinner. You get to decide, but choose your colleagues well, because your choices can affect the impact (positive or negative) of the group.

Whom you choose is up to you, and this choice is linked to the second helpful activity on which you can focus: Avoid negative professional influences. Surrounding yourself with ethical, competent, and enthusiastic professionals increases your likelihood of feeling the same. Connecting yourself to cynical, bored professionals hastens your feelings of burnout. One of our recent graduates accepted a job at a local high school. She was eager to begin her work and viewed school counseling as a noble profession. During her first few weeks, a senior school counselor took her under her wing as a mentor to orient her to the new position. The new counselor quickly learned that her mentor had a different view of school counseling. The mentor spent her days talking to her boyfriend on the phone and shopping online. She left for lunch off campus at 11:00 am and often did not return until after 1:00 pm. When the new counselor asked if she could start a divorce support group for the ninth-grade class, the mentor said, "Oh, we don't do stuff like that here." Basically, the mentor never saw students, except for scheduling and some advising.

The new counselor was mature enough to realize that her mentor's view of counseling was going to have a negative effect on her own development. It was too late to find another job, so she chose to do two things. First, she created a networking group of new school counselors from area schools. That afforded her some positive support. Second, she interacted with the other school counselor only on an as-needed basis. When she had new ideas, she either enacted them on her own or went through her supervisor. The key is that she recognized the negative influence and took responsibility for her own career growth.

The third suggestion for preventing burnout is to commit to theory development. We believe that too much emphasis has been placed on theoretical integration and eclecticism. Theory represents a consistent philosophical framework designed to organize the complex information provided by the client. Trying to pick and choose from all the theories leaves the counselor confused as to the method of the picking and choosing. For novice counselors (and many "experts," for that matter) deciding what to do becomes a random process rather than a cohesive one. For this reason, we encourage our students to choose the theory that bests resonates from their own philosophical beliefs about people and how change occurs. Once a congruence has been found between theory and counselor, then expansion, not contraction, can occur.

The advantages of theoretical consistency go beyond clinical impact. Boy and Pine (1980) list the following as benefits to the counselor as a developing professional:

- Enables the counselor to review research by others employing the approach and make modifications based on that research.
- Enables the counselor to conduct personal research contributing to the effectiveness of the approach.
- Provides the counselor with a consistent base from which modifications can occur.
- Enables the counselor to contribute to the advancement of knowledge regarding the theory.
- Presents a behavioral consistency influencing the client's pattern of responses.
- Presents the client with a professionally responsible approach possessing goals for which there is supporting research.

(pp. 162–163)

In the service of preventing burnout, theory provides not only a road map that decreases the experiences of feeling lost but also a framework for new counselors to grow and contribute to the field through original research. In these two arenas, theory provides a backdrop for personal and professional growth, keys to avoiding boredom and burnout.

Last, to truly combat the consequences of our profession, it is vital that every mental health professional works to develop a wellness plan. Wellness is both a personal benefit and professional/ethical mandate. Section C of the American Counseling Association Code of Ethics (ACA, 2005) states that counselors should "engage in self-care activities to maintain and promote their emotional, physical, mental, and spiritual well-being to best meet their professional responsibilities." Research also shows that counseling students experience threats to wellness as a part of their training and need to develop methods for creating and maintaining wellness as a part of their professional skillset (Roach & Young, 2007).

So, what are the elements of a good wellness plan? Good question! Plenty of models exist that provide a structured way to assist you in developing a comprehensive plan that works best for you. In general, a plan should be comprised of activities that attend to your emotional, physical, cognitive, spiritual, relational, and structural needs. The plan should also have strategies that take into account possible threats to the plan. It should also be flexible. It should evolve with your professional self, and activities can be added or deleted to meet your needs. We encourage you to think of developing wellness as an evolution of finding things that work for you and amending your plan to fit your current life. It should not be a static plan, but is instead one that is fluid and responsive. In fact, not revising your plan can be a good warning sign of stagnation and burnout.

Summary

As you begin this phase of your training, expect to experience a range of emotions. While counseling can be deeply rewarding, it can also challenge you in complicated and often personal ways. Since effective counselors must merge who they are with what they know, your professional identity and clinical style will differ from others. If you think of this unique outcome as an opportunity rather than a source of frustration, you will be in a better psychological position to reap the full range of benefits that practicum and internship afford. Almost all that is accomplished in counselor formation occurs through various relationships. By taking the necessary steps to make these relationships healthy and productive, you can expect to gain much from your experiences.

Chris, the counseling student described in the introduction to this chapter, eventually redirected the frustration and confusion he experienced into useful insights about himself and his work with clients. He achieved this outcome by taking the risk of letting others help him and support him in accomplishing his professional goals. His fear of not being as good as he thought he was did not block him from taking the steps that he needed to begin the process of becoming as skilled as he could be. It is no less important for you to search for and participate fully in a professional community. Do so by recognizing that the professional community places dual demands upon you: You are expected to give back as much as you obtain. Finally, recall that you are traveling a path that all who provide mental health services have traveled, albeit in their own way, before you.

Reflection Questions

1. Why do you believe Chris, the student described in the introduction, encountered so much difficulty with his transition to clinical training?
2. What do you expect to gain from clinical training?
3. What personal characteristics do you possess that will enhance your efforts to help others? Which will interfere?
4. Under what conditions would you pursue personal counseling?
5. Of the five relationships you must manage in clinical training, which will be easiest for you? Which will be most difficult? Why?
6. Consider your professional network at the present time. Who among your colleagues would you choose as a consultant? What are the characteristics of those you chose that make them good supports?
7. Where are you in Watts' theory development process? What steps can you take right now to make progress?
8. What is your wellness plan? What do you see as some main personal vulnerabilities to burnout?

References

American Counseling Association (ACA). (2005). *Code of ethics and standards of practice.* Retrieved March 15, 2017 from www.counseling.org

Auxier, C. R., Hughes, F. R., & Kline, W. B. (2003). Identity development in counselors-in-training. *Counselor Education and Supervision, 43,* 25–38.

Baldwin, S.A., & Imed, Z.E. (2015). Therapist effects: Findings and variables. In M. J. Lambert (Ed.), *Bergin and Garfield's handbook of psychotherapy and behavior change* (6th ed., pp. 258–397). New York: Wiley.

Boy, A. V., & Pine, G. J. (1980). Avoiding counselor burnout through role renewal. *Personnel and Guidance Journal, 59,* 161–163.

Edelwich, J., & Brodsky, A. (1980). *Burn–out: Stages of disillusionment in the helping professions.* New York: Human Services Press.

Fall, K. A., Holden, J. M., & Marquis, A. (2017). *Theoretical models of counseling and Psychotherapy* (3rd ed.). New York: Routledge.

Gibson, R. L., & Mitchell, M. M. (2008). *Introduction to guidance and counseling* (7th ed.). Columbus, OH: PHI Learning.

Kesler, K. D. (1990). Burnout: A multimodal approach to assessment and resolution. *Elementary School Guidance and Counseling, 24,* 303–311.

Kiser, P. M. (2015). *Getting the most from your human service internship: Learning from experience* (2nd ed.). Belmont, CA: Wadsworth.

Norcross, J. C., & Lambert, M. J. (2011). Evidence-based therapy relationships. In J. C. Norcross (Ed.), *Psychotherapy relationships that work: Therapist contributions and responsiveness to patients* (2nd ed., pp. 3–16). New York: Oxford.

Osborn, C. J. (2004). Seven salutary suggestions for counselor stamina. *Journal of Counseling and Development, 82,* 319–328.

Roach, L. F., &, M. E. Young (2007). Do counselor education programs promote wellness in their students? *Counselor Education and Supervision, 47,* 29–45.

Skovholt, T. M., & Ronnestad, M. H. (1992). Themes in therapist and counselor development. *Journal of Counseling & Development, 70,* 505–515.

Watts, R. E. (1993). Developing a personal theory of counseling. *Texas Counseling Association Journal, 21,* 103–104.

2

ETHICS OF PRACTICE FOR ADVANCED CLINICAL WORK

Anthony enjoyed the ethics courses more than any of the other graduate counseling courses he had taken. The idea that the study of philosophy, values, and logic could produce practical recommendations such as standards of professional behavior intrigued him. Undergraduate experiences in his chosen minor led him to believe that the study of philosophy was more about debate and the exploration of abstract ideas than it was about developing concrete recommendations for patterns of appropriate professional conduct. His undergraduate minor in philosophy propelled an academic interest in counseling ethics, but his personal and professional desire to complete his clinical training in a way that honored the ethical codes of his chosen profession created a different type of pressure upon him. He understood that what was once an academic exercise was now something that must be upheld and guaranteed to each client with whom he worked. Anthony also knew that he could not achieve this goal alone. He knew that it was impossible to develop a code that could identify all possible situations along with the correct action to be taken in each. Whereas some students may have been put off by the idea that ethical decision-making required input from and dialogue with others, Anthony looked forward to it. For him, the topic of counseling ethics was going to become a living and dynamic process.

Jennifer, one of Anthony's classmates, and Anthony were assigned to the same site. They liked and respected one another and were frankly happy to have been placed together at the same mental health center. Although this center had been popular with students from Anthony's program, it had been several years since anyone had been assigned there for clinical training. Anthony was relieved that at least he knew one other person who would be working with him during the semester. After participating in a day-long orientation, Anthony and Jennifer were introduced to their supervisor, Dr. Palant. Dr. Palant scheduled the students for their weekly hour-long individual supervision sessions and reminded them that she would be available for consultation whenever either of them felt the need. She stressed the point that they were now working under supervision and that they should never feel that they had to make important decisions about their clients without input and support from their supervisor. Anthony quickly realized that he had entered into a training relationship that honored the fact that ethical and clinical decisions needed to be explored and discussed. Jennifer read the situation differently. She seemed almost offended by Dr. Palant's offer. She insisted to Anthony that she was quite capable of making many, if not all, of the decisions on her own. When he asked what she would do if she was uncertain or if she encountered a situation that was more serious than she felt she could manage, she abruptly said, "I'll ask you for help." While he was flattered that she had such confidence in him, her reply also made him anxious.

In the first day of his highly anticipated clinical experience, Anthony was face-to-face with an important and worrisome ethical dilemma. Should he (a) contact his site supervisor and inform her of the problem, (b) remain silent about the situation and hope that Jennifer never needed to talk to him, (c) meet with and describe the situation to his on-campus faculty adviser, (d) talk directly to the faculty practicum instructor, (e) discuss the situation with another student in his program, or (f) meet with Jennifer? The options overwhelmed Anthony; worry about getting Jennifer into trouble if he told others about her position made him as anxious as did the fear that she would go to him for help or ask no one for help when she really did need to talk to her supervisors. It was not just Jennifer that Anthony was worried about. Jennifer's decisions could be potentially hazardous to her clients.

While Anthony knew that the codes would not contain specific information about how to handle this identical situation, they would offer some guidance as to how he might proceed. He was certain that it would be improper for Jennifer to avoid sharing important information about her clients with Dr. Palant. What he did not know was how he should proceed—that is, until he read the following section from the code:

Informal Resolution. When counselors have reasonable cause to believe that another counselor is violating an ethical standard, they attempt to first resolve the issue informally with the other counselor if feasible, providing that such action does not violate confidentiality rights that may be involved.

(ACA, 2005, H.2.b)

Although Anthony found it difficult, he was able to meet with and talk frankly to Jennifer. He shared his concerns about being asked to assume responsibilities that he was not trained or prepared for and his fears that clients' concerns would not be properly addressed if Jennifer's supervisor were not involved. Jennifer instantly understood what she had done and what she would do about it. She recognized that because of her fears associated with asking people for help, she had placed Anthony in an awkward situation and risked not being as effective with her clients as she could be. She apologized and assured him that she would share her reservations about talking to Dr. Palant the next time that all three of them met.

Although the circumstances produced much discomfort, the outcome was even better than Anthony expected. Restored faith in his classmate, confidence in the process, and comfort with his supervisor buoyed him as he awaited the inevitable next ethical dilemma. Knowing where to find answers to important clinical/ethical concerns, knowing whom to talk to, and knowing what steps to follow did not make the decisions any easier, but they did combine to form a process that increased his confidence in being able to face the next ethical concern.

Introduction

Anthony encounters an ethical dilemma within days of beginning his field placement. His choice to consult the code, develop a plan of action, and then take the necessary steps to resolve the problem is emblematic of a pattern that is repeated countless times by all mental health professionals. We chose to cover ethics early in the text because we want to make the point that ethical concerns should guide *all* decision-making. The choice of where you complete your clinical training is as much an ethical issue as is any other aspect of your work as a counselor. To further emphasize the point, ethics are so fundamental to the profession that we must turn to a discussion of them at the earliest possible opportunity. In this text, it is Chapter 2.

Many graduate programs that focus on mental health services include at least one course in ethics. You may have taken such a survey course where the codes, decision-making models, and numerous case examples were covered. These courses offer valuable insights and information along with useful examples drawn from the experience of others. Clinical training, on the other hand, offers opportunities to synthesize what you learned from studying ethics with what you will personally confront as you gain clinical experience. Studying ethics and acting ethically offer different but equally valuable challenges.

We would be surprised, and even a little worried, if students reported that they were not concerned about the challenge of managing ethical issues. After all, ethical codes deal more with concepts than with specific acts, so an amount of ambiguity is inherent. Uncertainty about such important issues frustrates novices as well as experienced mental health professionals. Since codes are based upon a values consensus, ambiguity is unavoidable, for several reasons. First, while specific prohibitions do exist (e.g., sexual relations with clients), most of the code contains language that must be interpreted. Consider the comment made by one internship student:

> I guess I always thought that ethical issues would be more clear-cut in my day-to-day counseling. After my ethics class, I remember feeling like all I had to do is consult the code, as if it was a rule book, a reference manual that I could consult if I had an issue. Within my first month I got a sense of just how gray the clinical/ethical world can be. I would have a question, consult my "rule book" and I was shocked at how little guidance was given. I didn't realize that most of these issues are not answered by a simple "yes" or "no." In ethics class, every case had a clear answer; in the clinical world, it seems much more confusing.

Second, human behaviors always fall along a continuum where lines of demarcation between what is ethical and what is not are often blurry. Where is it appropriate to draw the line regarding, for example, physical contact between a counselor and client? Is a handshake prohibited? How about a pat on the back? Is it appropriate to hug clients? It may surprise you to know that practitioners will have different answers for each of these questions.

Finally, behavior has to be interpreted within the context in which it exists. For example, sharing personal information with members of an adult client's family would be a clear violation of confidentiality. On the other hand, if the client had threatened self-injury or suicide, such a disclosure would be an ethical mandate. Ford (1995) discusses the complexity of making ethical decisions, offers a caution to those of us who help students become counselors, and draws a reasonable conclusion about how students should think about the process in stating that

> instructors might be concerned about making ethical behavior appear so complex and difficult that students will instead take refuge in cynicism [Abeles, 1980]. Students must understand that behaving ethically is neither easy nor impossible; it is both difficult and possible.
>
> (p. 5)

Ironically, regarding ethics, your lack of clinical experience can actually be beneficial. As a novice, you may be more attuned than your veteran counterparts to the internal physical and emotional changes that signal the presence of ethical concerns. Seasoned counselors run the risk of becoming cavalier about ethical concerns. Counseling can become routine to the extent that the internal emotional responses that alert us as an ethical dilemma begins to unfold now lack the impact they once had. Since it is crucial for counselors to be able to identify these internal emotional responses, we think that it helps to have a personally meaningful way to refer to them. To this end, we sometimes apply an animal metaphor suggested by several students who said that when they encountered ethical concerns, it felt as if *ferrets* were darting about inside of them. The metaphor is sensible because nausea and fluttering are examples of the gastrointestinal sensations often associated with anxiety. Counselors would be likely to have similar reactions in situations where ethical concerns were present. It would be a good idea to identify a metaphor for these reactions that makes sense to you. It can help you properly identify when ethical concerns are looming. Regardless of the metaphor you select, it is important to keep in mind the idea that "if it does not feel right, it probably is not right." As a counselor you will need to "trust your gut" as matters of ethical concern unfold. Consider the scenario in Box 2.1 and test your ferret.

Box 2.1 It's Just Coffee

Read the following case and note where your "ferret" starts to get agitated.

I have a long commute to my private practice every morning. On Tuesdays, I have an early couple's appointment, 8:00 am. It is my routine to stop at the same coffee shop every morning and get a cup of coffee to wake my brain up for the day's activities. One Tuesday, as I am making my way to the office, I stop at an intersection and calmly wait for the red light. As I look over, I see Stan, one part of my 8:00 couple's appointment, sitting next to me at the light. He rolls down his window, motions for me to do the same, and states, "Hey, you're out early!" I reply, "Yeah, I'm just going to grab some coffee before I get started." He nods knowingly and says, "You going to CC's?" I nod and he adds, "Great! I'll meet you there." He rolls his window up, light turns green and off we go.

I arrive to the coffee shop and there he is waiting for me at the front of the store. He smiles warmly at me as he opens the door. As we stand in line, he talks about the football game that weekend, his work and a vacation that the family has planned for the summer. When we get to the counter, he says, "I'll get you coffee." I tell me and the cashier that I'll go ahead and pay for my own. We have a brief debate before he finally acquiesces. We stand at the counter and make our coffee and finally I tell him I will see him later.

At 8:00 Stan and Lori arrive at the appointment. As they sit down to start the session, Stan says, "I told him all about our vacation this summer so he already knows about that." She seems confused and replies, "When did this happen?"

Putting the pieces together that we have touched upon thus far, to achieve the level of ethical practice required of practicum and internship students you will need to:

- Be sensitive to your reactions and to those of your client (Trust the ferret!).
- Couple the goals of helping your client with protecting your client's rights and well-being.
- Thoroughly familiarize yourself with the code of ethics.
- Know and be able to use at least one ethical decision-making model.
- Be prepared to consult with others regularly and openly.

Relationships Governed by the Ethical Codes

Within the mental health profession, codes of ethics vary by profession (counseling, psychology, social work, psychiatry) and by the relationships that they govern (counselor–client, agency–client, supervisor–supervisee, etc.). While counselor–client codes receive the most attention, it is equally important to explore the codes that govern the relationships between you and your supervisor, field site, and college or university.

Counselor–Client

During your work with clients, you are expected to know the ethical code that guides your clinical work. Your decision to enter the practical component of your training affirms that you understand and have accepted this responsibility. We offer a limited review of ethics, selecting those areas of the code that are particularly important to students completing practicum or internship under university and field-site supervision. It is also important to understand that no single part of the code should be more or less important than another to you.

Several codes of ethics exist for mental health professionals. While you are expected to be thoroughly familiar with the codes that govern your specific mental health subdiscipline, studying other codes can be helpful. Once you know your group's code, you might want to make comparisons to others. You can do so by selecting such common issues as confidentiality, dual relationships, and informed consent and then comparing how other codes deal with these universal concerns.

Variations from one code to another probably result from the subjectivity inherent in the underlying principles upon which most, if not all, mental health codes of ethics are based: *respect for autonomy, nonmaleficence, beneficence, justice, and fidelity* (see Kitchener, 1984 for a more complete discussion of these principles). In addition, codes of ethics are subject to change since they are linked to continuously evolving social and professional norms. Codes of professional conduct form (a) the interrelationship of the values of society and the values of the profession and (b) a consensus that emerges between society and the empirical practices of the mental health professions. Community standards for treatment are therefore dynamic. For example, the standard of *informed consent*, a concept based on the principle of respect for autonomy, illustrates how codes change in response to evolving social and clinical concerns. Informed consent stipulates that the client is given sufficient information upon which to base a decision about his or her care. Such information might include a description of the counselor's training and experience, risks associated with different courses of treatment, and expected outcomes. While this seems sensible, it has not always been the standard for treatment. Between 50 and 100 years ago, health professionals regularly withheld information from those being treated under the assumption that potentially disturbing information would be detrimental to the effort to cure them. Under such a community standard, it might be considered unethical to tell a cancer patient, for example, that he or she had a fatal illness. What's more, treatment decisions were regularly made with little input from the person being treated. Over time, this "doctor knows best" approach has evolved into its polar opposite: informed consent. This example underscores just how greatly values evolve over time and how necessary it is for these changes to guide practice.

While an in-depth discussion of counseling ethics is beyond the scope of this book, we offer a review of several concerns: informed consent, confidentiality, professional boundaries, and clinical competence.

Informed Consent

Respect for autonomy is the principle that mostly underlies the concept of informed consent. Clients have a right and a responsibility to make independent decisions about their care; their choices must therefore be based upon complete and open disclosure of the methods used and the possible outcomes (positive and negative) anticipated. Counselors are obliged and ethically bound to provide their potential charges with a wide range of information. The counselor disclosure statement (CDS) is becoming an increasingly common way to inform clients. CDSs specify, in writing, the nature of the relationship between the client and the counselor. They are contracts that: (a) inform clients about the counseling process, (b) identify the counselor's professional training, clinical experience, and licensure status, (c) establish clinical and ethical boundaries, (d) identify courses of action when particular conditions exist, and (e) clarify expectations. CDSs honor many ethical mandates, including, for example, informed consent, limits of confidentiality, and duty to warn. The CDS is given to clients at the beginning of the first meeting or in advance of that meeting. In this way, clients are free to review the parameters of the relationship in advance of its formation. Student CDSs are especially useful because they specify from the outset that the client will receive counseling services from a practicum or internship student who is working under the supervision of a licensed professional.

The Louisiana Counselor Licensure Law and the rules stemming from that law require that counselors complete a CDS that includes specific information about each of the following topics:

1. Counselor Identifying Information
2. Qualifications
   Current graduate student working under supervision, completing practicum/internship
3. Description of the Counseling Relationship
4. Areas of Expertise
5. Fee Scales
6. An Explanation of the Types of Services Offered and Clients Served
7. Code of Conduct
8. Privileged Communication
9. Emergency Situations
10. Client Responsibilities
11. Physical Health Considerations
12. Potential Counseling Risks
13. Confirming Signatures of Client and Counselor (Supervisor and Counselor Intern)

> AUTHORITY NOTE: Promulgated in accordance with R.S. 37.1101_1115.
> HISTORICAL NOTE: Promulgated by the Department of Health and Hospitals, Board of Examiners, LR 15:627 (August 1989), amended LR 20 (May 1994).

Before CDSs were mandated, few if any counselors wrote and distributed them. In fact, many experienced professionals balked at having to design these forms once licensing boards required them. Despite the objections, counselors quickly realized that completing a CDS turned out to be a valuable exercise. It provides an opportunity to (a) reflect upon your choice of a counseling theory, (b) clearly define skills, abilities, and limitations, (c) consider many practical aspects of the counseling process, including limits to confidentiality, billing, scheduling, and client and counselor expectations, and (d) apply the ethical codes that govern practice. Preparing a CDS is an excellent way for you to explore ethical concerns before meeting with clients, and it will help you formulate answers to many questions that commonly arise in the course of providing counseling services. As a part of your clinical training, we encourage you to prepare a rough draft, have it reviewed by other students, and complete a final draft based upon those peer recommendations. The time that you invest in this assignment will pay many dividends. And the final product, a written CDS, will benefit your clients. A sample CDS is provided in Box 2.2.

Box 2.2 A Sample Counselor Disclosure Statement

Jackson Murphy, Ph.D., LPC
512 December Ave, Suite 504
Austin, TX 78704

Counselor Disclosure Statement

Qualifications: I am a Licensed Professional Counselor (16009). I received my Ph.D. from the Counselor Education and Supervision program at the University of North Texas. For over a decade, I have worked with adults, adolescents in children in both individual and group counseling.

Nature of Counseling:

I work with clients who believe they have the capacity to solve their own problems with my assistance. Within this approach, we will struggle together, as equals, with any problems you choose to bring into therapy with the goal being that of you finding your own path to greater independence, growth and social interest. Because I believe all behavior is goal directed, my role is to facilitate your insight through mutually examining your current goals of behavior, your beliefs surrounding these goals, explore how these goals are/ are not fitting your needs, and to collaboratively set new goals according to your specifications. Throughout the collaborative process, I will provide clarification, encouragement, tentative hypotheses and interpretations to facilitate your movement toward your selected goals.

Although our sessions may be intimate psychologically, ours is strictly a professional relationship rather than a social one. Our contact will be limited to group counseling sessions you arrange with me except in case of emergency when you may contact the answering service (812-XXXX) and I will get back to you as soon as possible. If in immediate distress please call the local 24 hour hotline number (512) 987-XXXX.

Expectations of you, as a client include: active participation in the counseling process, arrive to appointments on time, attend sessions as scheduled, inform me of any other ongoing counseling, to keep me up to date on any medications you may be taking, and to have a physical if you have not had one in the last year.

Confidentiality: Most of our communication is confidential, but the following exceptions to confidentiality do exist: a) I determine you are a danger to yourself or others; b) you disclose abuse, neglect, or exploitation of a child, elderly, or disabled person; c) you disclose sexual contact with another mental health professional; d) I am ordered by a court to disclose information; e) you give me written consent to release information; or g) I am otherwise required by law to release information. I routinely consult with other licensed colleagues regarding cases. In the event that I consult on your case, all identifying information is excluded to protect your confidentiality.

Fees: In return for a fee of $100 per session, I agree to provide counseling services for you. The fee for each session will be due and must be paid at the conclusion of each session. Cash, personal checks, or credit cards are acceptable for payment. I currently do not file for reimbursement from health insurance companies. In the event that you choose to cancel an appointment, you must call 24 hours in advance or you will be responsible for the normal session fee.

Referrals and Complaints: Should you and/or I believe that a referral is needed, I will provide alternatives including programs and/or people who may be available to assist you. You will be responsible for contacting and evaluating those referrals and alternatives. At any time you may initiate a discussion of possible positive or negative effects of entering, not entering, continuing, or discontinuing counseling. While benefits are desirable, specific results are not guaranteed. In fact, during counseling, issues may be uncovered that were not expected and the change process itself can be taxing emotionally and/or physically. I encourage you to discuss any issues of discomfort with the group.

I assure you that my services will be rendered in a professional manner consistent with accepted legal and ethical standards as set by the Texas Licensing Board, a copy of which is available on request. If at any time for any reason you are dissatisfied with my services, let me know. I will gladly discuss any perceived problem or issue and willingly work with you to resolve any concern you may have. If we cannot resolve your concerns together, you may contact the appropriate licensing board listed below:

Texas State Board of Examiners of Professional Counselors
Texas Department of State Health Services
Mail Code 1982
P.O. Box 149347
Austin, Texas 78714–9347

By your signature below, you are indicating that you have read and understood this statement, or that any questions you had about this statement were answered to your satisfaction, and that you were furnished with a copy of this statement. By my signature, I verify the accuracy of this statement and acknowledge my commitment to conform to its specifications.

Client's Signature	Counselor's Signature
Date	Date

Confidentiality

The confidentiality of the counseling relationship forms one pillar of its effectiveness. With such a guarantee, clients become free to expose troubling concerns and experiences that would under other circumstances remain suppressed or avoided. While confidentiality is based on several principles, fidelity, or "faithfulness to promises made and to the truth" (Welfel, 2016, p. 37) is particularly important. Clients expect, and counselors must deliver, confidential treatment. The promise that counselors make in this regard demands scrupulous adherence to the standards that govern the protection of their clients' information and identities. While your family doctor may say hello at a social gathering, as a mental health professional you are not free to publicly identify yourself to clients. A simple greeting would unwittingly identify the other as receiving mental health services. We have rarely been able to successfully predict which of our clients will speak to us in public and which will not. To emphasize the point, we offer the following situation, which happened to one of us. A counselor was invited to serve on a board for a local community service program. The president introduced him to each member with brief, informal, threesome meetings. As he moved about the room, the counselor was surprised to discover that one of his clients was a board member of the organization. Had the counselor known beforehand that the client was on the board, he would not have accepted the invitation. As the president at last introduced the counselor to his own client, the counselor looked for some signal from the client, who quickly responded by saying that he was happy to meet the new member and asked him what type of work he did. The counselor asked the same question in return. The two men shook hands, parted, and headed for their respective seats. The next day, during the regularly scheduled counseling session, the client thanked the counselor for maintaining the confidentiality of their relationship.

Absent guarantees of confidentiality, many clients would be reluctant to explore important experiences and reactions in their lives. According to Jourard and Landsman (1980), self-disclosures are critical to the client's growth and development. They maintained that sharing information in the presence of a trusted "other" had two beneficial effects. While the counselor's empathic understanding of the client's concerns seemed the most obvious, the fact that the clients heard themselves more completely when concerns were uttered in the presence of another turned out to be the more curative force. Counselors and clients eventually use such information to develop plans to ameliorate difficulties and to access emotions that would otherwise be avoided.

Confidentiality has limits, and the management of them becomes yet another challenge of the ethics governing this aspect of the counseling relationship. Most legal jurisdictions and ethical codes stipulate that observing confidences cannot endanger the life of the client or the client's relation-ships. Counselors have a duty to warn if a real danger exists regarding the client's own life or the possibility that the client would injure someone else. This duty to warn is to a large extent based upon the interrelated concepts of nonmaleficence (doing no harm) and beneficence (doing good). Because counselors are, and should be, mandatory reporters of abuse toward chil-dren, older people, and people with disabilities, clients need to be aware of this limit to confidentiality as they enter the counseling relationship. Deciding whether a reportable threat to another person exists requires care-ful assessment, consultation, and action. You are working under supervi-sion, however, so these decisions will always be made in consultation with supervisors. No one looks forward to making such a report, but openness, support, and experience make the difficult accomplishable. The fact that this possibility was covered in the CDS and discussed early in the counseling process helps. Fidelity, faithfulness to promises made, ultimately carries the counselor through this difficult process because "clients tend to trust truth-ful and honest counselors, even if the truth is painful or difficult" (Cava-nagh & Levitov, 2001, p. 62). And such life-and-death concerns demand that you faithfully take steps to directly protect your client's life or others in his or her life. Protocols for assessing suicide and homicide risk are available and should be obtained from site and university supervisors.

While the ethic of confidentiality governs the sharing of information from a professional standpoint, privileged communication is the legal standard. Courts can and sometimes do subpoena records and counselors. Though the client owns the "privilege," such requests must be immediately dis-cussed with the client because it is ultimately the judge who will determine whether the information and/or your testimony is required. There is little that counselors can do to prevent divulging such information if they are ordered to do so, beyond asserting their client's right to privileged com-munication. Supervision, consultation, and a phone call to the American Counseling Association's legal hotline are all important steps when legal action produces confidentiality and privileged-communication concerns.

While we are covering this subject, we would like to stress the fact that the client actually "owns" the information and can therefore dictate where and how it will be shared. Though not a limit to confidentiality, a client's request for his or her counselor to disclose information to others is actu-ally quite common. The client may ask you to speak, for example, to an employer, another health care worker, or school officials (in the case of minors). The client's decision for you to take this action must be codified by completing a *release*, a written and signed document that stipulates to whom you can speak and in some cases what you are allowed to discuss. Clients will often ask to you discuss the decision to release information and to explore possible problems that may arise.

Confidentiality is a ubiquitous concern. Our lives as counselors are filled with occasions where the confidentiality of our clients must be fiercely protected. We quickly learn catchphrases like "I cannot confirm or deny . . ." as we respond to inevitable telephone and personal requests for information from others. We develop styles of interacting with other professionals that protect client identities. We limit what we say and where we say it. And we develop methods to guard the records and information that we obtain from our clients. Unfortunately, breaches of confidentiality sometimes occur. The principle of fidelity guides us under these circumstances as well. Being truthful to our clients, even in situations where the promise of confidentiality was not kept, is particularly important.

Professional Boundaries

Dual relationship is the term often applied to clinical situations in which counselors inappropriately choose to begin counseling relationships with clients with whom they have a conflict of interest or in which clinical boundaries slip and produce inappropriate counselor–client relationships. Both unethical situations harm clients. The principle of nonmaleficence is most applicable here because the term means to do no harm or to protect clients from harm.

Counselors do not offer services to friends or family members. They resist counseling people with whom they have other types of relationships. For example, sanctions against dual relationships protect students from obtaining counseling from their professors. Supervision is not counseling. Each has a different set of goals and different means. Blurring the boundary between teacher and counselor is especially worrisome for students in the clinical portion of their training. As a supervisee, you should be alert to improper invitations to shift from supervision to counseling.

Establishing and maintaining appropriate boundaries are essential clinical tasks to learn. The idea of a "slippery slope" is often used to describe boundary infractions that appear insignificant but actually mark the beginning of a serious change in the therapeutic alliance. Unfortunately, counselors who take part in the erosion of these boundaries usually presume that they are exhibiting noble intentions as they unwittingly participate in what will eventually lead to countertherapeutic, in some cases dangerous, outcomes. Evidence that boundaries were poorly established from the beginning of the therapeutic alliance almost always surfaces when histories of problem-laden therapies are studied.

Implementing a course of action that focuses on the establishment and maintenance of boundaries is complicated by the fact that clients, for the most part, know almost nothing about mental health ethics. This naïveté produces confusion when your clients apply what they know about relationships in general to the counseling relationship. As a counselor, you may surprise or even insult them with your responses. For example, a client, after offering many deeply personal replies to your questions, may become frustrated when you correctly "process" rather than answer his or her questions about your personal life. You are appropriately more interested in discussing your client's need to know about you than in actually answering the questions, but the shift from what is commonly expected in "real-life" interactions still feels awkward to the client. Although you may respond to client questions with versions of the statement "This therapy is about you and should not focus on my life," the client may remain confused because such questions about you as counselor seem completely benign and consistent with social convention. Professional counseling relationships proceed in this unbalanced way so that ultimately clients share more and more detailed information about their emotional, social, vocational, and spiritual lives yet learn next to nothing about their counselors beyond that which can be obtained from reading the disclosure statement. The imbalance is striking to clients because people have come to expect others to share and risk as much as they do. Indeed, in life outside of the therapy office, such a one-sided relationship is uncommon.

In addition, human beings quite naturally respond to others with a deepening sense of emotional closeness as more-intimate parts of the self are shared. Unfortunately, clients can easily mistake this form of closeness for the type found in a close personal friendship or love relationship in which, unlike in the counseling relationship, both people share equally. If counselors and clients misinterpret the "contrived" closeness that clients experience from sharing so much of themselves for something other than a therapeutic or clinical relationship, serious problems develop. You will need to approach this aspect of the therapeutic alliance with caution and clarity so as not to allow your client to confuse counseling with the types of social relationships that form between people who mutually choose to share and respond to one another out of love or friendship. The value of appropriate boundaries for all counseling relationships cannot be overstated.

Clients can become frustrated, even hurt, when counselors correctly enforce various clinical boundaries. Such situations are often difficult for counselors and clients. Gift-giving is an excellent example of a potentially difficult-to-enforce ethical boundary. In general, people (counselors), are not comfortable with refusing gifts nor are they (clients) accustomed to having their gifts refused. Thus, managing ethical sanctions against accepting gifts from clients may feel unnatural and needlessly difficult. Counselors fear their clients' reactions when they return a gift; clients feel predictably hurt when their gifts are refused. Despite the discomfort, the need to maintain this boundary persists. Accepting gifts invites the client to change the nature and structure of the counseling relationship from well-bounded and professional to informal, casual, and friendly. If the gift is a sign of appreciation, it would be clinically preferable if the client used such an occasion to more completely appreciate the self rather than another. In any event, managing the boundary of gift-giving becomes much easier after one or two experiences. You will find that being empathic and being firm are not mutually exclusive events. In most cases clients, even those who might initially appear hurt by your refusal of a gift, at some point express their appreciation for how you were able to maintain critical boundaries that in hindsight make better sense to them.

Counselors set boundaries with their clients by communicating with them. Therefore, our nonverbal reactions are as important as what we say. Skilled counselors learn to be consistent in both realms of interaction. Mixed messages are especially destructive to boundaries. Depending to some extent upon the client, something as seemingly minor as a pat on a client's shoulder as he or she leaves a session could undo what was verbally emphasized as the importance of a well-bounded professional relationship. Clients also need to know why such boundaries are important to the counseling process. For example, no clinician would question why a counselor would refuse an offer to come to a client's house for dinner. Counselors understand that the dinner would mark a change in the relationship from a professional alliance to a casual friendship. They recognize the worrisome decrease in objectivity, the countertherapeutic changes in expectations of the client for his or her counselor, and the plethora of confidentiality issues that would surface. Experienced clinicians may even recognize that the client's invitation may be caused by undisclosed anxieties that the client believes could be resolved by being friendly with his or her counselor. Clients, of course, have no recognition of these and other factors, so the counselor is ultimately responsible for not only maintaining the boundary but for explaining the benefits accrued from doing so. When counselors tell clients that they are ethically prohibited from, for example, accepting an invitation to dinner, they have only partially responded. It is important for the client to know why in some detail.

Consider the case of a client who unproductively began and ended counseling relationships with a number of counselors and was eventually referred to yet another counselor. During the intake interviews, the client discussed a long list of failed personal relationships in which she ended up feeling used and disrespected. While she did not identify the feelings, her loneliness and sadness were palpable. Note here that her personal history and her counseling history cued the counselor to relationship problems that signaled the potential for boundary problems in the newly forming counseling relationship. When the client asked the counselor for a hug and kiss good-bye at the end of the session, it came as no surprise. The counselor correctly declined and told the client that this issue would be the first order of business when they met for the next regularly scheduled meeting. The client returned predictably hurt and angry. The counselor accepted that this was how she felt and responded by telling her that counseling must be a professional, well-bounded relationship and that the hug and kiss would have seriously interfered with that important goal. The counselor expressed having far too much respect for her and her struggles to allow the erosion of boundaries that were critical to her efforts to heal. The counselor explained that the hug and kiss might have reduced some level of her loneliness, but this counseling effort would be focused on more important and far-reaching goals, such as developing requisite skills for the formation of close personal relationships in her private life. The counselor knew that the client had a long history of repeating unproductive relationships, and allowing her to inadvertently do the same thing to the counseling relationship would have been counterproductive, disrespectful, and unethical. Once the counselor explained this last set of insights to her, she seemed to understand and appreciate the course that the counselor took with her. While her loneliness persisted, the groundwork had been laid so that she would be able use the counseling relationship to help herself on her journey to find intimacy in her personal life. This client, like most, encountered distortions and difficulties in her relationships with many people in her life. That she would inadvertently make similar problematic choices in a counseling relationship should not be a surprise; it is a major reason why counselors must scrupulously manage boundaries.

You can develop and maintain appropriate boundaries if you are willing to carefully honor them from the very outset of the counseling relationship and if you recognize the value of screening for potential dual relationships. Proper boundaries and clearly defined goals build trust and openness, critical elements of any effective clinical relationship.

Clinical Competence

One of the most common issues mental health professionals face is trying to answer the question, "Am I any good at this?" Rooted in this question are many other concerns related to competency. Ethical guidelines compel us to do good and do no harm, yet if you asked many counselors at any point if they really knew whether they were making a difference in the lives of their clients, you might get a troubled look. Consider this thoughtful remark from one seasoned professional:

> My most nagging doubt about my profession is whether or not I am positively impacting my clients. There are sessions when I feel like I am right on, but I don't really know if the client is getting it. There have also been numerous occasions when I thought the session went horribly wrong and the client comes in the next week and says it was the best session ever. In times like that, I really wonder if I truly understand what works about this process.

After having trained many students, we recognize that your lack of experience fills you with (a) questions about what to do, when to do it, and how it should be done and (b) predictable worry about the fact that your clients are being treated by you, a counselor in training. Your supervisors respond to your inexperience with their own set of concerns coupled with an ethical and professional mandate to create a safe environment for you to grow into a mental health professional. Your relationships to your university, field site, and supervisors have been carefully defined so that you can gain the requisite work experiences with actual clients and so that clients will be helped in the process. All professions recognize the risks and benefits that exist when theoretically trained but inexperienced clinicians enter this phase of their professional education. Every trained mental health professional began by working with a first client in a practicum setting that was designed to accommodate the client's needs and the counselor's lack of experience.

There are two main elements of competency: *internal feelings of inferiority*, which are subjective and *measures of competency*, which are objective. The internal feelings of inferiority are a normal part of life. Dealt with in a healthy way, these feelings can motivate you to stretch yourself and continue to grow. At your current level of professional development, these inferiority feelings related to competency may seem to color every moment while in practice. Consider some of these concerns that arise in any group supervision session:

"What do I do if my client . . ."

- questions my training?
- has an issue I have never worked with before?
- is different from me (gender, ethnicity, religion, age, sexual orientation)?
- gets angry in session?
- doesn't talk much or talks too much?
- is offensive/irritating/boring and I don't like him/her?
- doesn't come back and won't return my calls?

Such questions are common at the beginning of all counseling relationships; they are just more disturbing at the beginning of your training. Your heightened sensitivity is useful because it motivates answers to questions that help you properly assess your level of competence and clarify the amount of supervision that you will need to carry out specific clinical assignments. We hope that in your supervision courses and post-master's experience, you work with a supervisor who helps you gain a sense of comfort with your areas for growth and to understand that competent practitioners always look for ways to improve. Because your feelings of inferiority are normal, it is not so much a question of whether you have them but what you choose to do with them. That question brings us to the objective measures of competency.

Throughout your program of study, we are assuming you have been thoroughly evaluated based on your ability in basic and advanced skills. Formal coursework assessments (both formative and summative), comprehensive exams, and licensing exams all represent methods of competency assessment. When you are "out in the real world," what do you do? In discussing ways to assess competency, we like to use the triad of competency model (see Figure 2.1). To illustrate the model, we will use the case of George. George is a new professional counselor who wants to start a group for adolescent girls to discuss issues of forming healthy relationships. How does George know he is competent to facilitate this kind of group?

The first leg of the triad is formal education. Formal education includes taking a graduate-level course or an extended workshop on the topic. Formal education activities expose the professional to relevant literature, experiential activities, and opportunities to ask an expert (the instructor) questions to enhance the learning experience. In the example of George, he

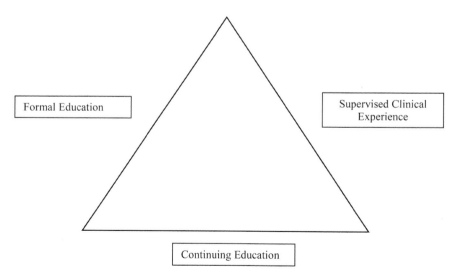

Figure 2.1. Triad of competency

would consider the courses he has taken in his graduate training. He, like most counselors, took a course in group counseling, so that would meet this aspect of competency for group. He has also taken courses in lifespan theory, where he learned about adolescent development. He seems to have this leg of the triad under control.

The second leg of the triad is supervised clinical experience. Supervised clinical experience means that you have practice working with the modality or population and that your practice has been supervised by someone with more experience than you have with the modality or population. If George had facilitated groups while he was seeking licensure, he might have felt more competent than if he had not, due to the feedback he received during supervision. If George is licensed and has not received any supervised experience related to group (modality) and/or population (adolescent girls), George can work on this leg of the triad in two ways. The first way is to seek a co-leader for the group who is competent. Using a co-leader can give George some in vivo training and feedback from someone who possesses more expertise. Along with the co-leader experience, George can participate in pre-group planning and post-session feedback sessions with his co-leader to improve his level of competency.

The second way for George to obtain supervised clinical experience is to seek a colleague to supervise his group work. If George is licensed, he may feel embarrassed to seek supervision from a colleague, but it is the ethical and professional thing to do. George can pay attention to his feelings of inferiority ("I am supposed to be competent. What if my colleague thinks I'm an idiot for asking for help?") and handle them in appropriate ways. On a personal note, we have found that our faith in other professionals increases when they ask for help because it is an indication that they know how to access help when they need it. It is those who do not ask for help whom we worry about.

The third leg of the triad is continuing education. Dedicating your professional career to continuous growth allows the dynamic of competency to be ever expanding rather than a static process. The exciting part of the field of counseling is that we do not, nor will we ever, know everything there is to know about human behavior. Therefore, competency is always changing, and we must seek out experiences that add depth to our professional knowledge. There are several ways to increase one's competency through continuing education. Licensing boards require a certain number of CEUs (continuing education units) per licensing cycle. CEUs can be obtained by attending conferences at the state, regional, or national level. Conferences provide excellent opportunities to learn a wide array of advanced clinical skills, get a refresher on old skills, and be exposed to new ideas.

You can also attend workshops that are held in your city or area. If you are licensed, you will soon receive countless flyers advertising these workshops. In addition to live continuing education, belonging to professional organizations allows you to receive professional journals filled with the latest research and ideas. Many of the professional journals allow the reader to fill out a form and answer some questions for CEU credit. George can use continuing education to broaden his understanding of groups and adolescent girls. He can attend conferences dedicated to the practice of group work or read journal articles detailing various group protocols when working with adolescents. As George continues to grow, his competency level will grow too, and both George and his clientele will benefit.

Ultimately, the issue of clinical competence helps us determine to whom we should provide service and who should be referred to other clinicians who possess treatment alternatives more appropriate to the particular client's needs. Unfortunately, competence is an important concern that can be easily and improperly influenced by clients themselves. During the evaluation process or when new information becomes available, a counselor may correctly determine that the client's needs call for a different type of mental health professional or someone with an expertise in a different area. Some clients balk at the recommendation and respond by insisting that the counselor continue to counsel them. Of course, a common and problematic situation develops if the counselor acquiesces. Problems like this are not specific to counseling. Family medicine and internal medicine physicians are also subject to patients asking them to continue treatment even though the need for a referral to a specialist is indicated. Counselors must not only demonstrate competence in correctly identifying whom they can appropriately help but also demonstrate competence in effecting appropriate referrals.

Although site and university supervisors identify the types of clients that are appropriate for you and your level of expertise, you need to be aware of your concerns and be willing to share them with those who are responsible for your work. The ideal situation exists when you and your supervisor are in agreement about the types of clients that are appropriate for you. When supervisors feel that you are more skillful and competent than you think you are, they are obliged to help you recognize the gap and adapt to it. When you feel that you are more skilled and competent than your supervisors believe you are, another set of problems develops. In this situation, one of two concerns may exist: (a) your supervisors have misjudged your skill set, or (b) you have an exaggerated self-assessment. The former is remedied by allowing supervisors to gain more experience of your work, but the latter is a problem that can worsen rapidly and significantly. Self-assessment and assessments completed by others are covered in Chapter 4. In any event, a harmony of opinion between you and your supervisor(s) concerning your level of competence is in all ways essential.

Student–Institution

To minimize risk to clients and to ensure that counseling students obtain worthwhile clinical experiences, the education of counselors is guided by an elaborate set of ethics and policies. We have reviewed some of the ethical requirements that govern the counselor–client relationship, and we now turn to those that govern the relationship between the student and the college, university, or agency. As we review these codes and standards, you will see that the same five principles that guide the counselor–client relationship have a place in the student–institution relationship. Universities and their faculties as well as agencies and their site supervisors must also abide by codes of supervisory ethics and standards for supervision that form obligations to their counseling interns and to the clients who are served by them. An example of such standards and codes of conduct can be found in the published standards of the Council for the Accreditation of Counseling and Related Educational Programs (CACREP).

Accredited counseling programs abide by a range of standards that include, for example, class size for practicum classes (five students), internship classes (ten students), amount of supervision, type of supervision, and standards for performance. The "Clinical Instruction" section of the CACREP (2016) standards opens with the following:

> Clinical instruction includes supervised practica and internships that have been completed within a student's program of study. Practicum

and internship requirements are considered to be the most critical experience elements in the program. All faculty, including clinical instruction faculty and supervisors, are clearly committed to preparing professional counselors and promoting the development of the student's professional counselor identity.

The short goal statement offers a glimpse into a collection of standards that are both comprehensive and specific. For example, the number of hours completed at the field site, amount of time devoted to direct client contact, and individual/group supervision activities are all covered. Course syllabi are often designed around these criteria, so your review of them will offer an opportunity to identify the source of the requirements and a chance to determine how consistent your course requirements are to the CACREP standards. We would specifically recommend that you review Sections H through M in these standards. Becoming familiar with these CACREP standards can be very helpful when questions or concerns arise about course requirements, training experiences, and evaluation methods.

Student–Supervisor

Mental health codes of ethics usually include sections that address clinical supervision. Of course, evidence of the same five basic principles can be easily identified. The Approved Clinical Supervisor Code of Ethics offered by the Center for Credentialing and Education (2005) provides one set of particularly useful specifications. You can quickly relate one or more of the five principles to each numbered statement in the list. Item number 1 emphasizes respect for autonomy. In item 13, justice, "the expectation that counselors will act fairly and equitably" (Cavanagh & Levitov, 2001, p. 61), is prominent. Counselors act justly when they understand and appropriately respond to cultural differences and the influence that such differences may have on the counseling relationship. See if you can identify which principles form the basis of the remainder:

1. Ensure that supervisees inform clients of their professional status (e.g., intern) and of all conditions of supervision.
    Supervisors need to ensure that supervisees inform their clients of any status other than being fully qualified for independent practice or licensed. For example, supervisees need to inform their clients

if they are a student, intern, trainee or, if licensed with restrictions, the nature of those restrictions (e.g., associate or conditional). In addition, clients must be informed of the requirements of supervision (e.g., the audio taping of all clinical sessions for purposes of supervision).

2. Ensure that clients have been informed of their rights to confidentiality and privileged communication when applicable. Clients also should be informed of the limits of confidentiality and privileged communication.

    The general limits of confidentiality are when harm to self or others is threatened; when the abuse of children, elders or disabled persons is suspected; and in cases when the court compels the mental health professional to testify and break confidentiality. These are generally accepted limits to confidentiality and privileged communication, but they may be modified by state or federal statute.

3. Inform supervisees about the process of supervision, including supervision goals, case management procedures, and the supervisor's preferred supervision model(s).

4. Keep and secure supervision records and consider all information gained in supervision as confidential.

5. Avoid all dual relationships with supervisees that may interfere with the supervisor's professional judgment or exploit the supervisee.

    Any sexual, romantic, or intimate relationship is considered to be a violation. Sexual relationship means sexual conduct, sexual harassment, or sexual bias toward a supervisee by a supervisor.

6. Establish procedures with their supervisees for handling crisis situations.

7. Provide supervisees with adequate and timely feedback as part of an established evaluation plan.

8. Render assistance to any supervisee who is unable to provide competent counseling services to clients.

9. Intervene in any situation where the supervisee is impaired and the client is at risk.

10. Refrain from endorsing an impaired supervisee when such impairment deems it unlikely that the supervisee can provide adequate counseling services.

11. Supervisors offer only supervision for professional services for which they are trained or have supervised experience. Supervision should

not include assistance in diagnosis, assessment, or treatment without prior training or supervision. Supervisors are responsible for correcting any misrepresentations of the qualifications of others.

12. Ensure that supervisees are aware of the current ethical standards related to their professional practice, as well as legal standards that regulate the practice of counseling.

13. Engage supervisees in an examination of cultural issues that might affect supervision and/or counseling.

14. Ensure that both supervisees and clients are aware of their rights and of due process procedures, and that you as supervisor are ultimately responsible for the client.

15. It is considered unethical for an Approved Clinical Supervisor to supervise a relative or immediate family member.

(Center for Credentialing and Education, 2005)

The Approved Clinical Supervisor code defines the nature of the relationship between counselors and their supervisors. It outlines what to expect from a supervisor, the supervisory relationship, and how to properly inform clients of your status as a person working under the supervision of a licensed professional. The parallels between aspects of the code governing counselor–client relationships and counselor–supervisor relationships are obvious. Dual relationships (item 15) are identified as problematic, and sanctions are imposed in both types of relationships. Issues of confidentiality, informed consent, and clinical competence are all included.

Making Ethical Decisions

While understanding and knowing the codes that govern practice and training are essential, they are not sufficient. You must be able to apply them effectively and willing to do so consistently. To achieve that end, researchers have developed protocols for ethical decision-making. Each of the following models offers a slightly different, sequentially ordered protocol for effective, ethical decision-making. Each begins by directing you to determine whether an ethical concern exists and ends with implementing an appropriate course of action.

Hybrid Model

This type of hybrid decision-making model is offered by Skovholt and Rivers (2004, p. 360) and based in part upon that of Corey, Corey, and Callanan (2014) and Kottler and Brown (2014).

1. Determine that an ethical and/or legal issue exists.
2. Frame the issue.
3. Review ethical guidelines, laws, policies of the work setting, and helping literature.
4. Consult with supervisors, colleagues, and/or other professionals.
5. Consider personal values.
6. Identify and consider various options for resolution.
7. Make a decision and act on it.
8. Accurately and fully document the issue, including all steps and actions taken.
9. Process the experience with supervisors and colleagues.

American Counseling Association Model

1. Identify the problem and define it.
2. Apply the proper Code of Ethics.
3. Access the nature and depth of the problem.
4. Generate potential courses of action.
5. After carefully considering potential consequences for each option, select a course of action.
6. Evaluate the selected course of action.
7. Implement the course of action.

(Forrester-Miller & Davis, 2016)

Employing a Model

Employing one of the available ethical decision-making models is an activity that will be repeated throughout the course of your career as a clinician. Disciplined attention to each of the steps will make it easier to integrate this approach into your clinical work; practice will increase your ability to make good decisions. We do not believe that one of the two protocols presented is necessarily better than the other, so we would encourage you to practice using both until you determine a preference based on your experience with them. You might start by identifying similarities and differences and then, having done so, hypothesize about why such differences exist. Once you understand the two models, analyze a potential ethical dilemma using each. This is a particularly effective exercise if you use it as an opportunity to work with peers. A good starting point would be the example situation offered at the beginning of this chapter.

Summary

Codes of ethics governing the counselor–client relationship are essential for obvious reasons. While this area of ethics usually gets the lion's share of attention, we also wanted to make you aware of and discuss the codes that govern the other important relationships in your life as a practicum and internship student. In doing so, we were able to illustrate that the same five basic principles influence all three relationship areas: counselor–client, student–supervisor, and student–institution.

We sought to demonstrate that ethics form one cornerstone of the profession and the counseling process. While it may not be easy to consistently follow the requirements of the codes, it is accomplishable and vital. We stressed the importance of openness and the need for supervision at this stage of your professional development. We know that ethical concerns can be worrisome, but we hope that you will also develop a sense of comfort from the idea that codes seek to ensure the proper treatment of those you counsel and those who are responsible for you as you learn to be a counselor.

This chapter on ethics is included early in the text because we believe that ethics should guide not only the counseling process but the counselor training process as well. We stress this point when we suggest that the selection of a field site is as much an ethical decision as it is an academic one. For example, you can easily recognize why a field site where you will be supervised by an old friend is problematic. However, it may be more difficult to recognize that certain settings may not be appropriate for you given the scope of your training or the fact that some supervision practices, accepted by the site due to their efficiency, may not be ethical or the best for your professional development. You will need to know a good deal about yourself and about the type of work done at sites you might possibly select if you are going to make a sound, ethical choice.

Reflection Questions

1. What reactions (feelings and thoughts) surfaced as you read Anthony's story in the introduction to this chapter?
2. What internal sensations do you experience that signal the presence of a potential ethical concern?
3. While the philosophical principles that underlie ethics have persisted for decades, mental health ethics are dynamic (evolving) rather than static (fixed). Why is this so, and what challenges does it place upon you as a clinician?
4. Under what conditions do you think you might be susceptible to allowing professional boundaries to inappropriately slip or erode?
5. What characteristics would you look for in a supervisor you were about to select for a discussion about a serious ethical concern?
6. What is the difference between thinking ethically and acting ethically?
7. What are some of your identified areas of competency? Within these areas, how do you meet the elements of the triad of competency?
8. What effect has reading this chapter had on your understanding of the opening story?

References

Abeles, N. (1980). Teaching ethical principles by means of value confrontations. *Psychotherapy: Theory, Research and Practice, 17*, 384–391.

American Counseling Association (ACA). (2005). *Code of ethics and standards of practice.* Retrieved March 15, 2017 from www.counseling.org

Cavanagh, M. E., & Levitov, J. E. (2001). *The counseling experience: A theoretical and practical approach (2nd ed.).* Prospect Heights, IL: Waveland.

Center for Credentialing and Education. (2005). *Approved clinical supervisor code of ethics.* Retrieved from www.cce-global.org

Corey, G., Corey, M. S., & Callanan, P. (2014). *Issues and ethics in the helping professions* (9th ed.). Pacific Grove, CA: Brooks/Cole.

Council for Accreditation of Counseling and Related Educational Programs (CACREP). (2016). *2016 CACREP standards.*

Ford, G. G. (1995). Teaching psychology students to reason ethically. Poster session presented at the annual meeting of the American Psychological Society, New York, NY.

Forrester-Miller, H. & Davis, T. (2016). *A practitioner's guide to ethical decision making.* Alexandria, VA: American Counseling Association.

Jourard, S. M., & Landsman, T. (1980). *Healthy personality* (4th ed.). New York: Macmillan.

Kitchener, K. S. (1984). Intuition, critical evaluation, and ethical principles: The foundation for ethical decisions in counseling psychology. *Counseling Psychologist, 12*(3), 43–55.

Kottler, J. A., & Brown, R. W. (2014). *Introduction to therapeutic counseling: Voices from the field* (8th ed.). Pacific Grove, CA: Brooks/Cole.

Skovholt, D. A. & Rivers, T. M. (2004). *Skills and strategies for the helping professions.* Denver, CO: Love Publishing.

Welfel, R. R. (2016). *Ethics in counseling and psychotherapy: Standards, research and emerging issues.* (6th ed.). Pacific Grove, CA: Brooks/Cole.

3

CLINICAL SUPERVISION
Developing a Collaborative Team

It was not until Jana received word that the pretrial diversion program had accepted her for internship that she realized how much she wanted to work there. She hoped to eventually seek employment as a federal probation officer, and the pretrial diversion program was just the sort of training experience she needed. Jana knew a great deal about the program because two of her friends completed internships there. She especially liked that she would be working with first-time offenders. She knew that second chances were rare in life, so helping offenders take advantage of this opportunity could be rewarding and challenging. If these clients successfully completed the program, their arrest records would be expunged or erased.

During the program orientation, Jana learned about the criminal justice system, office policies and procedures, and the counseling strategies that the staff identified as useful when working with offenders. Although it was all fascinating, it was also intimidating. Jana did not know Della, her assigned supervisor, and none of the other students Jana knew had ever worked with her. The idea of reporting to someone about whom she had almost no information became a source of concern. This person would be supervising her work, directing many of her activities, and evaluating her performance. Jana had no idea what to expect, and she was worried. At the same time, she trusted and liked her university practicum instructor, so his comments *about how good Della was as a supervisor provided some hope. There was a lot riding on this final component of Jana's training.*

Introduction

Jana's concerns about her supervisor are understandable. As we stressed in Chapter 1, advanced clinical courses function as a result of a collection of important relationships. This chapter explores arguably the most critical pair: the supervisor–supervisee relationship. In some clinical courses, there are at least two such relationships because you will have both a field-site supervisor and a faculty supervisor (course instructor). We will define supervision as well as identify the ethical and clinical boundaries of this relationship. And because supervision is a collaborative process, we include steps that you can take to improve your clinical, personal, and professional results.

Clinical training is the point where students rely heavily upon the professional relationships they have developed with professors and the relationships they will develop with site supervisors. A successful supervisor-supervisee relationship relies upon appropriate levels of openness and understanding. Teachers and students must work cooperatively for an extended period of time to develop this level of professional interdependence. If you already know and trust your assigned site supervisor the transition will be easier than if you are meeting the supervisor for the first time. Students appreciate the fact that they are entering this phase of their training with someone who taught them in other classes, may have provided academic advising and with whom they have had other professional contact. Faculty also appreciate the advantage of knowing the students they will be supervising and they recognize that an excellent way of assessing the effectiveness of their programs is by observing students in the final, clinical portion of their training. For these reasons, we especially enjoy working with our students as they complete practicum and internships. If you begin your supervised clinical experience with someone your have worked with previously, the learning curve is predictably steeper but accomplishable.

Supervisory relationships and experiences form novices into counselors and ensure an appropriate level of care to the clients with whom students work. Whenever we reflect on our own professional development, we first recall the cadre of supervisors who guided and supported our efforts at becoming a counselor. Mostly we were supervised by one person at a time, but one of us during a postdoctoral internship reported to five supervisors. Yet even the potentially frustrating situation of sorting through contradictory recommendations proved remarkably helpful. In the end, the tactical complications produced by multiple supervisors proved a minor inconvenience when measured against what was learned from the professional community these five experienced clinicians created. Indeed, skilled supervision is a precious and critical component of the counselor formation process.

Clinical Supervision

Defined

Bradley, Ladany, Hendricks, Whiting, and Rhode (2010) defined clinical supervision as:

> A didactic and interpersonal activity whereby the supervisor facilitates the provision of feedback to one or more supervisees. This feedback can pertain to the work in supervision, the supervisee(s), the supervisee's clients, or the supervisor, and can positively or negatively influence supervisee counselor competency and client outcome.
>
> (p. 3)

The definition identifies the relational aspects as well as the possible foci of supervision. It also notes the range of impact that supervision can have on supervisee development and client growth.

Bernard and Goodyear (2018) offered the following description as they sought to define supervision:

> An intervention provided by a more senior member of a profession to a more junior member or members of that same profession. This relationship is evaluative, extends over time, and has the simultaneous purposes of enhancing the professional functioning of the more junior person(s), monitoring the quality of professional services offered to the client(s) she, he or they see(s), and serving as a gatekeeper of those who are to enter the profession.
>
> (p. 6)

This definition reflects the ethical and clinical concerns that evolved with respect to counseling in general and clinical training specifically. The relationship between an experienced practitioner and a novice seeking to enter the profession must always address the student's need for experiences whereby he or she can develop requisite clinical skills and competencies while protecting the safety and well-being of his or her clients. Supervisors are ethically and legally responsible for the care of the supervisee's client, but their responsibilities also extend to their supervisees and to the counseling profession.

The definitions also surface the existence of a potentially problematic dual relationship. On the one hand, supervisors seek to enhance their charges' professional and personal growth, yet on the other hand, they must evaluate them and make judgments about their suitability as professionals. This suitability to the profession also includes an assessment of how psychologically healthy or safe it is for certain supervisees to provide mental health services to their clients. Offering counseling services to clients brings with it risks to the counselor's mental health and psychological well-being. Supervisors must occasionally intervene in ways that protect the student from such psychological risks or injuries.

Consider one supervisee who began working with a family where the father's drinking problem was negatively affecting everyone. This supervisee had experienced a similar problem in his own family of origin. On the one hand, his personal experiences could be invaluable to the family he was charged to help but on the other such a family posed personal and psychological risks. In this particular case the supervisee began to suffer psychological symptoms. He obtained personal counseling and he continued to work with the family. The outcome: He gained valuable insights about himself, resolved the internal conflict, and ended up helping the family in ways he never dreamed possible. The example illustrates that such "problems" are often resolved with positive results, especially when supervisory efforts are simultaneously augmented externally with effective counseling.

Supervision is a process with a broad scope of concerns and some of these concerns may tend to conflict with others. Supervision is a delicately balanced process. By recognizing the need to manage these complexities and identifying methods to do so, you will be in a better position to cooperate effectively. At this point in your training it should not be a surprise that we begin to manage these potential problems by establishing and maintaining the unique boundaries that differentiate supervisory, consulting, and counseling relationships.

Delineating Supervision, Consultation, and Counseling

Because the types of relationships formed and the goals of supervision, consultation, and counseling are different, confusing one for another or allowing one to shift into another will produce problems. You and your supervisors will need to understand the differences and consistently recognize the boundaries that differentiate each type. The distinction between supervision and consultation is easily made. In *supervision* the supervisor has ethical and legal responsibility for the client even though he or she is not directly treating the client. You work under supervision when you are a student, when you are completing required hours for licensure, and when you learn new techniques and procedures.

Consultation also relies upon interaction with an experienced clinician, but in contrast to supervision, the consultee retains sole responsibility for the client from ethical, legal, and clinical standpoints. Experienced counselors regularly use consultants to assess their clinical judgments and to ensure that clients are treated effectively and ethically. Consultants are expected to share the most up-to-date and sound information they possess and identify the limits of their knowledge. Licensed mental health professionals are expected to regularly consult with other professionals throughout the course of their professional lives. This type of consultation forms one of the pillars that define a community standard of treatment. Students are often surprised to learn that their supervisors, along with the cadre of trained counselors that work around them, regardless of how experienced they are, consistently consult with other trained counselors.

Although it is fairly simple to discriminate between supervision and counseling, erecting and maintaining the appropriate boundaries that prevent supervision from morphing into counseling can be complicated. During supervision, many of the supervisee's personal issues may arise. This is actually a desirable trend because surfacing such issues motivates us to (a) learn more about ourselves, (b) resolve our psychological struggles, and, in turn, (c) improve our ability to be helpful to others. But the supervisee's personal issues must be addressed in a counselor–client relationship, not in the supervisor–supervisee setting. So-called shifts to *counseling*, in which the supervisor becomes the counselor and the student becomes the client, are particularly worrisome and should always be avoided. Cautions against such a shift are couched in the restrictions that prohibit dual relationships. Being a teacher, a supervisor, and a counselor to the same person will produce conflicts. While a supervisee's desire to speak more deeply about a personal issue that is directly affecting the supervisee's ability to work effectively with his or her client may be greeted with interest by the supervisor, it must be referred to another setting where the supervisee can meet privately with a counselor. Since all supervisors are also counselors, they must remain vigilant to such boundary problems. They can easily develop clinical interests in their supervisees that will interrupt supervision. Such limits should be discussed early in the supervisor–supervisee relationship so that when even a minuscule erosion occurs, both parties will be prepared to identify the change and take appropriate corrective action.

So, what do you do when the supervisory relationship begins to slip into counseling? Ideally, both parties will be aware of the shift, but at a minimum it requires only one person to notice and bring it into the discussion. At this point, ethical supervisors will first focus on how the supervisee's behaviors impact the work with the client, instead of the more counseling-oriented behavior of delving into the personal issues that underlie the current behavior. If the supervisee is able to see the dynamics clearly, then work can continue to progress as usual. If the supervisee is struggling to explore from this perspective, or if the issues seem to be serious (awareness is not enough to hold the boundary), then a referral to personal counseling is warranted.

Goals of Supervision

Like most human endeavors, supervision works best with clearly defined goals whereby progress can be easily measured and correctives rapidly implemented. Bradley et al. (2010) summarized the three main goals of counseling supervision:

1. Facilitation of counselor professional and personal development
2. Promotion of counseling competencies
3. Promotion of accountable counseling services and programs.

(p. 6)

The transition from student to clinician requires success in all three areas. Counseling is a theoretically and ethically bound process that relies upon the proper use of a diverse collection of tools (skills, abilities, and attitudes) that reside within the counselor. Such broad-based goals are essential because client personalities and the struggles they confront differ markedly. The larger the skill set, the wider the range of clients you will be able help. Thus, you should expect supervision to improve your ability to make clinical sense of an ever-widening collection of client issues and to tailor your interventions by correctly selecting from the many skills that are available to you. Supervision helps you correctly negotiate the gaps between what you know, what you need to know, and what you should actually do as you respond to the challenge of clinical work.

Stages of Supervision

Because supervision is a relational process, it follows predictable stages that mirror what one would expect in the counseling relationship. For example, Beitman's (1987) stages of psychotherapy (engagement, pattern search, change, and termination) can be adapted to the supervisor–supervisee relationship, though the topics and focus would of course differ from those found in a counseling relationship. To begin with, engagement is no less important in the supervisory relationship, but the purpose of that relationship is different. A relationship bound by trust, respect, and a shared sense of purpose makes it possible for supervisees to discuss sensitive information that must be revealed if the supervisee is to improve. Absent a strong relationship, supervisees will be reluctant to talk about the embarrassing or difficult situations that often arise during counseling sessions. Imagine how difficult it might be for you to share information about a counseling session that you know contained errors in judgment or clinical interventions without some sense that you would be accepted, respected, and guided toward an appropriate resolution. Research (see, e.g., Barnes, 2004; Mehr, Ladany, & Caskie, 2010; Mehr, Ladany, & Caskie, 2015) shows that fear and shame associated with actual as well as presumed errors and concerns about being evaluated negatively consistently block trainees from disclosing as much as they should. Clients are not likely to speak about deeper or more embarrassing experiences if their level of engagement with their counselor is not sufficient with respect to trust, understanding, and confidence that the disclosure will be used productively. Supervisees will also avoid such discussion if they do not feel the relationship can properly manage the sensitive information and because they may fear that negative evaluations will jeopardize passing the course or, worse, being blocked from entering the counseling profession at all! It is not surprising that according to Ronnestad and Skovholt (1993):

> In supervision, the anxious student may tend to discuss in supervision only clients who show good progress, choose themes in which he or she is functioning well, or choose a mode of presenting data that allows full control over what the supervisor learns. For example, video or audio-taping may be resisted. This is a delicate area that demands tactful handling by the supervisor. Fortunately, this changes with increased experience.
>
> (p. 398)

The importance of the supervisor–supervisee relationship is further emphasized when you consider how much important information can be screened from the supervisor when supervisee fears and anxiety are not properly managed.

Ultimately, you can use Beitman's (1987) stages to assess the nature or level of your relationship with your supervisor and the stages of development to identify your level at any particular point in your clinical training. As we intimated earlier, it would be difficult, if not impossible, to achieve higher levels of professional development without a commensurate supervisor–supervisee relationship. For example, to traverse the change stage of the developmental process, the supervisory relationship would need to have evolved through the pattern search stage. At this level, the relationship would have developed enough trust and confidence to manage the anxieties that would interfere with exploring alternatives, assessing efficacy, and internalizing those that should be incorporated into an integrated personal approach.

Problems often arise when supervisor and supervisee try to accomplish a developmental task without having achieved the necessary relationship level. When this does happen, a quick assessment can guide both participants to a serviceable solution. If, for example, the student is trying to accomplish a developmental task that requires perhaps more "engagement" or "pattern search," the supervisor and supervisee can redeploy their efforts at enhancing the supervisory relationship (engagement) or developing more alternatives (pattern search) and then return to the developmental task. While we know that this may sound simplistic, in practice it really does work. Students will even use these exact terms during supervision meetings. An intern once responded to a recommendation made by a classmate by saying, "I need more pattern search before I commit to following the recommendation." The class knew what the student meant and immediately cooperated by offering additional patterns (in this case, treatment suggestions) and waiting for the student to find one that formed a better match.

Evaluation and Anxiety

Obtaining regular, clear, honest feedback about your progress is vital as you refine your diagnostic and treatment skills and as you work cooperatively with others. Unfortunately, this important element of training in supervision can also be a source of anxiety. Trainees want to do well, they want to safely help their clients, and they want their efforts to be seen positively by their peers and supervisors. While anxiety at appropriate levels is necessary to motivate change, excessive levels adversely affect performance. Such evaluation-related fear can result from the climate created by supervisors in the individual and group settings and they can result from an individual student's personal life history where evaluation was associated with harsh or painful outcomes. Personal counseling would most benefit the latter source while careful attention to the creation of a safe learning environment, focused on continuous improvement, would be most helpful for the former. Since the environment and the student are closely entwined, efforts at helping both sources may be needed.

A careful explanation of the evaluation process and clear examples of how inevitable difficulties will be remedied will help you to use the evaluation process to improve your work. In the next chapter we cover various evaluation methods and illustrate how these methods can be used to systematically improve outcomes and develop more effective strategies. For the most part, students look forward to the evaluation component because they see it as the most direct route to becoming skilled clinicians. Over time you will become increasingly comfortable with this component of your training, mostly because experiencing the process helps you to gain comfort with it. You realize sharing your concerns with others helps you to understand the depth of the issue with which you are struggling and once you implement the suggestions, the results are rewarding. Counselors are very much like clients in this respect. Clients are not likely to share their struggles if they feel there is little to gain from doing so. And counselors are understandably reluctant to discuss difficulties in their work with clients until they realize the benefit to doing so.

We honor this important concern about the value of assessment in the next chapter by illustrating the importance of both summative and formative evaluations and by stressing the importance formative evaluations. Summative assessments are familiar to all of us who have ever taken a midterm of final examination. Formative assessments, on the other hand, are evaluation tools used to guide students as they develop on a continuum toward mastery of a skill or theory. Such assessments simultaneously define an area of concern and strategies for improving. Their use is critical to successful supervision because they foster an environment that reduces fear and focuses on continuous improvement.

Bret, a first term intern, had been worried about his work with a new client, a woman that had been ordered into treatment because of a substance abuse problem. Bret watched as his classmates discussed their cases, all of whom seemed to be highly engaged and motivated to change. After talking to another student from his supervision site, an intern who was completing the last course in the sequence, he decided to share his concerns with his classmates during group supervision. His more experienced class mate shared that initially he had similar reservations but the results were so uniformly positive that he began to look forward to his supervision times. This more experienced intern felt that his concerns were always greeted with interest and understanding and perhaps more importantly, suggestions were useful and implementable. Apparently worries associated with being judged by others were far less painful than struggling with a clinical concern alone. Bret presented the case during a group supervision class. His supervisor explained that working with clients who are ordered into treatment included a very special set of issues that had not been covered in previous coursework. Armed with a couple of studies about counseling such clients, encouragement from other students in the class, and a promise to return next week with any additional concerns, Bret prepared for the next session. The outcome surprised him and it had a calming effect. Some anxiety persisted but he actually looked forward to his next supervision session. He now had a plan and he had support.

Supervision Processes

In your advanced clinical courses, you can expect to be supervised in individual, triadic, and group formats. The CACREP (2016) standards require a variety of these supervision modalities for advanced clinical students. The research literature supports the unique aspects and efficacy of each approach and each are valuable, and some supervision goals may be better achieved in one type over another (Borders et al., 2012; Carter, Enyedy, Goodyear, Arcinue, & Puri, 2009; Hein, Lawson, & Rodriguez, 2011; Lietz, 2008; Linton & Hedstrom, 2006).

Supervision sessions usually include case presentations, reviews of recorded (audio and video) sessions, reviews of verbatims (when recording is not permitted), general or specific emergent site or agency concerns, ethical or clinical emergencies, and topics of special interest (e.g., new techniques, counseling theory, community mental health concerns). Student presentations on these topics usually generate rich discussions that help clarify and expand the student's concerns and questions. The clearly defined issues can now be linked to clinical treatment alternatives. Group supervision has the advantage of a larger pool of people from which to draw suggestions, but individual supervision can also produce a rich collection of useful interventions, especially if supervisor and supervisee share the responsibility. Triadic supervision provides a nice middle ground between the two other approaches.

Since alternatives are useful only if they are implemented, the supervisory process explores why the student should make adjustments to the counseling process and how these alternatives could be carried out. It can be difficult to adjust your view of the client's issues and challenging to enact new clinical interventions. Simulations and role-playing exercises may be used at this point because they offer a serviceable model of specific options, and they can bring to the surface unanticipated client reactions that will need to be managed. For example, consider the case of a practicum student whose client does not allow him to speak. Each session is basically a monologue. Whenever the student does try to interrupt, the client quickly speaks louder and faster, blunting every effort to enter into a dialogue. During group supervision, the student is comforted by the unanimous support from classmates, all of whom confirm how difficult the client is to engage. The student also explains that it would feel very rude to interrupt the client with any more force than that which has not as yet worked. The student asks for answers to two specific questions. Why would people block a counselor from dialoguing with them? What should be done to interrupt this countertherapeutic situation? Group discussion not only helped the student understand that the client's undisclosed fears would be causing the engagement block but also produced several ways of confronting the client. A role-play exercise was the only other step that the student needed before being able to enter the new insight into the client's struggle and implement the confrontation. The exercise was repeated several times so that the student could practice responding to several client responses to being confronted.

The choice of how to carry out role plays and simulations should include student input. You may end up playing the part of your client, portraying the counselor while another student plays the role of the client, or simply observing while two other students assume the roles of counselor and client. No matter the format, this exchange of information is quite useful—it forms the content of supervision. But human encounters always create process concerns in addition to the content. These process concerns are equally important in supervision. Two such processes—*parallel process* and *countertransference*—are uniquely important in supervision. When properly managed, they enhance students' clinical skills.

Parallel Process

Parallel process occurs when a particular element of the counselor–client relationship replicates itself in the supervisor–supervisee relationship. This remarkable effect occurs frequently but can easily go undetected. Experienced supervisors train themselves to notice when parallel process events occur and to use the material the events create as they dialogue with their supervisees. Parallel process affords the supervisor an *in vivo* teaching tool that if properly managed can have a profound positive influence on their supervisees. We recall an incident not too many years ago in which a supervisee, while reviewing a case during group supervision, became noticeably frustrated with and demanding of the supervisor. He turned to the class and said, "I am getting nowhere with the people I am trying to help, and supervision is a waste of time!" The other students' nods of understanding seemed to calm him some, but the frustration was still palpable. One student asked him if he still wanted to discuss the case he had been scheduled to present. He said he did, composed himself a bit more, and began the case presentation. He offered the usual basic information about the client and then stated that "the client was very angry at" him. The client told him that he was not helping at all and demanded that he immediately become much more proactive in solving his problems for him or he would ask for another counselor. The student closed by saying that he did not know what to do, but he had to do something or he was going to "lose" the client.

Parallel process had been discussed earlier in the term, but the intensity of this supervisee's experience made it almost impossible to recognize. Such emotionally intense situations are common reasons why parallel process can be difficult for supervisees and supervisors to detect. In our real-life example, the supervisor also had difficulty identifying the parallel process because of his own emotional reaction to seemingly having failed his supervisee. The client's highly charged demand for answers and for someone to be responsible for him had fired through his counselor (the supervisee) and was making its way to the supervisor. Once the supervisor's own defensiveness subsided, he was able to correctly label the parallel process and invite the supervisee to join him as they worked their way through the concerns together and eventually back to a useful way of properly managing the client's issues. The successful resolution of this episode produced many desirable results. The supervisee left the session with a better understanding of his client, some strategies for increasing client responsibility and accountability, greater confidence in his ability to be helpful, and more willingness to identify and work through the next inevitable parallel process issue. Because the other members of the class vicariously experienced the parallel process concerns, they became more skilled at identifying and resolving them.

According to Borders & Leddick (1987), "[t]he 'reflection process' [Searles, 1955] refers to the supervisee unconsciously behaving like the client in an effort to communicate subtle client dynamics to the supervisor" (p. 44). The previous illustration, though not too subtle, is a good example of a "reflection process." However, the reflection process is not the only parallel process effect. According to Doehrman (1976), parallel process could also explain why some counselors assume the role of their supervisors when counseling their clients. More recently, research by Tracey, Bludworth, and Glidden-Tracey (2012) noted evidence that supervisees adopt the behavior of their clients in supervision and this often creates a pull for supervisors to move into the counselor role. Supervisors, if aware of the parallel process dynamics, can intervene with the supervisee in the way that would be most therapeutic for the client, as the supervisee is likely to soak up that response. The parallel process can be discussed later for maximum learning.

Being aware of parallel process is equally important because it can inadvertently interfere with your overall effectiveness with your client. A student who was confused about her client's psychological problems asked her supervisor for help in developing a good diagnosis and treatment plan for a particularly challenging client. Although the client was a new transfer to her, the client had been seen at the clinic for several years by various counselors but experienced only minor improvement in her condition. A rich discussion ensued, replete with important hypothetical explanations about the client's problems, conclusive diagnostic findings, and several potentially successful treatment plans. Unfortunately, the discussion between the supervisor and the supervisee was replicated when the counselor met with the client. On the recording, the pair sounded like two experienced professionals talking about someone they were about to help. Years of therapy made the client psychologically savvy enough to switch the counseling session to a consultation. Unearthing this parallel process produced many interesting and ultimately useful insights. The student realized that the client had actually participated in similar countertherapeutic encounters with previous counselors. Once the student understood her contribution to the parallel process, she successfully helped the client recognize and own her part in the problematic encounter. This parallel process encounter eventually paved the way for the student to help a client who had floundered in several previous attempts by other counselors.

As we have illustrated, during individual supervision, the supervisor's response will, to a great extent, determine whether the parallel process issues will be handled in a helpful or a problematic way. A supervisor who acts defensively will only increase the frustration levels and prolong the deleterious effects of the parallel process encounter. Working cooperatively, on the other hand, offers the supervisee a model for dealing more effectively with the client and a chance to learn more about himself or herself as a counselor. The onus for a successful outcome rests on the supervisor and his or her skills in managing encounters enriched by parallel process. We need also mention that group supervision offers the opportunity for other students to help detect and resolve parallel process concerns. Supervisors appreciate the value of multiple observers, so they encourage all members of the group to be sensitive to parallel process concerns whenever and with whomever they arise.

Countertransference

The tendency for clients to project feelings from another relationship in their life onto the counselor is legendary. But countertransference, the process of the counselor projecting onto the client, is an equally important clinical concern—one that is often identified and tended to by supervisors. Countertransference is not, in and of itself, a problem, but how you react to these feelings can be.

Consider an overly dependent client who in the course of a session asks the counselor a number of questions that urge the counselor to take responsibility for choices that should fall to the client. Assume also that the counselor, when confronted with these questions, unwittingly *reacts* in a directive and paternalistic way. In this example, the counselor "acts out" the countertransference, and as a result, the client experiences yet another unhealthy relationship where someone (in this case the counselor) jumps in and takes responsibility, eventually making choices that the client should have.

Unfortunately, in this example, countertransference directs the counselor's behavior. Had the counselor recognized the countertransferential feelings and talked them out instead of acted them out, the client would have benefited from the countertransference-propelled interaction. A more aware counselor would have told the client, "I know it would be wrong to do so, but for some reason I feel like I want to give you advice and make decisions for you." The client might have responded by saying, "You know, this happens to me a lot but no one has ever said that it was wrong to do so, like you just did." The client might even have asked the most therapeutic questions, "What do I do that invites people to criticize, direct, and take responsibility for me? Why do I do this? What can I do to change?" This example stresses the point that countertransference should not be avoided but rather should be carefully identified and diligently talked through with clients. Countertransference offers clients important clues to how they are perceived by others and where they may need to focus their energies. And, for the counselor, it can highlight personal concerns that may need to be addressed in the counselor's individual or group therapy.

Implementing Supervisory Suggestions

A portion of weekly supervision time should be allocated to discussions regarding the implementation of recommendations and suggestions. You should always be prepared to: (a) describe how you tailored your clinical efforts in light of what you learned during supervision, (b) discuss the steps you took to carry out recommendations, and (c) provide an assessment of how efficacious the changes actually were. You often have some latitude in how you carry out general suggestions, but you must also be prepared to act when a specific course of action is needed. There are situations in which you must carry out a specific set of instructions ordered by your site or faculty supervisor. For example, during a case presentation, your supervisor confirms that the information shared by your client meets the criteria for a compulsory report to child-abuse authorities. You would be expected to discuss your concerns, if any, about this course of action and then immediately carry out the request as is consistent with the agency or site policies. While you may feel uncomfortable about having to make the report or you may judge the situation as less severe and not warranting such a report, you are still required to proceed. Students sometimes respond to such feelings or thoughts by delaying action or ignoring what they have been told to do. When a student senses that this may be happening, and we know that it can hard to recognize, it is vitally important to discuss the reluctance immediately with a supervisor. We recall one case where a student had delayed acting for a full week. During the next group supervision, he revealed that he had not complied with the supervisor's request. He was directed to immediately leave class, report to the field site, obtain the client file, call in the report, and have the field supervisor call to confirm that all of the steps had been completed. Although supervision is normally a collaborative experience that produces alternative courses of action whereby students choose among the options, there are times when a prescribed set of steps must be followed.

Maximizing Supervision Effectiveness

Many students, and a surprising number of supervisors, take something of a passive stance with respect to supervision. Absent directions to do otherwise, students will often do little to prepare for supervision sessions. And supervisors may leave the responsibility of what will be discussed completely in the hands of the students, many of whom have not thought much about what they need from the process and how they plan to go about getting this help. Students may also lose sight of the fact that there are steps that they can personally take to reduce heightened levels of fear and anxiety that can adversely affect their participation. With the potential for these problematic situations to occur, we offer several strategies that you can use to ensure that your supervisory experiences deliver all that you want and need from them. Beinart (2003) offers the following useful suggestions:

> Supervisees need to take responsibility for taking an active part in supervision. This involves playing a part in a collaborative relationship, showing interest and enthusiasm, identifying needs clearly, arriving at a supervision meeting properly prepared having thought through issues and priorities, being open and receptive to feedback and being prepared to give clear and honest feedback to the supervisor. It is not helpful when supervisees fail to raise issues that they are struggling with, get defensive when offered feedback or do not take the advice of their supervisor without good reason or discussion.
>
> (p. 50)

The author's recommendations can be converted into action once you understand the forces that affect supervision and identify the methods and strategies that must be implemented. These suggestions not only improve the amount and quality of information shared, but they also positively affect the process and enhance the supervisor–supervisee relationship. We suggest a protocol for planning out your specific supervision experiences as well as methods for managing the anxiety that inhibits professional growth and eventually developing requisite levels of self efficacy.

Box 3.1 What are you looking for in a supervisee? Our perspectives

Dr. Fall: I see supervision as a collaborative relationship, so I want supervisees who are willing to take responsibility for their growth process. Unlike coursework where I, as the professor, am primarily responsible for creating the class, imparting information and evaluating learning, advanced clinical courses represent a shift in the learning environment. This shift is characterized by a focus on relationships as the agent of change. In supervision, I want supervisees to be aware of our developing relationship and participate in that process by being willing to share meaningful aspects of their work, both positive and areas for growth. I think supervisees should set the agenda for supervision sessions and identify what they want to get out of our meetings.

Dr. Levitov: Ideal supervisees should exhibit several important traits. Not only a basic understanding of counseling ethics but an enthusiasm for exploring ethical issues coupled with a willingness to take any necessary steps to carry out an ethical course of conduct collectively form one pillar found in an ideal supervisee. Empathy for and a willingness to understand others and their life struggles forms yet another pillar. Such empathy and understanding should also extend to counseling classmates and coworkers. A basic knowledge of counseling theory and a willingness to more deeply explore a range of treatment options forms yet another pillar. Finally, supervisees should also be willing to explore the influence their own lives may play in their efforts to successfully help others. These traits are equally important and essential to success in clinical training.

This about your own development. How close are you to the ideal expressed in these perspectives?

Planning for Supervision

Perhaps the best way to prepare for supervision is to follow a protocol that directs you to answer a number of important clinical questions about the client and the course of treatment. Preparing these responses will ensure that you will be able to deliver the prerequisite information that your supervisors and classmates will need if they are going to be helpful to you. And as you prepare the case material, you will also be able to more accurately identify the questions to which you will be seeking answers during supervision. This level of preparation includes properly formed and focused clinical questions and the ability to share a sufficient amount of background information. You and your audience will be in a much better position to explore the concerns and make good recommendations.

Box 3.2 is an example of a case presentation form that may be used to organize pertinent case information. There are many types of case presentation forms and supporting documents. Box 3.2 should be treated as a draft document because you will need to modify it to meet your specific site and supervision needs. You should also feel free to add other sources of information (e.g., genograms, test results, therapy summaries) that you deem helpful, in formats that honor confidentiality concerns. The best way to prepare good materials is to carefully anticipate what you will be asked and what you will want to know. Most students become efficient after preparing only a few consultations.

Box 3.2. Sample case presentation form

Name:_____ Date of presentation:_____

Name or Client ID:_____ Date of session:_____

Type of presentation (Circle one):
Audiotape   Videotape   Written Verbatim   Written Case Presentation

Presenting concern(s) bringing client to counseling (in client's words):
_____
_____

Your theoretical orientation: _____

Your perception of the client's concerns based upon your theoretical orientation:
_____
_____

Client's identified counseling goals:
1._____
2._____
3._____
4._____

Number of times client has been seen:_____

Relevant clinical history and background (Attach a genogram for family issues):

_____

_____

_____

_____

Diagnosis:

_____

_____

Perceived strengths and resources:

_____

_____

_____

Specific issues and questions to be discussed in supervision:

1._____

2._____

3._____

4._____

Recommendations suggested during supervision:

1._____

2._____

3._____

4._____

Changes implemented and assessment of effectiveness:

Useful (y/n)

1._____

2._____

3._____

4._____

Follow-up questions:

1._____

2._____

3._____

4._____

Counselor Self-Efficacy

Counselor self-efficacy (CSE), as described by Barnes (2004), forms the final goal for students working under supervision. CSE is defined by Larson and Daniels (1998) as "one's belief or judgments about her or his capabilities to effectively counsel a client in the near future" (p. 180). A series of effective counseling experiences, support from supervisors, an enlarged pool of counseling skills, varied opportunities to make and evaluate clinical judgments, knowing and applying protocols (e.g., suicide assessment, child abuse assessment), and useful formative evaluations combine to increase levels of CSE.

CSE is important for two reasons. First, CSE helps students evolve through the developmental stages of counselor growth. Second, advanced clinical students who have higher levels of CSE can integrate evaluative information more effectively (Barnes, 2004; Larson and Daniels, 1998), have greater positive client outcomes (Bakar, Zakaria, & Mohamed, 2011), and manage anxiety more effectively, (Lent et al., 2009). The question is not whether CSE is vital to your growth as a counselor, but how you can capitalize on all of your clinical and educational experiences in order to maximize your CSE potential while in graduate school.

CSE plays a significant role in supervision and the extent to which you will be able to use the wealth of information that supervision produces. Ikonomopoulos, Vela, Smith, and Dell'Aquila, (2016) demonstrated that combining direct counseling services and quality supervision experiences increases CSE, which is great news, as you should be experiencing all three in your advanced clinical courses. You can do a great deal to increase CSE by identifying what you specifically need to build your confidence in working with clients and describing how you will obtain it. Supervisors appreciate supervisees who have thought their way through these questions and who have some idea of what would be helpful for them.

Since developing CSE has risks attached to it, there are steps that supervisors can take to help students more safely expose themselves to the situations that develop CSE. According to Barnes (2004):

> Modeling an appreciation for constructive feedback, or observations of strengths and areas in need of continued growth, is important to facilitating trainee self-reflection. This can be accomplished by establishing a collaborative environment in which the supervisor or counselor educator seeks constructive feedback from the trainee about his or her experiences in supervision or training during each session.
>
> (p. 63)

This type of modeling guides students by introducing a common style of communicating as they share and integrate feedback. While being able to communicate productively with supervisors and other clinicians is essential during clinical training, your need for these skills will persist throughout your life as a mental health professional. Consultation and supervision require that you communicate with professionals and integrate what you learn in essentially the same way.

Della had supervised many internships during her 15-year tenure in the program. She appreciated Jana's enthusiasm, knowing that it would carry her through challenges she would soon face. Della also knew that she would have to support, understand, and encourage Jana if their supervisor–supervisee relationship was going to form the foundation for the positive clinical outcomes that they both anticipated.

Della and Jana met about a week after orientation for the first of many weekly supervision sessions. Della explained how important it would be for Jana to feel comfortable discussing all aspects of her work in the program. She told Jana that creating a climate of openness would be a responsibility shared by both of them. Della told Jana that she would also have to rely upon her to provide feedback concerning how effective the supervision sessions were and identifying areas that might need improvement. Della closed by telling Jana that she hoped that they would be able to form something called "a professional community." Della defined the term to mean a collection of professionals, all of whom are focused on self-improvement and share the common goal of delivering quality and ethical care to clients. She emphasized the need for mutual respect and understanding coupled with a willingness to confront difficulties and resolve differences. This type of working relationship, formed from optimism and encouragement, would be a unique opportunity for Jana. Della's introduction reduced Jana's anxiety and buoyed her spirits. She felt confident that their working relationship would be able to resolve the inevitable difficulties, improve her skills as a counselor, and introduce her to a profession where consulting with other professionals will continue throughout her career.

Summary

Supervision is a process that is based upon a clearly defined and well-bounded relationship between a supervisor and one or more supervisees. Because there are risks associated with novices providing treatment, supervisors assume an impressive range of responsibilities. They are responsible not only for their supervisees but also for their supervisees' clients. And supervisors are responsible to the counseling profession. They are expected to make decisions and to act in the interest of the client, the supervisee, and the profession. In the last case, supervisors may be seen as "gatekeepers," individuals who seek to ensure that only competent clinicians are allowed to enter the ranks of the profession.

Supervision is a relationship that follows predictable stages and needs to be properly cultivated. It is also a relationship that if not properly managed can erode into counseling. Students and supervisors risk serious problems if such a dual relationship occurs. When effective, supervision helps manage fear and anxiety, and it offers new ways of understanding clients, treatment alternatives, a source of very useful evaluative information, and a setting in which to openly discuss a range of professional topics (e.g., ethics, counseling theory, research).

As a participant in the process, you can do a great deal to improve outcomes. You can carefully prepare for all of the events in which you participate during clinical training. A shared sense of responsibility helps, as does a willingness to be open, involved, and engaged. You can train yourself to be an active participant by managing fears and anxieties, learning about parallel process, studying the effects of countertransference, modifying the supervision form to meet your particular needs, and being an active participant. Supervision is a precious opportunity for growth, and there is much that you can do to enhance your involvement in it.

Reflection Questions

1. What steps would you take to ensure that a supervisory relationship did not become a counseling relationship?
2. What behaviors might you see in yourself if you were at the "counselor stance" level of development?
3. What steps could you take to ensure that you would be able to benefit from evaluations and assessments of your work as a clinician?
4. What would be appropriate fears or anxieties for students about to begin their clinical training?
5. How could you tell if levels of anxiety had increased to the point that they would affect your work? What would you do?
6. What will you do to ensure that you receive the maximum benefit from your practicum or internship?
7. Who would you talk to and what would you say if you felt that there were problems with the quality and type of supervision you were receiving?

References

Bakar, A. R., Zakaria, N. S., & Mohamed, S. (2011). Malaysian counselors' self-efficacy: Implication for career counseling. *The International Journal of Business and Management, 6*, 141–147.

Barnes, K. L. (2004). Applying self-efficacy theory to counselor training: A comparison of two approaches. *Counselor Education and Supervision, 44*, 56–69.

Beinart, H. (2003). Models of supervision and the supervisory relationship and their evidence base. In I. Fleming & L. Steen (Eds), *Supervision and clinical psychology: Theory, practice and perspectives* (pp. 36–50). Hove: Brunner-Routledge.

Beitman, B. D. (1987). *The structure of individual psychotherapy.* New York: Guilford.

Bernard, J. M., & Goodyear, R. G. (2018). *Fundamentals of clinical supervision* (6th ed.). New York: Pearson.

Borders, L. D., Welfare, L. E., Greason, P. B., Paladino, D. A., Mobley, A. K., Villalba, J. A., & Wester, K. L. (2012). Individual and triadic and group: Supervisee and supervisor perceptions of each modality. *Counselor Education and Supervision, 51*(4), 281–295.

Borders, L. D., & Leddick, G. R. (1987). *Handbook of counseling supervision*. Alexandria, VA: Association for Counselor Education & Supervision.

Bradley, L. J., Ladany, N., Hendricks, B., Whiting, P. P., & Rhode, K. (2010). Overview of counseling supervision. In N. Ladany and L. J. Bradley (Eds.), *Counselor Supervision* (4th ed, pp. 3–13). New York: Routledge.

Council for Accreditation of Counseling and Related Educational Programs (CACREP). (2016). *2016 CACREP standards*.

Carter, J. W., Enyedy, K. C., Goodyear, R. K., Arcinue, F., & Puri, N. N. (2009). Concept mapping of the events supervisees find helpful in group supervision. *Training And Education in Professional Psychology, 3*(1), 1–9.

Doehrman, M. J. (1976). Parallel processes in supervision and psychotherapy. *Bulletin of the Menninger Clinic, 40,* 1–104.

Hein, S. F., Lawson, G., & Rodriguez, C. (2011). Supervisee compatibility and its influence on triadic supervision: An examination of doctoral student supervisors' perspectives. *Counselor Education and Supervision, 50,* 422–436.

Ikonomopoulos, J., Vela, J. C., Smith, W. D., & Dell'Aquila, J. (2016). Examining the practicum experience to increase counseling students' self-efficacy. *Professional Counselor, 6*(2), 161–173.

Larson, L. M., & Daniels, J. A. (1998). Review of the counseling self-efficacy literature. *Counseling Psychologist, 26,* 179–218.

Lent, R. W., Cinamon, R. G., Bryan, N. A., Jezzi, M. M., Martin, H. M., & Lim, R. (2009). Perceived sources of changes in trainees' self-efficacy beliefs. *Psychotherapy: Theory, Research, Practice, Training, 46,* 317–327.

Lietz, C. A. (2008). Implementation of Group Supervision in Child Welfare: Findings from Arizona's Supervision Circle Project. *Child Welfare, 87*(6), 31–48.

Linton, J. M., & Hedstrom, S. M. (2006). An Exploratory Qualitative Investigation of Group Processes in Group Supervision: Perceptions of Masters-Level Practicum Students. *Journal for Specialists in Group Work, 31*(1), 51–72.

Mehr, K. E., Ladany, N., & Caskie, G. I. L. (2010). Trainee nondisclosure in supervision: What are they not telling you? *Counselling & Psychotherapy Research, 10,* 103–113.

Mehr, K. E., Ladany, N., & Caskie, G. L. (2015). Factors influencing trainee willingness to disclose in supervision. *Training and Education in Professional Psychology, 9*(1), 44–51.

Ronnestad, M. H., & Skovholt, T. M. (1993). Supervision of beginning and advanced graduate students of counseling and psychotherapy. *Journal of Counseling & Development, 71*, 396–405.

Searles, H. F. (1955). The informational value of the supervisor's emotional experiences. *Psychiatry: Journal for the Study of Interpersonal Processes, 18*, 135–146.

Tracey, T. G., Bludworth, J., & Glidden-Tracey, C. E. (2012). Are there parallel processes in psychotherapy supervision? An empirical examination. *Psychotherapy, 49*(3), 330–343.

4

AM I DOING THIS RIGHT? FORMATIVE AND SUMMATIVE ASSESSMENT

Dylan's internship site provided services to individuals with substance abuse problems. Several months' worth of successful interventions improved Dylan's confidence and increased comfort levels with his clients. Unfortunately, his very first client, after several months of successful work on a long-standing substance abuse problem, telephoned him to let him know that he had begun to experience an unexpected and worrisome return of the same symptoms that originally brought him into counseling. Though Dylan knew that such relapses are especially common in substance abuse treatment, he was still worried. He was also uncertain about how to approach his client in light of this new information. At the beginning of their next counseling session, only a day or two after the phone call, the client opened with, "I'm slipping, but this time I know what to do: I have to return to the same basics that we spoke of when I first came into counseling!" Surprised that he had so quickly come to rely on the products of the counseling relationship, Dylan asked him what specifically he meant by the comment.

He answered without hesitation; he had been mulling over options for a while. He offered the following steps:

1. Attend at least three AA meetings per week
2. Contact his sponsor daily
3. Return to complete his unfinished "third step"
4. Reassess his progress in counseling
5. Channel unproductive worry and anxiety into actions that would benefit his long-term goal of sobriety

This level of problem-solving arose in stark contrast to the chaos and uncertainty with which he presented when first entering counseling. Dylan realized that his client's decision-making was no longer clouded. Actions were no longer hampered by the gridlock that forms from anxiety, uncertainty, and an inability to identify useful alternatives. Dylan recognized that his client could now not only sense when things were beginning to move in an undesirable direction but also identify and implement steps to improve his situation. This client had developed an effective system that he could activate on his own. The client reported that confidence and hopefulness now replaced his crippling fears because he now had an effective way to recognize when something was wrong, and he even knew what to do about it.

Introduction

The example offers you two valuable messages: We cannot fix what we cannot see, and we will not see that which we do not believe can be fixed. These points are equally important to you as a counseling student. You will, if you are not already, be making a number of key decisions about your professional future. To make good choices you will need to acquire accurate information, accept criticism, and act on what you learn. These skills are vital as you make decisions ranging from where you choose to complete your practicum or internship to determining your effectiveness as a counselor and isolating specific areas where improvement is needed. Throughout your professional life you will be expected to regularly assess the quality of your work and develop effective ways of ensuring that you are delivering services that meet acceptable standards of treatment. Knowing and using evaluation and assessment skills can prepare you for the professional journey of improving yourself and your ability to be helpful to the clients you serve.

Having spent so much time in schools and colleges, you understand how motivated people can be to obtain good evaluations (e.g., grades), how difficult it may be to be open to criticism, and how valuable positive and negative observations can be to your personal growth. As a counseling student, you may also recognize the existence of internal forces that inhibit people from being able to attend to and process information that they may perceive as threatening to their self-concept or self-worth. These so-called defense mechanisms affect all human beings to some extent. At one extreme, heavily defended people cannot process anything that is contrary to their self-perception. Their chances of benefiting from criticism are seriously impaired. This depth of self-protection would make it difficult, if not impossible, to successfully complete clinical training. Clinical training demands a much greater level of vulnerability than participation in content courses.

It is no surprise that *evaluation* and *assessment* are terms that many people greet with feelings of uneasiness and defensiveness. In an attempt to ease these predictable defensive reactions and improve the chances that students will be able to hear and act upon appropriate concerns, we often focus more on what can be done to improve instead of fixating on the deficiency.

We encountered this valuable approach while one of us was serving on a team that was preparing materials for a university-wide accreditation process. We on the team knew, going into the assessment, that there were deficiencies. We also knew that being defensive about them was not going to improve our situation and that a rigid stance would only worsen the situation. Early in the meeting, one member of the team openly shared the dimensions of the problem with the assessment group. The assessment group leader thought for a moment and then said: "We are not as concerned with the deficiency as we are with what you are doing to remedy it." We had been working on the resolution for some time, so the discussion immediately moved to the correctives and what we expected to happen once all the changes were implemented. Though this example refers to an organizational problem, you can be equally effective by employing the same problem-solving approach to help yourself and your clients. It honors the existence of areas where improvement is needed but does not stall at the point where the potential to tumble into unproductive defensiveness is highest. We have encountered this reality in both clinical settings and organizations and concluded that to be able to improve, we must visit our deficiencies, but we must be careful not to unproductively dwell there.

Our practical approach links assessment, information verification, identification of alternatives, establishment of priorities, and measurement of the overall effectiveness of problem-solving efforts into an organized system. The model draws upon several recognized paradigms: *institutional effectiveness* (IE) and *outcomes assessment* (OA) (Nichols, 1991). These two systems establish and evaluate personal and organizational goals through *total quality management* (TQM) to create an organizational climate that fosters *continuous improvement* (Deming, 1986). Deming defined 14 steps that organizations must follow to achieve their goals. Four of these steps are particularly applicable to successful counselor formation. Offered in paraphrased form, they are:

1. Create constancy of purpose toward improvement.
2. Improve constantly and forever.
3. Drive out fear.
4. Institute education and self-improvement.

The combination of paradigms offers a model that is entirely consistent with the training of counseling students and the work of counselors in general.

While business management literature may seem an unlikely place from which to acquire theoretical models for helping counseling students maximize gains from experiential clinical training, TQM principles are actually quite applicable to mental health service agencies as well as to individual mental health professionals like you. OA coupled with select elements of TQM produces reliable methods to assess institutional and individual strengths and weaknesses, identify alternatives, create environments that are conducive to productive change, and ultimately assess outcomes. TQM recognizes the importance of the individual to the system and recognizes that any change must be supported by the entire organization if it is going to improve.

Institutional Effectiveness and Outcomes Assessment

Since the late 1980s, academic settings of all kinds have come to rely upon IE and OA methods to assess and improve quality (Nichols, 1991). This change in methodology was considered a landmark event because assessment efforts moved from questions about what academic institutions provided to students (and to what extent), to questions of whether the desired results (outcomes) were actually being achieved. To accomplish this paradigm shift, institutions were first required to develop comprehensive mission statements. These mission statements were then translated into a number of highly specific goals. Finally, each goal was further defined by the creation of one or more measurable outcome objectives. The process of developing mission statements, goals, and outcome objectives is repeated in each academic and administrative unit of the institution, all of which must be aligned with the university-wide mission statement. The approach emphasizes the need for a high level of specificity and "measurable" outcome objectives.

IE and OA, though usually applied to academic settings, can easily be adapted to assess centers that offer mental health services and mental health training as well as to individual mental health service providers. As a student engaged in clinical training, you will find that the process of identifying an overall mission, specifying related goals, and creating measurable outcome objectives can help focus and direct your efforts to improve your clinical skills.

A realistic mission statement for an internship student, completing a community counseling program, might read as follows:

> Through participation in a range of supervised clinical experiences I seek a level of proficiency that ensures that all clients in my care receive ethical and effective treatment. I recognize the need for supervision and look forward to full and open participation in a consultative process that will, in varying forms, span my career as a counselor. I expect to synthesize all elements of clinical training so that I can form a professional identity and adopt a professional demeanor that is consistent with existing standards for community counselors.

As we mentioned earlier, the mission statement becomes the genesis for a number of goals. To illustrate, we have slightly modified the CACREP Knowledge and Skill Requirements for Community Counselors into clinical training goals that correspond to the previously noted mission statement. Additionally, we have included one or more sample outcome objectives for each of the goals. We understand that you and your professors might develop goals and objectives that are different from those listed here. Such differences are completely understandable because community counseling is a broad field where no single or universal set of priorities exists. Our only purpose here is to offer an example of goals and outcome objectives on which to base a discussion of how models of assessment can be usefully applied.

Goals and Sample Outcome Objectives

1. Become familiar with typical characteristics of individuals and communities served by a variety of institutions and agencies that offer community counseling services;

   1.1 Describe the characteristics of the individuals served at your proposed or current field site.
   1.2 Identify one or more agencies that provide services to a similar population.

2. Know and be able to apply models, methods, and principles of program development and service delivery for a clientele based on assumptions of human and organizational development, including prevention, implementation of support groups, peer facilitation training, parent education, career/occupational information and counseling, and encouragement of self-help;

   2.1 Correctly identify a client's level of human and organizational development.
   2.2 Properly apply delivery systems that are deemed appropriate to the client's needs.
   2.3 Correctly assess the effectiveness of the system and make recommendations accordingly.

3. Implement effective strategies for promoting client understanding of and access to community resources;

   3.1 Identify at least three community resources that would be helpful to a particular client.
   3.2 Offer the options to the client by the use of a clinical approach that ensures the greatest likelihood that the client will acquire the community resource.

4. Know and be able to apply principles and models of biopsychosocial assessment, case conceptualization, theories of human development, and concepts of normalcy and psychopathology leading to diagnoses and appropriate counseling plans;

    4.1 Correctly conceptualize the client by identifying his or her stage(s) of development, level of psychopathology, social concerns, vocational issues, and areas of identified strengths.
    4.2 Develop and implement a treatment plan that improves the client's biopsychosocial condition.

5. Know and be able to apply the principles of diagnosis and the use of current diagnostic tools, including the current edition of the *Diagnostic and Statistical Manual*;

    5.1 Offer a correct diagnosis for the client.
    5.2 Demonstrate the combined use of interview, psychological test, and consultation information in making the diagnosis.
    5.3 Offer at least one additional diagnostic explanation for the client's condition.

6. Develop effective strategies for client advocacy in public policy and other matters of equity and accessibility;

    6.1 Identify at least three areas where improvements in equity and accessibility could be made within the agency or school.
    6.2 With permission and supervision, implement one of the noted improvements.
    6.3 Correctly assess the effect of the change.

7. Apply appropriate individual, couple, family, group, and systems modalities for initiating, maintaining, and terminating counseling, including the use of crisis intervention and brief, intermediate, and long-term approaches.

    7.1 Correctly identify an appropriate treatment for the client.
    7.2 Provide an acceptable rationale for the treatment choice.
    7.3 Identify expected therapeutic milestones.
    7.4 Demonstrate the ability to shift approaches when conditions warrant a change (e.g., moving to a crisis intervention approach from an intermediate therapy approach following the death of the client's spouse).

7.5 Correctly assess the effectiveness of the intervention or mode of treatment selected.

7.6 Correctly identify alternative approaches that may be needed if a predictable change occurs in the client's life (e.g. the diagnosis of a serious health problem following symptoms that were not initially considered life-threatening at the time the therapy began).

7.7 Correctly assess the efficacy of the change.

(Adapted from CACREP Standards, Section C; Knowledge and Skill Requirements for Community Counselors)

An in-depth discussion of the preceding goals and objectives would be our first choice for a beneficial exercise. Of course, we will have to leave that activity to you and to those with whom you are training. On the other hand, we can use the matrix to make some observations that will help clarify the assessment issues that form the focus of this chapter. The first and perhaps most important conclusion that emerges from a review of the sample outcome objectives is the fact that for the most part, subjective criteria form the basis for determining whether a particular objective is met. Although more-objective criteria might be desirable, according to Bernard and Goodyear (1992), "our profession is plagued with a certain degree of ambiguity that limits us as evaluators . . . We are still unsure about what in therapy is therapeutic" (p. 106). Thus, clearly defined conclusions about what is right and what is wrong, what works and what does not, become difficult to glean. Counselors are faced with alternatives that must be weighed, actively discussed, and continuously assessed. Whereas experienced counselors may find this reality inspiring, you may find it troubling. Such subjectivity can produce levels of uncertainty about how best to help your clients and worries about what you specifically may need to do to successfully complete your clinical training.

The review of the objectives offers one other conclusion. To be effective, you will need to manage an impressive range of responsibilities, be able to apply the information you have learned, and acquire many new skills. Stated from an educational perspective, you will achieve a level of mastery that spans all of the categories that form Bloom's taxonomy: knowledge, comprehension, application, analysis, synthesis, and evaluation (see Bloom, 1984; Bloom, Englehart, Furst, Hill, & Krathwohl, 1956). Abilities in each category of the taxonomy are vital to the task of helping supervisors teach students to translate theory into effective clinical practice. (For a more detailed discussion, see Granello, 2000). Table 4.1 offers examples of the skills associated with each of the categories of the taxonomy. It illustrates the range of cognitive abilities required for clinical practice.

If the evaluation of clinical training poses unique challenges, what methods should be used to properly manage what J. Bernard and Goodyear (1992) refer to as "the burden of evaluation" (p. 106)? The most basic answer to this question is to (a) rely upon a model that uses formative rather than summative evaluation and (b) create working and learning

Table 4.1 Counseling Skills Across Bloom's Taxonomy

Bloom's Categories	Skills	Examples
Knowledge	What When Name	Recall of information related to client or case
	List Define	Knowledge of core classroom-based information
Understanding	Summarize Describe Why	Summarize facts related to the case
	Paraphrase Interpret	Predict consequences of interventions
		Show comprehension of importance of data collection
Application	Apply Demonstrate Construct	Use research to make clinical decisions and decide on interventions
	Interpret Practice	Apply theories to current cases Problem solve difficult client issues
Analysis	Analyze Classify	Identify patterns of behavior in clients
	Compare Contrast Experiment	Identify parts of client history that are relevant to presenting problem
		Compare and contrast similar interventions with different clients

Bloom's Categories	Skills	Examples
Synthesis	Create Combine Integrate Design	Combine information from different academic courses to apply to real-world problems
	Generalize Hypothesize Construct	Conceptualize case, bringing together all relevant information
	Summarize	Design an intervention that uses all of the client's resources
Evaluate	Appraise Assess	Articulate a rationale for interventions
	Defend Evaluate Recommend	Assess the value or significance of a particular theory or intervention
	Critique	Make choices based on reasoned arguments

Note. Adapted from Granello (2000).

environments that manage fear, encourage self-assessment, and foster continuous improvement as an overarching goal.

Formative and Summative Evaluations

Educators make choices about which type of evaluation to employ by determining which one is more suitable to the material being taught and by defining the overarching goal of the assessment. According to Royse, Thyer, Padgett, and Logan (2006), "[f]ormative evaluations are employed to adjust and enhance interventions" (p. 116). On the other hand, summative evaluation is "evaluation designed to present conclusions about the merit or worth of an object and recommendations about whether it should be retained, altered, or eliminated" (Joint Commission on Standards for Educational Evaluation, 1981, p. 156). One common example of a summative evaluation is the final grade in a course. Summative evaluations, though clearly unavoidable, are much less useful to you at this stage of your training assuming you define usefulness as the extent to which assessment information can be used to identify deficiencies and illustrate specific ways in which you can improve.

Within the context of student clinical training, formative evaluation offers many important advantages. With a focus on adjusting and enhancing interventions, you can easily see the value of a process that establishes a continuous loop in which evaluation information guides decision-making, development of serviceable alternatives, implementation of treatments, and assessment of effectiveness. Relying upon formative evaluation techniques will not, by itself, ensure successful acquisition of clinical skills. Subjective assessments, the complexity of the material that must be mastered, and the challenge of properly caring for a client as you learn, cause emotional reactions that can blunt your efforts to develop into a skilled counselor.

Total Quality Management

When individuals are afraid, they are unable to experience other feelings, motivation diminishes, creativity decreases, and problem-solving skills are impaired. The effect of fear is universal—it is individually and collectively stifling. The management of fear is obviously an important and common counseling initiative, so why seek suggestions from a seemingly unrelated management initiative like TQM? The answer is that TQM deals with the issue of fear in a practical way; it recognizes how reliance upon shared goals and objectives can reduce the fears that hamper success, and it endorses the concept of continuous improvement. According to Suarez (1993), "The elimination of fear is necessary to create an environment of trust and cooperation, essential ingredients to initiating and sustaining a total quality effort, pursuing continuous improvement, encouraging innovation" (p. 1). Dr. W. Edwards Deming (1986) not only identified the management of fear as a fundamental requirement but also placed the responsibility for locating and correcting sources of fear squarely on the shoulders of managers and supervisors.

Since communication is such a central part of clinical training, Suarez's (1993) conclusion about the trust that can replace fear in the workplace is particularly applicable: "In general, the higher the trust, the more open the communication, and the more stable and predictable the cooperation.

On the other hand, low trust leads to uncertainty and defensive behaviors" (p. 63). Because uncertainty and the likelihood for defensiveness are already high given the training task and the setting where interns and practicum students work, methods for managing both are vital. In summary, TQM principles aid clinical training efforts because they:

- direct professors and site supervisors to recognize the importance of a shared vision for training that includes mission, goals, and objectives
- direct those who are responsible for training to bear the responsibility for managing fear within the work setting and the classroom
- foster a climate of continuous improvement

Once a mission, goals, and objectives are agreed upon and supervisors have assumed their responsibilities (e.g., reducing fear and guidance), practicum and internship students face the task of continuous improvement. This task relies heavily upon knowing and properly employing assessment and evaluation tools. How you obtain information, how you verify its integrity, how you apply it, and how well you understand potential blocks to obtaining such information become central to learning.

Sources of Evaluation Information

As a counseling intern working with clients, you rely upon many sources of evaluation information. The intake interview is arguably the most basic, important, and widely used tool at your disposal. When clients share their inner experience, we become privy to the unique patterns that form and maintain the person we are trying to assist. The client's history, assumptions about the world, feelings, concerns, and perceived strengths and weaknesses are all essential requirements for any enterprise focused on helping someone make important life changes. You would be lost and unable to help without this critical information the client provides. At the same time, you also have the advantage of obtaining information from additional sources. Psychological, vocational, and academic testing can often identify important aspects of the client's life that are not as easily or directly obtained from interviews. Finally, information gained from others' experience of the client can also be incorporated as you complete the picture that forms from the constellation of evaluative information about the client.

As a practicum or internship student enrolled in a graduate program, you will have access to many similar sources of evaluation information in seeking information about your own skills and abilities. Assessment information obtained from various types of tests, supervisors and professors, peers, clients, and yourself can be used in combination to help you develop strategies to accomplish your goals, assess your progress, improve your clinical skills, and make wise career decisions.

Tests and Assessments

Just as various test instruments exist to aid clients, similar tools are available to help practicum and internship students. As OA worked its way through schools and colleges, a wide range of outcome instruments developed. Multiple examples of such tools can be found on the World Wide Web by completing searches for "client satisfaction surveys." Supervisor assessment forms as well as students' assessments of their supervisors can also be found in the same way. These forms are regularly updated so searches should be repeated with some frequency.

The clinical use of testing emphasizes the mechanics of test construction, norming information, and the conditions under which tests should be administered. As a graduate student who has taken at least one measurement and assessment course, you realize the importance of establishing reliability and validity for any measurement or assessment effort. Both concepts are easily defined. *Reliability* refers to the extent to which tests measure consistently. *Validity* refers to the extent to which a test measures what it purports to measure. According to Henerson, Morris, and Fitz-Gibbon (1987), "validity and reliability help to determine the amount of faith people should place in an evaluation instrument" (p. 133). The process of establishing reliability and validity for paper-and-pencil instruments is fairly straightforward. We need not proceed any deeper into specific forms of reliability and validity, but it would be valuable to discuss some of the special challenges associated with assessing clinical or counseling outcomes.

Problems emerge when we shift our interests to traits that are more subjective, elusive, and difficult to define but no less important to assess. The truth is that we are regularly faced with the prospect of trying to measure such subjective or elusive constructs as feelings, intentions, or qualities of interaction. Measuring attitudes (our own as well as those of our clients), for example, is a highly subjective and complicated process. As Henerson, Morris, and Fitz-Gibbon (1987) state:

> The task of measuring attitudes is not a simple one. What's more, attempting to demonstrate attitude change, as some evaluations require, is probably the most difficult of all evaluation tasks. Why is this so?
>
> To begin with, the concept of attitude, like many abstract concepts, is a creation—a construct. As such it is a tool that serves the human need to see order and consistency in what people say, think and do, so that given certain behaviors, predictions can be made about future behaviors. An attitude is not something we can examine and measure in the same way we can examine the cells of a person's skin or measure the rate of her heartbeat. We can only infer that a person has attitudes by her words and actions.
>
> (pp. 11–12)

Fortunately, techniques do exist for measuring such constructs. In fact, qualitative methods were actually developed in part to solve this problem. *Process evaluation* is one such example of a qualitative tool that emphasizes "looking at how a product or outcome is produced rather than looking at the product itself; that is, it is an analysis of the processes whereby a program produces the results it does" (Patton, 1987, p. 23). Such a method is particularly well-suited to assessing process-rich enterprises like counselor training and counseling.

One additional qualitative approach is worth including. Patton (1987) recognized that "not only will outcomes vary along specific common dimensions, but outcomes will be qualitatively different and will involve qualitatively different dimensions for different clients" (p. 24). The idea that individualized outcomes can and should be measured parallels basic counseling expectations. Data collection techniques for either of the two approaches would include the use of interviews, direct observations, and the analysis of written documents (e.g., case notes) or psychological reports. Qualitative methods can be applied so that the unit of analysis becomes an individual and, in our case, that individual could be a client or practicum or internship student. That qualitative methods offer an alternative in situations where quantitative methods cannot be applied is but one piece of the evaluation puzzle. In a larger sense, reliance upon qualitative methods encourages a desirable paradigm shift in which the importance of process is elevated and the use of formative evaluation emphasized. Both of these by-products are equally important and vital to the clinical training assessment model offered in this chapter.

Supervisor or Professor Assessments

While supervision was covered in detail in Chapter 3, several comments about supervisor assessments are worth including here. Many universities use a summative assessment instrument of one type or another on which to base judgments about final grades. It is crucial to obtain a copy of that instrument as soon as possible. Most supervisors and instructors recognize this fact and include a copy of it in the course syllabus or in the agency orientation materials. If it is not there, ask for it because you will need to take into account the agency and school performance criteria as you begin the process of developing your own goals and outcome objectives.

You should also be mindful of the fact that those who supervise your work are faced with two tasks that often create a dilemma for them. As people interested and involved in your development as a counselor, they assume a clearly formative role in your efforts to become a skilled clinician, but on the other hand, they are expected to provide a summative evaluation in the form of a final grade or perhaps a determination of whether you are ready to move to the next level of your training. You have a vested interest in both of these tasks and should do all that you can to ensure that the formative assessments are directly linked to the summative evaluations. Developing and sharing goals and outcome objectives with supervisors, asking for help from them, and being clear about the fact that you cannot work in a setting that cultivates fear, are all important tasks. While an imbalance of power between supervisors and students exists, the need to be clear about your needs and willing to share your concerns should not be diminished. While Deming maintains that managers must be responsible for managing fear in the workplace, your need to identify conditions that are interfering with your ability to achieve agreed-upon outcomes is equally important.

Peer Assessments

Counseling accreditation standards mandate group supervision, and so you will meet weekly with other students in your practicum or internship. Peers often offer suggestions, ask questions, and in some cases offer assessment information during the classes led by the professor or supervisor. Such peer comments can be useful as you refine your skills and develop treatment alternatives for your clients.

Threats to objectivity of course exist. Fellow students may be uncomfortable offering critical comments for many reasons. They may worry that such comments might negatively influence the way in which others, including the supervisor, perceive them in the supervision group. They may fear that what they say could cause you or other members of the group to treat them more harshly. And friendships with other students (peers) may interfere with their ability to be completely honest about perceived difficulties. It would be unwise to rely upon peer evaluations alone as a basis for determining the extent to which you are achieving your clinical goals and growing as a professional. While obvious limitations exist, peer comments do occupy a place within the rubric of evaluation sources. If you recognize that peer comments are often censored and that peers may be more likely to take sides with you when differences of opinion exist between you and a common supervisor, you will be in a better position to accurately assess the level of influence to assign to peer assessments.

Client Assessment

Though clients are not commonly seen as sources of practicum or internship student assessment information, in terms of OA principles, they are probably an ideal resource. Unfortunately, not all agencies and schools collect this type of information, although the process is becoming more common. During a postdoctoral internship in a local university hospital setting, all clients were asked to complete a simple questionnaire either following formal termination or after they stopped returning for counseling sessions on their own. Completed surveys, whenever they were received, became a focus of weekly individual supervision sessions. This process identified both areas where improvement was needed and clinical strengths. As the intern's collection of evaluations grew, the supervisor and the intern together were able to identify patterns that described how the intern was perceived by clients, and they were able to assess the efficacy of interventions from the client's perspective. While we cannot overestimate the value of such client assessments to one's development as a counselor, students often find the idea of client evaluations intimidating and anxiety provoking.

Useful survey instruments exist, and they should be included in the list of assessment sources for all advanced clinical students. The University of

Table 4.2
COUNSELOR EDUCATION
UNIVERSITY OF NORTH TEXAS
COUNSELING & HUMAN DEVELOPMENT CENTER
COUNSELING EXPERIENCE EVALUATION

Thank you for coming to the Counseling and Human Development Center. Through your use of this setting, your counselor has gained important professional experience. Now that you have completed your last session with your counselor, we are interested in your evaluation of this experience. Please do not put your name on this sheet. Feedback sheets will be collected by the instructor throughout the semester and shown to the counselor at the end of the term.

Your counselor's first name _____ Number of sessions attended __

You came to this Center by way of: Self-referral_____
                                    Counseling class _____
                                    Other _____(Please explain briefly)

Please respond to each statement:

	TO A LOW DEGREE					TO A HIGH DEGREE
My counselor . . .	1	2	3	4	5	6
seemed calm/relaxed	___	___	___	___	___	___
seemed confident	___	___	___	___	___	___
helped me feel comfortable	___	___	___	___	___	___
clearly explained expectations	___	___	___	___	___	___
seemed organized	___	___	___	___	___	___
conveyed acceptance of me	___	___	___	___	___	___
took an interest in me	___	___	___	___	___	___

seemed real-not playing a role   ___ ___ ___ ___ ___ ___

was warm/caring   ___ ___ ___ ___ ___ ___

seemed to understand me   ___ ___ ___ ___ ___ ___

was honest and direct   ___ ___ ___ ___ ___ ___

was supportive   ___ ___ ___ ___ ___ ___

helped me think about myself   ___ ___ ___ ___ ___ ___

helped me express my feelings   ___ ___ ___ ___ ___ ___

helped me make progress with
the concerns for which I came
to counseling   ___ ___ ___ ___ ___ ___

What one thing did you like most about your counselor?

What one thing did you like least about your counselor?

If you were considering ongoing counseling, would you seek out this counselor? In answering this question, please do **not** consider such factors as location, cost, etc.; please consider **only** the quality of the experience you had with this counselor.

a. definitely.   }
b. probably.   }
c. uncertain.   }   If you would like to explain your answer further,
d. probably not. }   please feel free to do so below.
e. definitely not. }

North Texas counselor evaluation form is just one example of a useful tool for obtaining client assessments of practicum and internship students.

While this form includes a number of Likert-styled items and sections for open responses, you might wish to develop a form of your own, once again relying upon objectives that you have specifically developed.

Assessment instruments have also been researched and developed to provide session-by-session information about the client's status and change process. Some common assessment tools include the Beck Depression Inventory II (Beck, Steer, & Brown, 1996), the Symptom Checklist 90-R (Derogatis, 2006), and the OQ-45.2 (Lambert et al., 1996). Some of these instruments can be used in an electronic format that charts elements of change in an easy-to-read format that is useful for clients and counselors.

Some counselors have perfected an exit interview format that they use during the last session with a client to obtain assessment information. Asking clients what they found helpful, what they thought interfered with progress, and what they wished had been different during their counseling experience can provide useful insights. Objectivity and frankness are again issues of concern. It may be difficult for some clients to be as direct in person as they might be on an anonymously completed evaluation form. While the questions are important and probably should be asked, we are only suggesting that you would need to be cautious about conclusions given the potential threats that exist to reliability, validity, and objectivity. On the other hand, in cases where a client would be willing to or actually asks to share evaluative information about the counselor with the counselor's supervisor, some of the noted threats could be reduced. While this does occasionally occur, it is uncommon. We are sure that there are additional but as yet undeveloped routes to obtain client views of the counselors who work with them. You may be able to develop creative and ethical ways to acquire this valuable information.

Self-Assessment

At the end of each clinical course, supervisors usually ask students what they believe they have accomplished and what they hope to improve upon in the clinical course they are next scheduled to take. The students' answers are always interesting, useful, and indicative of the fact that they have thought about the questions. Unfortunately, supervisors rarely have

sufficient time to learn what specific information led them to their conclusions; what information, if any, they felt they needed but were unable
to obtain; and how they actually assessed the accuracy of their conclusions.
While you may experience the same time limitations in your own clinical
courses, we hope this section may encourage and guide you to reflect more
deeply on the sources of information and the efficacy of your own evaluative conclusions.

Human beings, like most living organisms, tend toward homeostasis,
or balanced states. In nature, such a balanced state is usually considered
healthy or adaptive. However, such is not necessarily the case in human
beings. Unfortunately, regardless of how healthy or unhealthy a particular social or psychological homeostasis may be, individuals will tend to
behave in ways that maintain that balance. This concept offers one serviceable explanation of why behaviors persist even when the people expressing
the desire for change report great pain and distress from remaining in that
balanced but unhealthy state. Fear of change and fear of the unknown are
common explanations for the maintenance of behavior patterns that produce such self-destructive behavior. It is this tendency to homeostasis that
must be considered when thinking about the process of self-assessment.

It is difficult for individuals to attend to information that has the potential to seriously interfere with the way they see themselves. Unfortunately,
many students enter clinical training clinging to the hope that who they
are, how they are, and what they are will be affirmed as ideally suited to
the role of counselor. Much like the clients they serve, the drive to cling to
a homeostasis forces them to look away from themselves and toward others
with expectations that they will be affirmed and change will become the
responsibility of those around them. To be sure, this predisposition interferes with the goal of continuous improvement and the pillars that form the
concept of counselor formation.

Evolutionary information is the term that we apply to previously unknown facts
that have the potential to change the way in which you perceive yourself, the
world around you, and your thoughts and actions. The counseling process
seeks to offer such information to clients, and in turn, we believe that clinical training should do the same. How, then, do you as a student manage the
drive to homeostasis and eventually overcome blocks to obtaining the evolutionary information that produces self-improvement? Fear management
is probably the most basic concern in the process. As discussed, faculty and

supervisors will need to take the initiative here in ensuring a psychologically safe environment. But if fears persist even though the environment appears safe, outside therapy often helps. Attitude adjustments are also helpful. For example, it would be wise to think of all evaluative information as formative rather than summative. In this way you may be in a better position to avoid highly defensive reactions to what you may misperceive as indictments rather than suggestions for improvement. Also, many people will not consider something that interferes with their self-assessment if they feel that they will be hopelessly mired once the information is delivered and internalized. For this reason, formative assessment information should include recommendations for change and encouragement that the change is accomplishable. As we noted earlier, it does not help to unproductively dwell on a deficiency because doing so will eventually produce forms of defensiveness and rigidity that block internalization of the assessment information and stifle the pursuit of corrective action.

We are susceptible to perceptual bias in all of our endeavors, and we are especially biased when observing and evaluating ourselves. In other words, if objectivity is the major route to reduced perceptual bias and being objective about oneself is difficult if not impossible, then self-assessment must be saturated with perceptual bias.

Difficulties with objectivity notwithstanding, there are a couple of methods that can be used to improve your ability to self-assess. Bernstein and Lacomte (1979) offer the following series of questions that would need to be answered prior to group or individual supervision sessions:

1. What was I hearing my client say and/or observing my client do?
2. What was I thinking about my observations?
3. What were my alternatives to say or do at this point?
4. How did I choose from among the alternatives?
5. How do I intend to proceed with my selected response(s)?
6. What did I actually say or do?
7. What effect(s) did my response have on my client?
8. How, then, would I evaluate the effectiveness of my response?
9. What would I do differently now?

(pp. 71–73)

Answering the questions in advance of obtaining peer and supervisor remarks will provide you with an opportunity to compare your responses to those of others. Where you encounter sizable differences between your answers and the comments of others, you should recognize the difference and explore the processes you employed to obtain your conclusions. For example, you might hear your client asking what you understood to be a benign question, when she said, "What is the fastest way to get in touch with you if an emergency occurs?" Others listening to the tape conclude that the client is actually in crisis and desperately seeking immediate help. It would not suffice to simply note the difference, blindly follow whatever your supervisor might recommend, and move on. You will need to carefully explore exactly how you may have missed the client's deeper meaning and develop methods for improving your skills in this area. Situations where your perceptions differ markedly from others are usually unpleasant but extremely valuable. Exploring those internal forces that tend to distort your observations can improve your ability to more accurately access varied forms of client communication.

The second approach replaces Bernstein and Lacomte's questions with a collection of goals and outcome objectives that you personally develop in consultation with peers and supervisors. You then assess the extent to which you are able to achieve the desired outcomes as you review samples of your clinical work. This model allows you to identify areas that may need improvement and assess the impact of any changes you implement. The process can also be expanded to identify any needed modifications to your goals and outcome objectives.

For instance, one subset of the outcome objectives offered earlier in this chapter could be easily used to assess an intervention:

1. Correctly identify an appropriate treatment for the client.
2. Provide an acceptable rationale for the treatment choice.
3. Identify expected therapeutic milestones.
4. Demonstrate the ability to shift approaches when conditions warrant a change.
5. Correctly assess the effectiveness of the intervention or mode of treatment selected.
6. Correctly identify alternative approaches that may be needed if a predictable change occurs in the client's life.
7. Correctly assess the efficacy of the change.

Once you have evaluated yourself on each of these objectives, you will need to consult with others to confirm your conclusions. Let us assume that when answering the first objective you discover that the selected approach has not produced the desired results, and a revised diagnosis confirms that the approach and the rationale for using it proved to be incorrect. When you identify a more appropriate way of helping the client and then implement it, you are not only correcting problems identified in items 1 and 2 on the list but also meeting criteria in items 4, 5, 6, and 7. That these outcome objectives are so interdependent comes as no surprise; all are based upon one comprehensive mission statement. We can also use this example to demonstrate one other advantage of this self-assessment model. Let us assume that after making the identified changes you become worried about how long it took you to determine that you needed to alter your approach. Your concerns, further confirmed by a discussion with your site supervisor, eventually prompt a decision to modify outcome objective number 5 so that it now reads: "5. *After every third session*, correctly assess the effectiveness of the intervention or mode of treatment selected." Establishing a specific frequency for making the effectiveness assessment improves the outcome objective by responding to the noted deficiency. Additional modifications may be needed, but this is an expected result because the approach emphasizes continuous improvement. Ultimately, if you take the time to develop, modify, and pursue the goals and objectives that you create yourself, you will be in a much better position to properly utilize self-assessment tools.

Students at some universities obtain clinical, evaluation-training early in their course of study. For example, counseling graduate students at Loyola University New Orleans work with hired actors who serve as clients for them as they complete, among other courses, Counseling Practice. This course is normally offered during the student's second semester of their program. In this class, students record all of their sessions and obtain the following assessment information:

1. The instructor's assessment of a written verbatim analysis completed on a segment of one of the four tapes.
2. Peer assessment information obtained during peer consultations with other students who are "treating" the same client-actor.
3. In-class assessments from other students and the instructor when video-taped sessions are reviewed.
4. Summative evaluation information provided by the actors who served as their clients during the term. The actors meet individually with the

students who "treated" them during the term and answer questions about how the actors perceived the students' efforts to help them.

This counseling simulation that spans most of the semester not only gives students a unique opportunity to obtain a wealth of formative evaluation information, but it also gives them a chance to verify and implement their findings. With material as subjective as that which is contained in a series of counseling sessions, the task of verifying and interpreting data becomes complicated. Students eventually come to rely upon *triangulation*, a qualitative tool that causes the evaluator to take greater stock in a finding if its existence is verified by several unrelated sources. For example, if a student believed that he or she misinterpreted the client's meaning in a specific situation, next discovered that other people seeing the same client agreed that it was a misinterpretation, then had the misinterpretation confirmed by the instructor reviewing the videotape, and finally discovered during the last night of counselor–client (actor) meetings that the client felt misunderstood, the subjective observation would now have the status of an accurate conclusion because the finding had been triangulated using several sources.

If carefully defined goals and outcome objectives exist, the counselor has a good chance of taking this finding and using it to improve his or her skills. And all of this will be possible so long as fear is managed well enough to allow the student to risk identifying the deficiency and then to apply the principles that produce continuous improvement. In this summary we offer one micro-example of how data are collected, evaluated, and applied.

Ultimately all successful counselors apply models of assessment and improvement throughout their professional lives. It is best to consider this portion of your training an enduring component of your responsibilities as a trained, practicing clinician. As we noted earlier in the chapter, the goal of continuous improvement begins early in clinical training, but it spans the life of your work as a practicing clinician.

Reflection Questions

1. How would you modify the sample mission statement to more properly reflect your own training priorities?
2. What are some personal fears that could interfere with your ability to actively participate in assessment activities?

3. What steps would you expect an instructor or supervisor to take to create a learning environment where fear is properly managed? Describe the steps in detail.

4. How would you collect formative evaluation information, analyze the efficacy of the information, and then develop an intervention that would improve the deficiency identified in the evaluation? Provide a hypothetical example.

5. What personal attitudes do you possess that could interfere with self-assessment efforts?

6. What personal attitudes do you possess that make self-assessment and self-improvement more likely?

8. What is your personal reaction to the notion that evaluation and continuous improvement are goals that persist though out one's professional life.

References

Beck, A. T., Steer, R. A., & Brown, G. K. (1996). Beck Depression Inventory-II.

Bernard, J. M., & Goodyear, R. K. (1992). *Fundamentals of clinical supervision.* Boston, MA: Allyn and Bacon.

Bernstein, B. L., & Lacomte, C. (1979). Self-critique technique training in a competency-based practicum. *Counselor Education and Supervision, 19,* 69–76.

Bloom, B. S. (1984). *Taxonomy of educational objectives.* Boston, MA: Allyn & Bacon.

Bloom, B. S., Engelhart, M. D., Furst, F. J., Hill, W. H., & Krathwohl, D. R. (1956). *Taxonomy of educational objectives: Cognitive domain.* New York: McKay.

Deming, W. E. (1986). *Out of the crisis.* Cambridge, MA: Massachusetts Institute of Technology.

Derogatis, L. R. (2006). Symptom Checklist-90-R.

Granello, D. H. (2000). Encouraging the cognitive development of supervisees: Using Bloom's taxonomy in supervision. *Counselor Education and Supervision, 40,* 31–46.

Henerson, M. E., Morris, L. L., & Fitz-Gibbon, C. T. (1987). *How to measure attitudes.* Newbury Park, CA: Sage.

Joint Committee on Standards for Educational Evaluation. (1981). *Standards for evaluation of educational programs, projects, and materials.* New York: McGraw-Hill.

Lambert, M. J., Morton, J. S., Hatfield, D., Harmon, C., Hamilton, S., Reid, R. C., & Burlingame, G. M. (1996). OQ-45.2.

Nichols, J. O. (1991). *A practitioner's handbook for institutional effectiveness and student outcomes assessment implementation.* New York: Agathon Press.

Patton, M. Q. (1987). *How to use qualitative methods in evaluation.* Newbury Park, CA: Sage.

Royse, D., Thyer, B. A., Padgett, D. K., & Logan, T. K. (2006). *Program evaluation: An introduction* (4th ed.). Belmont, CA: Thomson Higher Education.

Suarez, J. G. (1993). *Managing fear in the workplace.* Arlington, VA: (TQLO Publication No. 93–01). Department of the Navy, Total Quality Leadership Office.

5

CLIENT INTAKE
First Steps in Forming the Alliance

One of the most fascinating aspects of the counseling profession lies within the energy of the first counseling session. As you wait for the client to show up, the countless possibilities for the emerging relationship may rush through your head. From the superficial curiosities ("I wonder what he will look like") to deeper reflections about self ("I wonder if she will think I'm a good counselor") to musings about the path counseling might take ("I wonder what the real issue will be"), all these thoughts occupy that space as you anticipate the first session. The inherent anxiety is a good thing because it aids in your ability to see each client as an individual, not just a "problem." When you allow yourself to anticipate, you open yourself up to an exciting part of counseling: the connection between two people who have never met and yet are about to embark together on a powerful journey of growth. This chapter explores the ways you can use the anxiety creatively to facilitate a solid foundation for counseling. As you will see, the first steps of counseling are filled with far more than superficial paperwork and history-taking. Done right, the first few sessions set the tone for the remainder of the journey.

The Importance of First Contact

Counseling begins from the first contact between client and counselor. For most, the first meeting is on the phone as the client attempts to set up an appointment. From that moment, both client and counselor are engaged in a parallel process of assessment and engagement. Consider the following excerpts and think about what the counselor and client might conclude from the interaction.

Phone Dialogue 1

Client:	Um . . . yeah. I don't know why I'm calling. My wife thinks I need to come in.
Counselor:	Would you like to make an appointment?
Client:	I guess. I don't know. I really don't have time, but I can try.

Phone Dialogue 2

Client (leaving message on machine):	Hi. My name is Amy and I would like to make an appointment. I need one as soon as possible. I'm really anxious and can't seem to get my life together and it's getting worse. Please call me back.
Counselor (calling back two days later):	Hi. I got your message and my next open appointment is in two weeks. Would you like me to pencil you in?

In these two brief interactions, you can probably draw some conclusions about the individuals. Without ever meeting the client in the first dialogue, what are your impressions? Most observers would say that this client is hesitant to enter counseling, and the main areas of potential resistance include feeling pressured into counseling and his time schedule. Paying attention to these dynamics may help you form the alliance with him and increase the likelihood of a positive counseling outcome.

From the client's perspective, in the second dialogue, what are some of your impressions of the counselor? The client may assume that the counselor will not be attentive due to the long wait for a return phone call or may even feel like the counselor's skills are weak based on the lack of concern in the face of urgent client symptoms. The client may feel ignored or not taken seriously, which could affect the alliance and even lead to the client not following through on the appointment.

Attending to the client's dynamics during the first contact can provide key information about the client, and being aware of your interaction can be a powerful first step in the alliance process. Once the client gets to the appointment, the therapeutic process can really get rolling. We believe that the first stage of counseling is designed to:

1. Gather information about the client. This information will help the counselor develop a phenomenological view of the client's world.
2. Orient the client to the process of counseling. The orientation includes both explicit activities, such as informed consent, and implicit actions, such as the way the dialogue progresses in the session.
3. Formulate tentative goals. Collaborative goal setting allows client and counselor to agree on some possible outcomes of counseling. Counselors use assessment, both formal and informal, to help facilitate realistic goal-setting.
4. Test the alliance. Not all counselors and clients are good matches. As the relationship develops, both parties need to decide if it has the potential for a good working relationship.

These steps in engagement of a client are congruent to the steps of a forming relationship between supervisee and supervisor. As you begin supervision, your supervisor will be exploring your style and skills in order to get a realistic picture of you. He or she will also orient you to the process of supervision, covering the topics discussed in Chapter 3. You will also learn a lot about the skill and manner of your supervisor through the supervisory dialogues. Together you will discuss goals for your training and determine whether the relationship is solid enough to provide an opportunity to work towards those goals.

First Meeting and the Purpose of Paperwork

On the day of the first session with a new client, most counselors report a sense of anxiety and nervous tension about the meeting. This feeling is normal; a person is about to come see you with expectations that you will help, but you know nothing about the person. The very fact that you have the privilege of connecting with another human being in this way may be anxiety provoking. Our first encouragement, which may seem like common sense, is to arrive early for the appointment. Clients may arrive late, but you must not because it conveys a lack of professionalism and a tone of disrespect for the client's issues. When the client arrives, greet him or her by introducing yourself and proceed to the next step in the process, which for most sites includes filling out paperwork.

Paperwork at some agencies can be overwhelming. We have worked in places where the forms clients have to fill out read like novellas. If the paperwork packet at your site is more than five pages long, you may explore the possibility of mailing the paperwork to your client prior to the first meeting or asking the client to come early to the first session to complete the necessary forms. All forms should serve a purpose in the treatment of the client. Although many sites contain many pieces of information, at a minimum the packet should include an informed consent document (professional disclosure statement), a consent to reveal confidential information form (to share pertinent information with other members of the client's treatment team—school counselors, psychiatrists, etc.), and a background information form.

While it may not be essential for clients to sign the release of confidential information form or fill out the background questionnaire immediately, it is important for the client to read, understand, and sign the informed consent document before discussing any issues. The professional disclosure statement, discussed in Chapter 2, orients the client to the boundaries of counseling, explains the role of the client and counselor, outlines fees and appointment issues, and specifies the exceptions to confidentiality. By reading the form and asking questions about the content, the client is able to make an informed choice about whether to participate in treatment. Not only does the discussion provide the client with needed information about the counseling process, it also provides an excellent opportunity for the counselor to engage the client in a cooperative relationship before the presenting problem emerges. Thus, the document becomes more than a piece a paper; it may also be considered a vital element of the engagement process. The other forms can also be used as methods of alliance building. Discussions about the consent to release confidential information can reveal other professionals who are working on the issue and the client's perception of their role in the process. Background information forms can provide jumping-off places for the dialogue. For example, most background forms cover broad topics such as presenting problem, medications, prior diagnoses, family constellation, and substance use, any of which can be places to begin the counseling (e.g., "I see that you mention you made the appointment to discuss your father's recent illness. Tell me a little more about that."). In addition to the general topics, it is also important to have a space on the background form for the client to note any feelings of suicide or homicide. These areas can be addressed at the very beginning of counseling to deal with or rule out a crisis situation.

The overarching goal of these first few minutes of the beginning session is to orient your client to the counseling process and begin the relationship formation. Using the paperwork as a means to initiate the dialogue serves the client and the alliance more effectively than does approaching the paperwork as a meaningless task: it is meaningless only if you fail to integrate the activity into the alliance process. Once the dialogue has begun, your understanding of the client can deepen.

Basic Elements of Alliance Formation

There is so much information about what to do with clients that it can feel overwhelming. In fact, trying to distill all the relevant information into one chapter was overwhelming to us! As we sat surrounded by the mountain of literature, we imagined that this is what it must feel like to students as they try to decide what to do to form a relationship with a client. We then thought about suggestions we give to our students: "Alliance forming is about the *relationship*. When you feel stuck, go back to the basics." So that's what we're going to do in this chapter: go back to the basics, that is, those popularized by Carl Rogers (1961), but widely accepted as alliance-building methods. We will use the elements of *empathy*, *unconditional positive regard*, and *congruence* to focus on the nature of alliance formation. Remember those?

Empathy

There is probably not another concept discussed in the counseling literature as universal as empathy. By now, you have probably discussed empathy in several of your courses, and if asked to describe it, you might say empathy is "being in touch with another person's feelings" or "walking in the client's shoes." Empathy has historically been viewed as an important part of the alliance-building between counselor and client. Rogers and Stevens (1967), who included empathy as one of the necessary and sufficient elements of change, clarify the concept in terms of the role of the counselor: "To sense the client's inner world of private personal meanings as if it were your own, but without losing the 'as if' quality, this is empathy, and this seems essential to a growth-promoting relationship" (pp. 92–93).

These two foundational quotations are instructive in how to form empathy in the client–counselor relationship. We must be able to touch the inner world of the client (e.g., see with his or her eyes) without losing our own sense of self in the process (e.g., the "as if" quality). At its most superficial, empathy can be experienced as an emotional connection between counselor and client: an acknowledgement of the affective domain of the client. Through that validation, the client feels understood. For example, consider the following exchange and comments:

Client: I am so tired of having to do all the work in my relationship.
Counselor: You feel frustrated over not being appreciated.
              (Counselor chooses to reflect the feeling of frustration felt empathically in the client's statement.)
Client: Yes! It seems like nobody ever gives me respect.
              (Client responds positively, feeling understood and validated.)

If we stopped here, the example would capture the essence of typical discussions regarding empathy. However, empathy can be viewed as more complex than a mere conveyance of emotional reflection. Barrett-Lennard (1981) defines empathy as a cyclical interchange between counselor and client and outlines a five-stage model that helps illuminate the complexities and pathways of empathy as an alliance-building skill. The five steps of the cycle will be briefly explored to add depth to your awareness of the role of empathy.

Step 1

The counselor actively attends to the client as the client actively expresses an aspect of self. In this step, the counselor is responsible for preparing for the client's self-expression through evidence of an *empathic set*, which is accomplished through being aware and attentive. The client is responsible for providing information—the stimuli for empathy. Simply put, the counselor must pay attention to the client, and the client has to say something to which the counselor can pay attention. Even though this step seems easy to accomplish, poor listening skills, stressful or emotional life distractions, or other factors can impede the counselor from being fully present for the client and thus disrupt the empathic connection before it has a chance to benefit the client.

Step 2

The counselor recognizes and can relate internally to the emotional content within the client's statements. Using intuitive sensing, counselors must attune themselves to the inner world of the client. It is here, in step 2, that you must place one foot firmly in your own experience to draw upon that knowledge as well as to anchor yourself and, at the same time, move the other foot into the world of the client by being curious about the client's own perspective. At first glance, this step might also seem easy, but consider the following client statement: "I am so upset that my husband left me." To adequately respond in an empathic manner, you first in your own mind connect and identify all the relevant emotions: pain, loneliness, sadness, anger, and so on. You mentally draw from analogous experiences in your own life to verify the accuracy of these initial feelings (this is the foot in your world). You then add in the context of what you know about the client, the client's nonverbal cues while speaking, and any other information regarding the client that may be pertinent (this represents the stepping into the client's world). Without internal reference to your own knowledge, it is impossible to intuit feelings of others. Without access to the client's world, you are left with only your own feelings, and the probability of empathic failure increases. Plainly, without both feet you are standing on shaky ground.

Step 3

The counselor conveys understanding of the client's emotional content. In this step, the counselor must frame a verbal response that demonstrates understanding of the client's world. The most common method is a reflection of feeling. Reflections of feeling can be phrased in a tentative ("You *seem* to feel disappointed") or certain ("You *are* disappointed") manner depending on the current state of the empathic connection. Tentative reflections carry less potency but may work well with beginning relationships or with clients who are suspicious, whereas reflections with a high degree of certainty convey more understanding and work well to deepen the empathic bond. It is also important to note that in addition to the counselor's words, the nonverbal communication is equally important in conveying empathy. Body posture, facial expression, and voice tone are all empathy-enhancing tools at this stage.

Step 4

The client attends to the counselor's response of understanding. This step is beyond the counselor's control. Obviously, most clients are in a state to hear what the counselor is saying, but some client factors may make the reception difficult, if not impossible. High levels of emotion might impede the listening skills of the client. For example, someone who is sobbing may miss what the counselor says. Severe psychopathology such as psychosis, panic attacks, or mania may make it difficult for the client to adequately receive the empathy of the counselor. Although the counselor cannot control these limitations, it is the counselor's responsibility to note these dynamics and work them into the treatment plan.

Step 5

The client provides feedback to the counselor regarding the accuracy of the counselor's statement and the resulting impact on the empathic connection between client and counselor. If accurate, the counselor's empathic reflection will allow the client to feel understood and validated, and thus the alliance will be enhanced. Often the feedback is offered with little more than a "Yes!" followed by deeper self-expression. It is the validation and understanding that facilitate the depth exploration. Even when the counselor's attempt is inaccurate, it still allows for a positive relationship impact, in that the reflection offers the client a chance to check the accuracy and correct the mistake. Feedback of this type often goes as follows:

Counselor: You seem angry about being betrayed.
Client: Not angry, I was livid! How could my lover do that to me?

This example illustrates how even perceived inaccuracies can be helpful to the alliance formation. The elegance in step 5 rests with the client's feedback, which allows for deeper understanding of the client's phenomenological worldview. The critical part of empathy is that the counselor is making a sincere attempt to understand the subjective view of the client, and the cycle demonstrates the unfolding of the process. As the counselor and client move together through the cycle, the alliance is formed.

Box 5.1 What so wrong with, "How Does That Make You Feel?"

If you have ever watched a movie with an actor playing the role of a mental health professional, you are bound to hear the therapist say, "How does that make you feel?" It is the cliché therapist response and is so ubiquitous it consistently finds its way into the tool kit of real life therapists, seasoned and novices alike. In our advanced clinical courses, we discourage our students from using this question for several reasons. In fact, rumor has it the uttering of this question in session will "make Dr. Fall's head explode". In truth, my head has never exploded, but there is a clinical rationale for why we believe this question should be avoided.

First, as a clinician who is attending to the client, you should have a sense of what the client is feeling. You may not know for certain, but that is fine. Certainty is not a requirement for empathy. The reflection of what you are sensing is important because it shows you are listening, which conveys interest and understanding. Asking the question, "How does that make you feel?" communicates none of these elements. In fact, it demonstrates empathic failure because you are basically saying to the client, "Although I have been sitting with you for five minutes listening to you speak, I cannot even guess at the feeling contained in your communication." So, think of it as a no-win question. It does not further the empathy cycle and may even leave your client feeling frustrated and ignored.

Second, in contrast to the no-win situation of "How does that make you feel", a reflection of feeling is a no-lose technique. If you are accurate in your empathy, and by accurate, we mean you really just need to be in the emotional ballpark, then your client feels understood and listened to by you. If, on the off chance you are inaccurate, your client will correct you and the communication cycle will continue! The interesting aspect is by virtue of your training and natural skill, you will be accurate almost 100% of the time. For example, can you ever imagine yourself doing this:

Client: I just felt so annoyed with boyfriend for not remembering my birthday! He never puts me first and only thinks about himself.

Counselor: You really felt prized by your boyfriend this week.

No, of course not! You can probably think of ten different feelings that you could reflect that would be accurate. So, our encouragement is for you to delete "How does that make you feel?" from your techniques. Your clients will thank you.

Unconditional Positive Regard

If empathy is the path to connecting with the client's world, unconditional positive regard is the way of accepting the client's right to see the world in his or her uniquely personal manner without judgment from the counselor. Rogers (1961) noted that unconditional positive regard is "a warm, positive and acceptant attitude toward what is in the client. It means an outgoing positive feeling without reservations, without evaluations" (p. 62).

In the beginning stage of counseling, clients are sensitive about disclosing embarrassing or shameful aspects of their life for fear that the counselor will reject or look down on them like so many people have done in the "real world." Conveying unconditional positive regard creates a safe environment for the client to discuss and explore painful parts of life, and it defines a unique aspect of the counseling relationship.

Much like empathy, unconditional positive regard is more complicated than most people suspect. It may seem intuitive that a counselor needs to accept the client and honor the client's right to a personal worldview, but clinical reality presents challenges to a counselor's ability to feel unconditional positive regard, most often when the client's worldview is significantly divergent form the counselor's own values. Issues such as parenting, domestic violence, religion, sexuality, and personal ethics all create potential rifts in the alliance due to problems with the counselor's ability to convey unconditional positive regard. Consider the following dialogue:

Client: I am so depressed. I can't believe all that has happened to me this year: the divorce, the lost job, my illness . . .

Counselor: It sounds like you have been through a lot over the past year. Tell me more about what that's been like for you.

Client: It's just wears me down. It's hard to go on day by day with all this on my back.

Counselor: I can see that your experiences have really taken their toll on you emotionally and physically.

Client: Thanks. It's nice to have a place to come and talk. Most people tell me to pull myself up and get on with my life. That just adds to the stress.

Counselor: Like you could just snap out of it, right?

Client: Right! I don't know, you know, sometimes I get so angry too.

Counselor: Tell me about the anger.

Client: Well, I used to be spiritual, you know, go to church and all that. But how could God turn his back on me? How could he let all this stuff happen to me?

Counselor: Well, maybe it's all happening for a reason.

Client: What?

Counselor: Well, I guess I am asking if now is the time to move away from something that has historically been a support for you.

Client: I guess I never viewed it as a support. If it was supporting me, why did I fall so hard?

The dialogue demonstrates how easily unconditional positive regard can begin to fade. In the first four interchanges, the counselor does a nice job of creating a safe environment for the client's expression. Notice how the counselor stays with the feelings, allows for deeper exploration, and connects with the client's perspective. Once religion enters the discussion, however, the counselor seems a bit shaken. The first response ("Well, maybe it's happening for a reason") seems to take the client by surprise. It's almost as if the counselor lost focus, as though the counselor was in tune with the client and then became momentarily distracted, and the distraction pulled the counselor back into the counselor's own world. The second comment is an attempt to reenter the client's world, but it is still rooted in the counselor's own belief system. It is as if the counselor's own possible belief that religion *should* be a support is interfering with the unconditional positive regard of the client's belief that religion has ceased to be a support.

Congruence

When a counselor is able to be genuine with the client, the client feels like he or she is relating to a real person. Rogers (1961) described congruence as a condition in which "the feelings the therapist is experiencing are available to him, available to his awareness, and he is able to live these feelings, be them, and able to communicate them if appropriate" (p. 61).

Many counselors impede congruence by erecting a rigid professional facade, placing extreme emotional distance between client and counselor. Hidden behind the impenetrable wall, the counselor may appear aloof and impersonal to the client. Counselors who adopt this approach have probably translated the "therapist as a blank screen" theme too literally. When counselors do not come across as real people to their clients, it makes it more difficult to relate and thus inhibits the relationship.

On the other hand, being too open and glib can be experienced by the client as abrasive or even cruel. Every counselor has thoughts and feelings during the course of the session that, if stated concretely, could be damaging to the client. For example, if the counselor is feeling bored in the session due to incessant client storytelling, then blurting out, "You are boring me to tears with your inane stories!" may be congruent, but it is not conducive to alliance-building. The art of congruence lies with being able to convey the emotion in a way that is helpful to the client.

Now that you are aware of some ways congruence can go wrong, let us explore some examples dealing with common, yet complicated, counseling situations related to congruence. The first example takes us back to the counselor feeling bored.

Client:	I don't know but when I was 15 I remember my mom took me to this weird store and we shopped for hours for little rabbit statues that were supposed to be made out of clay, but it seemed we never really found a rabbit made of clay but we did find some really neat clay statues of porcupines, or I guess, they really weren't statues, but more like figures because figures are smaller than statues and when I think of statues, I tend to think of museums and not so much about things that go in houses. Anyway . . .
Counselor 1 (too distant):	Uh-huh . . .
Counselor 2 (abrasive):	Stop! I can't take this anymore. You are rambling, and it's putting me to sleep.
Counselor 3 (appropriately congruent):	Let me jump in here a minute. I am sure there is something you really want me to know, but I am getting lost in all the words and details.

In the three examples, notice the difference in tone and probable client reactions. The too-distant example will likely produce more storytelling on the part of the client, and the boredom will morph into anger or resentment in the counselor. The abrasive response has a high probability of producing an embarrassed or defensive client response. The appropriately congruent response highlights the counselor emotion, and the counselor notes the reason (words and details) but takes responsibility for the feeling. This allows the client to feel less defensive and facilitates insight by offering multiple pathways of exploration, both within the counselor–client relationship and in relationships the client has outside of counseling.

Our second example deals with counselor fear.

| Male Client: | I think all women are full of crap. They just try to manipulate and screw men over. It makes me so angry I just want to strangle them sometimes. Don't get me wrong, I love the ladies, but down deep inside, I know I can't trust them. I never have met one I could trust or that didn't stab me in the |

	back. Every time I think of it, I just want to take it out on the first woman I see.
Female Counselor 1 (too distant):	I can tell you are really frustrated by the women who hurt you.
Female Counselor 2 (abrasive):	Well, I'm a woman! I feel threatened by you and want you out of my office!
Female Counselor 3 (appropriately congruent):	I have to say that I feel fearful and intimidated, being a woman and listening to your obvious anger, but I am also sensing a lot of hurt in your voice. I wonder if you could talk specifically about feelings of trust in our relationship.

In this example, the counselor's feelings of fear and intimidation are normal responses to the client's expression of disdain for women. The client is probably keenly aware that his behavior produces fear—some might say that is even his intent—so pretending to not have feelings could possibly lead the client directly to not trust the counselor. Being abrasive may honor the feelings, but they are communicated in a way that increases the chance of a hostile or defensive client reaction. The appropriately congruent response directly conveys the feelings of the counselor in a non-threatening manner and openly offers the client an opportunity to explore the feelings within the context of the relationship. While this approach does not guarantee the client will respond in a self-reflective manner, it does increase the probability that the dialogue that follows will be alliance enhancing rather than destructive.

Other Important Skills for Alliance Formation

Now that you have a deeper understanding of three important elements of building a therapeutic relationship, we can also explore a few other skills that will assist you in gaining an understanding of your client's world. These skills can be used in conjunction with empathy, unconditional positive regard, and congruence to set the stage for the next phase of the counseling process described in Chapter 6.

Questions

Most of us are taught that the easiest way to get information is to ask a question. However, counselors are aware that they want the engagement process to feel less like an interrogation and more like a dialogue. Knowing the difference between two types of questions can aid in the development of the alliance.

Closed-ended questions can be answered minimally, usually with such one-word answers as yes and no. Examples of closed-ended questions include:

Are you having trouble at school?
Do you ever feel like you don't belong?
Can you imagine yourself getting better?

Clients responding to these closed-ended questions with one-word answers will provide little real information for the counselor. Even worse, the lack of information often prompts the counselor to ask even more questions, often leading the interview to feel more like an interrogation than an engagement process. Put yourself in the client's seat and consider the following dialogue:

Counselor: Your mother asked you to come here today because of some issues you were having with your soccer coach. Is that accurate?
Client: Yeah, I guess.
Counselor: Do you think you have issues with your soccer coach?
Client: No.
Counselor: Are you having problems with your mom?
Client: No.
Counselor: Can you describe your relationship with anyone you might not get along with?
Client: Not really.
Counselor: Do you sometimes feel that no one really understands you?
Client: Yes.

OK, that's enough. We hope by now you get the idea how uncomfortable a long series of closed-ended questions can be for both client and counselor. Even if you are not feeling particularly uncomfortable, you probably see the limitations of the information gathered by closed-ended questions.

Conversely, *open-ended questions* encourage the client to answer with elaborated answers, allowing for greater detail and sharing. One type of open-ended question really isn't a question at all but more of a prompt for further exploration. This type begins with, "Tell me more about." Consider the same counselor invitation that was used on the closed-ended question example:

Counselor: Your mother asked you to come here today because of some issues you were having with your soccer coach. What do you think about your relationship with your coach?

Client: Umm, I don't know. I don't think I really have a problem with him.

Counselor: So you think everything is going pretty good. If there was something you could change about the relationship, what would it be?

Client: Well, he's pretty hard on me. When he yells at me, I just don't want to listen to him at all. I just tune him out and that really pisses him off.

Counselor: Tell me more about how you tune him out.

Client: I just hear him getting on me and it's like he isn't recognizing how hard I am working. He just wants to focus on the negative. It hurts, but I would never let him know that.

Counselor: What would happen if you did let him know?

Client: Oh man, I bet he would really get on me then, for being a wimp.

Did you notice how different the tone and amount of information gathered is when using open-ended questions? It feels much less like an interrogation session and allows both client and counselor many opportunities for discovery.

Use of Silence

Silence is not just something that occurs in counseling. It can be used as a tool to teach the client about the structure of counseling, can assist them in taking responsibility for contributing to counseling, and is vital to working out a therapeutic rhythm and flow to the developing counseling relationship. Counselors often find silence uncomfortable so it is important to be able to discern between unproductive and productive use of silence. Berg, Landreth, and Fall (2018) note that, "[s]ilence that conveys acceptance and support and that seems to be encouraging working through thoughts and feelings is constructive" (p. 139) and needs little interference from the counselor. In general, if the client seems to be pondering or reflecting or if the counselor has just asked a question, allow time for processing and let the client break the silence. By creating this space, the counselor achieves two goals: the client is given time to process and it teaches the client responsibility for the rhythm of the session, as the counselor will not rescue them by jumping in and stopping the process.

Interestingly, there has been some research on the specifics of silence in rapport building. Sharpley, Munro, and Elly (2005) studied the effect of initiated and terminated aspects of silence and found that

> Silences which were initiated and terminated by the client, and silences that were initiated by the counsellor and terminated by the client were most likely to contribute towards rapport. It seems inadvisable for counsellors to initiate silences and also terminate them, and counsellors should not terminate a silence initiated by their clients.
>
> (p. 158)

Similarly, Daniel, Folke, Lunn, Gondan, and Poulsen (2018) noted that unproductive silences were connected with less rapport while productive silences, especially in later stages of counseling, were associated with better rapport. These empirical findings support the notion that clinicians should be mindful of the type and purpose of the silence and to embrace the use of silence as a viable therapeutic technique.

Paraphrasing

Paraphrasing is a technique that acknowledges understanding of a client's behavior or thought process. While empathy focuses on the affective experience of the client, paraphrasing can help convey validation of the content of the client's story. Paraphrasing is an excellent skill to use to help the client key in on meaningful elements within all the billions of details of their life story and is instrumental in helping both client and counselor identify patterns that will be important later in counseling. Consider the following example:

Client: I don't know. I just feel so confused all the time. I'll be working on a project at home and a million things interrupt me. My mom will call on the phone and just go on and on about her day. I just can't tell her I need to go, so I might be on the phone for

	45 minutes. Then my boyfriend will come by and want to go grab some food and I feel bad about putting him off. I even get distracted by the television! Yesterday, I really needing to finish a report and *Jaws* was starting. I love that movie and ended up watching it instead of doing my report.
Counselor:	Let me jump in here and see if I am hearing you. It seems that you are having a difficult time setting boundaries and the choices you are making are really getting in the way of you attending to your work tasks.
Client:	Yes, now that I think about it. That is what I'm saying. It's me not saying no in every case. I know what I need to do, but I don't make that choice.
Counselor:	And then you blame the external factor: your mom, your boyfriend, *Jaws* . . .
Client (laughing):	Yes!

In this example of paraphrasing, it is important to note that the counselor emphasizes the client's behavior, not the behavior of other people. This internal focus assists in moving the person from an external locus of control to a heightened internal locus. This shift will not occur immediately, so it is vital for techniques in the beginning stage to set the norm for focusing on self.

Clarifying

Clarifying is a rapport-building technique that encourages a deeper level of awareness on the part of the client. It facilitates the client going deeper into their experience, tapping into the underlayers of cognition and emotion. Often clarification cab be expressed by encouraging the client to "Tell me more about . . .", but it can also single out elements of the client's story. Clarifying is especially important when the client uses vague language. For example, if the client says, "I just want to be happy," what does "happy" mean? The client has not defined it and so to gain understanding, the counselor must either make assumptions to fill in the blank or ask the client to clarify. Clarification is always better than assumption when trying to build data It is also possible that the client has not thought deeply about his or her own definition of happiness. In this case, asking the client to clarify is not only helpful for the counselor, but also provides a catalyst for greater client insight and awareness. As noted in other rapport-building techniques, modeling the process of counseling is important at this stage. Clarification sends the message to the client, "We go deep here." Consider the following example:

Client: I guess I just feel so irritated about what's going on in my relationship right now.

Counselor: Tell me more about the irritation.

Client: I feel trapped all the time. Like I can't breathe. Like every move I make is scrutinized and judged.

Counselor: When you feel smothered, tell me about your behaviors and how you react.

Client: I freeze. I ball up and I think I go into protective mode. My girlfriend says I get real distant, but I think I just don't know what to do.

In this example, the counselor uses the "Tell me more . . ." clarification to get the client to delve deeper into the concept of "irritation." The clarification allows the client to more clearly define where the irritation comes from, where it is localized, and some other feelings associated with it. The counselor then seeks to clarify what the client does with those feelings, to get some behavioral depth to the irritation. The client responds by illuminating a behavior of withdrawal, which may prove to be useful as the counselor looks for themes and possible elements of change.

Opening and Closing a Session

Knowing how to open and close a session is a vital part of setting the structure for the work done in session. It helps clients learn the rhythm and flow of the counseling and serves to focus the client on the issues at hand and also transition out of the session. In a sense it sets the boundaries for the counseling experience and, when those boundaries are consistent, the client will feel safe to explore deeply and honestly.

When opening a session, it is typical to start with something that will focus the client on the here and now. The client will be coming into the room fresh from the activities and distractions of everyday life. Some will enter counseling in crisis. You want to create an atmosphere of calm and readiness to begin the work of counseling. During your first session with the client, it is often a good idea to begin with a greeting and a brief orientation to the process of counseling. The client will have completed some paperwork, so going over any pertinent parts of the paperwork would be appropriate at this time. For example, an opening of a first session might go like this:

Counselor: Good morning. I want to welcome you to counseling and I am looking forward to getting to know you. Today, as this is our first session, we will go over the paperwork you just filled out and I'll answer any questions you have about that. We will then spend the remainder of the time today talking about you. I don't know anything about you at this point, so this session will be the start of a process which begins with you teaching me about your life and what you might like to change. We'll wrap up around 3:45 and spend the last five minutes making a plan for next week.

Later session openings will include summarizing previous work and touching base with any homework or processing items you asked the client to think about between sessions.

Counselor: Welcome back. I look forward to talking with you today. Last week we ended with the idea of you keeping a journal of the times you noticed yourself feeling anxious. I would like to know how that worked for you this week.

Counselor: Good morning. For the past few weeks we have been exploring your relationship with your current boyfriend. You had identified a pattern where you tend to avoid conflict in order to keep the peace. What thoughts have you had about the pattern this week?

Both examples help provide continuity of the counseling process. Even if the client reports not thinking about the material over the week, asking about it brings the norm of continuity into the client's awareness and increases the probability that the client will begin to carry the session work into life between sessions.

The main thing to remember about opening a session is that it should provide focus to the client. If you open with "So, what would you like to talk about today?", the client has no foundation to build on, no expectation of the process of counseling. When confronted with this complete lack of structure, you have a high probability of getting the response, "Uh, I don't really know where to begin," or beginning with a topic that will need to be redirected, for example, "I guess I want to talk about how my boss is a complete moron." By providing some guidance and direction, the client has a greater chance of understanding the expectations of the counseling world and can then get the most out of the experience.

In closing a session, the first rule is to give the client enough warning that the session is ending. Stopping a session abruptly can be jarring for clients and can leave them feeling exposed as they move out into the world. Consider the impact of the following exchange:

Client: I just felt so betrayed by my mother. I don't think I've ever allowed myself to admit I was angry at her and it feels like a relief but also like I am betraying her by feeling that way.
Counselor: Ooops! We are out of time. Let's pick up on that next week.

In general, give the client and yourself at least five minutes to sum up the session, provide the client with any homework or things to think about over the next week, and then end the session. For example, saying, "Riley, we have about five minutes left in our work today, so I would like to talk about how you might apply what you have learned today over the next week" is usually enough to shepherd the client into a more future-oriented frame of mind.

There are times when a client will disclose a new and deep aspect of him or herself in the last five minutes. These intense disclosures can be difficult for clinicians because there is a fear of hurting the client if you cut off the processing, so the tendency is to go over time, thus making the session boundary inconsistent. While counselor's must use their judgment, it is usually best to reassert the boundary. This teaches the client that important material needs to be brought up when the counselor and client have time to deal with the content. Reasserting the boundary teaches the client an important lesson about the culture of counseling and decreases the frequency of boundary testing. The following example is one way to deal with late disclosures.

Client: Before we go, I wanted to talk about something that I have been meaning to discuss, but just haven't had the guts. I was severely abused as a child and I have never really processed any of this.

Counselor: I want to acknowledge your courage in bringing this up in counseling. This is a good place to begin exploring your painful past and how it is impacting you currently. I am worried that we only have five minutes left today and I want to be able to give this issue the time it deserves. I would suggest we start with it next week so we have time and space to carefully unpack it.

One last point about closing a session during the rapport-building stage. Clients often come in to counseling not knowing what to expect from the process. Much of the alliance formation is about teaching them about the culture of counseling. As such, it is vital that you take time in the closing to sell the counseling process to them. The first step is to let them know that whatever occurred in the session was exactly what was supposed to happen as part of the process. This is important in the first few sessions where the focus will be on exploration. If the client is expecting that all their problems will be solved, they may leave feeling disappointed about what is occurring in the session. Letting them know that work is occurring will help instill hope in the counseling process and increases the chance they will return. It is also important to set another appointment and give them something to think about so a sense of continuity is created between the session times. For example:

Counselor: Thanks for summarizing for me. That is helpful. As we wrap up, I want to say that I thought we did good work today. I appreciate you telling me about yourself and I not only have a better sense of what is important to you, but we have also started to focus in on some things you want to change, namely the way you relate to your son. This is exactly where we need to be. For next week, I want you to notice the main ways you connect and disconnect with your son. We can explore that next week as well as continuing to learn about other relationships in your life. I'll see you next week at the same time!

Obviously, as you form the relationship with your client, you are going to utilize all of these skills and more to generate a therapeutic relationship. The main point of this chapter is that although the beginning stages of counseling are anxiety-provoking, forming an alliance is best constructed by remembering the basics. When you encounter new people, their life is known to them but is completely unknown to you. It's like sitting in front of one of those 3-D art posters. The entire picture is there, but you can't see it yet. To see it, the first step is not complicated: relax and don't try too hard to see it. Applying this approach to counseling is like letting the picture of the client's life unfold through the process of connecting.

The Other Side of Intimacy

This chapter has emphasized the necessity of developing an intimate rapport with your clients. The core techniques of empathic listening, reflection of feeling and content, summarization, and open-ended questions are all designed to facilitate the client's deeper exploration of self and provide the counselor with the information needed to help with that exploration. As the counselor actively listens to the client, the client unfolds his or her inner world, intimacy deepens, and the rapport occurs.

As a result of this process, a relationship develops that is far different from the relationships that form outside the counseling session. Counseling relationships and traditional relationships vary in three primary ways: (a) flow of communication, (b) depth of sharing, and (c) speed of intimacy development. Traditional relationships develop through mutual sharing; as each person shares meaningful aspects of self, the relationship deepens. In counseling, the flow of information goes only one way, client to counselor, and yet a form of intimacy develops between the two people. As a product of the one-way relationship, a power differential occurs as the counselor comes to know a lot about the client but the client knows little to nothing about the personal life of the counselor.

In addition to the unidirectional flow, counseling relationships also differ from traditional relationships in the depth and speed of sharing as well as in concomitant intimacy development. As you well know from your work with clients, they will share pieces of themselves that are extremely private, and they do so soon within the life-span of the therapeutic relationship. As you see more clients, you will be surprised how many times you hear, "I've never told this to anyone . . ." after knowing a client for only a session or two. We tell our students, "[p]sychological intimacy travels much faster than traditional intimacy," in our attempt to prepare them for the deep connection the client will feel as a result of rapport building.

In the context of this deeply intimate reaction, client and counselor create an atmosphere conducive to growth. However, clients are apt to respond to the felt sense of deep intimacy in ways that the individual normally responds to related intimacy levels in "real-world" relationships. For instance, clients who respond with avoidance or fear of intimacy in their personal relationships will respond in a congruent fashion to the intimacy in counseling. Many clients connect psychological intimacy with physical intimacy. For many people, the idea of responding to psychological closeness with physical closeness is very natural. Regardless of the response, it is the counselor's job to process the feelings and fold them into learning opportunities for the client.

In your time as a professional counselor, you will deal with client-to-counselor attraction on numerous occasions. Equally as frequent, you will also encounter times when you feel an attraction to one of your clients. Counselors are people, and as a function of our humanity, we enjoy the feeling of intimacy generated in the counseling session. We enjoy the fact that clients are willing to trust us, tell us their secrets, and even pay us for our time. We feel important, needed, and respected. For counselors who are not getting these needs met in outside relationships, the tendency to look to clients for fulfillment is strong. Being attracted to a client is not the unethical aspect—in fact, it is very normal. What differentiates unhealthy attraction from healthy attraction is how the counselor handles it. Because most counselors respond to the thought of being attracted to a client with denial and shame, we will first outline some warning signs of a developing yet unnoticed attraction, and then we will discuss some steps to manage the feelings.

Pope, Sonne, and Holroyd (1993) list several clues to what they term "unacknowledged sexual feelings." They are:

Dehumanization of the client and/or counselor: Dehumanization is a way to push the sexual feelings away and gain some emotional distance without actually dealing with the attraction. Dehumanizing clients comes in the form of beginning to see the client as a label, such as their diagnosis. Dehumanizing the counselor is characterized by a movement to a more aloof professional posture, such as being overly cognitive or playing the "expert."

Avoidance: Sometimes the counselor is so ashamed of the feelings the only thing to do (besides deal with them) is to avoid them by avoiding the client. Counselors can pick up on this clue if they find themselves "forgetting" to return phone calls from the client, or missing or canceling appointments.

Obsession and/or fantasies during sexual activities: Not being able to get thoughts of your client out of your head is one important sign that something is going on that needs to be explored. An extension of constantly thinking about the client would be when you think about your client as a sexual partner while masturbating or having sexual relations with your partner. Before you say, "That would never happen to me," Pope and Tabachnick [1993] conducted a national survey and noted that half the sample reported having sexual fantasies about their clients on rare occasions and a fourth responded that the fantasies were more frequent than rare.

Isolation of the client and/or counselor: The counselor may begin to isolate the client from family, friends and romantic ties by subtly encouraging the client to cut off communication with these individuals. An example would be the counselor stating, "You know, it sounds like you are very unhappy with the way your boyfriend is treating you. You feel he just doesn't listen or respect you. Maybe you are right in trying to disconnect from him for a while." By doing so, the client may become more reliant on the counselor for emotional support. Another clue to isolating the client would be the atmosphere of secrecy around the relationship or what occurs in counseling. Saying to the client, "I think we should keep this to ourselves because other people wouldn't understand" should be a clear sign that the relationship needs to be reexamined.

Isolation of the counselor occurs when the counselor knows something is not right, but cannot pinpoint the catalyst for the discomfort (the sexual attraction). Instead the counselor reports feeling "overwhelmed and stressed out" and as a result, often begins to pull away from support networks of colleagues and friends. The isolation may be interpreted as "they don't understand me" or "they would judge me" which in turn, propels the counselor deeper into the bond with the client who does "understand".

When the vigilant counselor notices the clues of attraction, steps must be taken to ensure that the attraction does not interfere with the counseling process. We are fairly certain that this issue was addressed in your counseling curriculum, but here are a few guidelines that may help you process the feeling as they arise.

1. <u>Define the scope of the issue:</u> In this stage, the counselor should explore and define the feelings associated with the attraction. These feelings can run the gamut from excitement and sexual lust to shame and fear. As the counselor examines the emotional landscape of the attraction, he or she can also look at the reasons for the feelings. Counselors can explore the reasons by asking questions such as:

   - What's going on in my intimate relationships right now? Do I feel loved? Do I feel respected? Do I feel needed?
   - What about the client do I find attractive? Is this a physical attraction? Emotional attraction? Intellectual attraction? Spiritual attraction?

   Often, the emotions detected that are associated with the attraction will be found to be absent in one's current relationships.

2. <u>Consult:</u> As mentioned, isolation is not only a clue to attraction but also can push the counselor closer to the client in unhealthy ways. Consulting a colleague about your feelings can give you an ally in preventing destructive contact with your client. The consultant can validate your perspective, give you insight on aspects of the relationship you might miss, and help you manage the feelings in a productive way.

3. <u>Seek personal counseling:</u> If the emotional strain is troubling to you, or if through your exploration you find elements missing in your current relationship, you should strongly consider working out those issues in your own counseling. As you know, getting your emotional needs met through your client is inappropriate, but finding ways to get what you want is a perfect arena for your personal counseling.

4. <u>Continue or refer:</u> As you move through this process, you will have to make a decision whether to continue seeing the client or refer the client to another mental health professional. Because attraction to clients is fairly common and normal, managing the feelings with these steps will allow most counselors to continue to work with the client as long as they continue to monitor the boundaries. In cases where the sexual attraction cannot be managed, the feelings will create an obstacle to the counseling and a referral must be made.

So what do you say after you've determined that you can't continue? Well, we believe that sexual attraction that creates an impasse in the counselor will often be felt by both parties as a "stuck place" in the counseling; a perceived lack of movement. The counselor can note the "stuckness" as the reason for referral. For example, "It seems like we are not making progress in our work. Perhaps this is as far as we can go." Getting client feedback is essential as well as a reevaluation of goals and appropriate referral based on those goals. The point here is that you can make the referral based on the process of counseling, rather than discussing the reason for the impasse, which is your issue, not the client's.

A Word About Premature Terminations

Often in the early phases of counseling, clients decide to not return. These "premature terminations" are usually not preceded by discussion or processing of the reasons for leaving. Instead, clients just stop coming. The consequence for ending counseling early leaves the client without help and support for the issues at hand. Researchers believe there are some ways to minimize premature termination. Some of the strategies include precounseling education, effective client screening, understanding client preferences for treatment, short-term treatment contracts, and appointment reminders (Murphy & Cannon, 1986; Reis & Brown, 1999; Swift & Callahan, 2008; Walitzer, Derman, & Connors, 1999). In addition, researchers note the importance of the counselor–client relationship, the ability of the counselor to access affective content of the client, and instilling hope in the therapeutic process, as viable methods for preventing client dropout (Ogrodniczuk, Joyce, & Piper, 2005; Swift & Greenberg, 2012; Swift & Greenberg, 2015).

In addition to the maladaptive effects premature termination may have on the client (Lampropoulos, 2010), the event may also impact the counselor in a negative manner. The abrupt ending of the counseling relationship can leave the counselor feeling incompetent, rejected, and hurt. As one intern reflected,

> I had only met with Josie twice, and I thought things were going well. Then she just stopped coming. She didn't call me to cancel. She just no-showed and did not return my calls. I have no idea why she stopped, and I keep thinking I did something wrong. It feels so unfinished. I can't believe I got dumped!

Premature termination is confusing and hits at the core of insecurity about your professional self. It is important to note that clients leave counseling early for a variety of reasons (Knox et al., 2011; Swift & Greenberg, 2012), and not all of them are counselor related. According to Garfield (1994), up to 57% of clients end treatment prematurely, with most completing no more than four sessions. Swift and Greenberg (2012) conducted a meta-analysis of 669 studies and found a much more optimistic 20% rate. Due to the uncertainty of the termination, it is a good idea to think about the many possible reasons and reflect on ways you can influence future clients to decrease the likelihood of clients leaving without processing.

Supervision provides an excellent venue for discussing the complex feelings associated with premature termination. Within group supervision, you will undoubtedly hear from other interns who have experienced the same issue and be comforted by the fact that you are not alone. Individual supervision can be used to explore deeper personal reflections about your professional identity and discuss plans for modifying the ways you form alliances with clients. By using supervision, the goal of learning to change what you can and becoming comfortable with what you cannot can be realized.

Summary

This chapter highlights the important elements of the beginning stages of alliance formation. From the initial contact with the client, the counselor has an opportunity to build rapport. Even tasks that might seem tedious, such as attending to paperwork, provide important information to both client and counselor about the process of counseling.

Three core concepts were used to define the basics of alliance formation: empathy, unconditional positive regard, and congruence. Although these are old news to you by now, they represent foundational pieces that will set the stage for success in the counseling relationship. As rapport deepens between counselor and client, the client feels more comfortable sharing important aspects of self that will increase the potential for exploration and growth. The cohesion between client and counselor decreases the probability of premature termination and facilitates movement to next stage of continued assessment, pattern search and goal setting.

Reflection Questions

1. What concerns do you imagine will surface as you prepare for the meeting with your first client?
2. Think about how you normally meet new people and get to know them. What aspects of your personal approach can be helpful to your professional approach to developing relationships with clients? Which aspects will not be useful?
3. How can you respond empathically to a client whom you have just met and hardly know?
4. How will you provide "unconditional positive regard" to your client as you listen to your client's difficulties or embarrassing moments?
5. What do you think it means for a counselor to rely heavily on closed-ended questions?
6. As counselors become more skilled, they tend to be able to engage with a wider range of clients. Why do you think that this change occurs?
7. What are some ways you would like to open a session? What do you think are the most important aspects to convey as you begin a session at the start of a counseling relationship?
8. What steps would you take to close your sessions? What are some problems that might occur as you try to end the session?
9. What are your concerns about premature termination? What would it say about your skill as a counselor if your client did not return?
10. How would you know you were attracted to your client? How would you know a client was attracted to you? What would you do in each situation?

References

Barret-Lennard, G. T. (1981). The empathy cycle: Refinement of a nuclear concept. *Journal of Counseling Psychology, 28,* 91–100.

Berg, R. C., Landreth, G. L., & Fall, K. A. (2018). *Group counseling: Concepts and procedures* (6th ed.). New York: Routledge.

Daniel, S. F., Folke, S., Lunn, S., Gondan, M., & Poulsen, S. (2018). Mind the gap: In-session silences are associated with client attachment insecurity, therapeutic alliance, and treatment outcome. *Psychotherapy Research, 28*(2), 203–216.

Garfield, S. L. (1994). Research on client variables in psychotherapy. In A. E. Bergin & S. L. Garfield (Eds.), *Handbook of psychotherapy and behavior change* (4th ed., pp. 190–228). New York: Wiley.

Knox, S., Adrians, N., Everson, E., Hess, S., Hill, C., & Crook-Lyon, R. (2011). Clients' perspectives on therapy termination. *Psychotherapy Research, 21,* 154–167.

Lampropoulos, G. K. (2010). Type of counseling termination and trainee therapist-client agreement about change. *Counselling Psychology Quarterly, 23,* 111–120.

Murphy, J. F., & Cannon, D. J. (1986). Avoiding early dropouts: Patient selection and preparation techniques. *Journal of Psychosocial Nursing and Mental Health Service, 24,* 21–26.

Ogrodniczuk, J. S., Joyce, A. S., & Piper, W. E. (2005). Strategies for reducing patient induced premature termination of psychotherapy. *Harvard Review of Psychiatry, 13,* 57–70.

Pope, K. S., Sonne, J. L., & Holroyd, J. (1993). *Sexual feelings in psychotherapy.* Washington, DC: American Psychological Association.

Pope, K. S., & Tabachnick, B. G. (1993). Therapists' anger, hate, fear, and sexual feelings: National survey of therapist responses, client characteristics, critical events, formal complaints, and training. *Professional Psychology: Research and Practice, 24,* 142–152.

Reis, B. F., & Brown, L. G. (1999). Reducing psychotherapy dropouts: Maximizing perspective convergence in the psychotherapy dyad. *Psychotherapy, 36,* 123–136.

Rogers, C. R. (1961). *On becoming a person.* Boston, MA: Houghton Mifflin.

Rogers, C. R., & Stevens, B. (1967). *Person to person: The problem of being human.* Lafayette, CA: Real People.

Sharpley, C. F., Munro, D. M., & Elly, M. J. (2005). Silence and rapport during initial interviews. *Counselling Psychology Quarterly, 18*(2), 149–159.

Swift, J. K., & Callahan, J. L. (2008). A delay-discounting measure of great expectations and the effectiveness of psychotherapy. *Professional Psychology: Research and Practice, 39,* 581–588.

Swift, J. K., & Greenberg, R. P. (2012). Premature discontinuation in adult psychotherapy: A meta-analysis. *Journal of Consulting and Clinical Psychology, 80,* 547–559.

Swift, J. K., & Greenberg, R. P. (2015). *Premature termination in psychotherapy: Strategies for engaging clients and improving outcomes.* Washington, DC: American Psychological Association.

Walitzer, K. S., Derman, K. H., & Connors, G. J. (1999). Strategies for preparing clients for treatment. *Behavioral Modification, 23,* 129–151.

6

IDENTIFYING PROBLEMS, ISSUES, RESOURCES, AND PATTERNS

In Chapter 5 we discussed ways to form a therapeutic alliance with the client. Utilizing empathy and a spirit of curiosity, counselors can enter the lives of individuals to facilitate change. Once you have the connection, a deeper level of exploration begins. As the landscape of the client's life unfolds, the counselor can recognize patterns that are unique to the client. In these patterns, the counselor can identify strengths and areas for growth. This chapter highlights some of the basic concepts associated with this part of the counseling process.

Assessment and Diagnosis

There are many schools of thought and external pressures (e.g., from insurance companies) that encourage counselors to begin the counseling process with a formal assessment and diagnosis process that guides

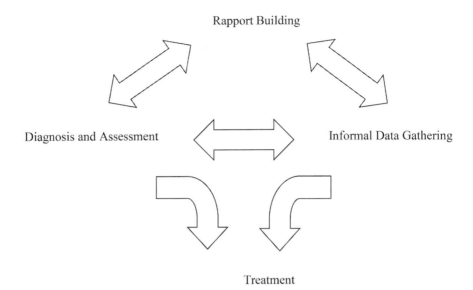

Rapport Building

Diagnosis and Assessment

Informal Data Gathering

Treatment

Figure 6.1 Connections among relationship building, assessment, and treatment.

treatment planning. Learning to use the *Diagnostic and Statistical Manual of Mental Disorders-5* was probably a part of your formal graduate training. While we believe that assessment and diagnosis are important, we also believe that the information can be incorporated into the counseling process so that it adds to the rapport building rather than detracts from it. In our own clinical practices, we have remarked on how the amount of paperwork has decreased the longer we have been in practice. We have found that it is sometimes just as efficient to get the information by dialoguing with the client.

A useful way for seeing how the elements of relationship building, assessment, diagnosis, and treatment connect is featured in Figure 6.1. This figure shows a cyclical process whereby each aspect of the cycle builds on itself to further the goal of treatment.

Assessment Tools

Formal assessment tools can serve as a valuable resource in complicated cases. Deciding when to use formal assessment tools requires deliberate decision-making on the part of the counselor. Seligman (1994) recommends that counselors consider these important points when deciding whether to use psychological testing:

- Consider what information and knowledge you are looking to find in the assessment.
- Consider whether your current informational sources (client, intake form, family members, external records) can provide the information you seek. If not, can the assessment provide the missing information?
- Consider the client's perspective regarding being "tested." If the client's reaction is apprehensive, working through those feelings and assessing the impact on the therapeutic relationship is important.
- Choose the tool that gives you the best chance of acquiring the information you need. Choose tools that provide reliable, valid, and meaningful data.
- Develop a method of incorporating the results into the counseling process. Think about how you are going to process the information with the client and be ready to discuss how it will benefit the client's treatment.

(pp. 69–72)

Once you weigh the benefits and disadvantages of testing, you probably have an idea of what testing should be done. The following are some of the common categories of assessments available. The list is brief, but you have already taken a course in assessment, so this should serve as a reminder and quick resource.

Personality tests

Personality instruments are designed to assess personal, emotional, social, and behavioral patterns of the individual. These tools are most often self-report–based, that is, taken by the client from the client's perspective. They can range from comprehensive instruments such as the Minnesota Multiphasic Personality Interview-II (MMPI-II) and the Myers-Briggs Type Indicator (MBTI) to more specifically focused instruments such as the Beck Depression Inventory (BDI) that addresses levels of mood disturbance. Also in this category are the projective personality tests such as the Thematic

Apperception Test (TAT) and the Rorschach Ink Blot Test. These tests are most often given as a part of a psychological testing battery administered by a psychologist. They are useful in providing information and clarification of personality patterns, especially with regard to diagnosable conditions.

Interest inventories

These assessments measure a client's likes and dislikes, primarily in work and academic pursuits. The Self-Directed Search (SDS), the Strong Camp-bell Interest Inventory, and the Kuder General Interest Survey, Form E are all examples of such inventories. These tests are widely used by counselors as methods for helping clients gain insight into their relative satisfaction or dissatisfaction with a chosen vocational or academic path.

Career development inventories

These assessments examine the client's progress along the accepted stages of career development, including associated attitudinal and cognitive factors. Whereas the interest inventories assess the content of career choice, career development inventories evaluate the process and the client's current place in that process. Examples of career development inventories include the Adult Career Concerns Inventory (ACCI), Career Decision Scale (CDS), Career Development Inventory (CDI), and Career Maturity Inventory (CMI). These tests are common in vocational counseling offices, especially on college campuses, and many can be accessed for online administration.

Measures of ability

These tests encompass all assessments of aptitude, achievement, and intelligence. Aptitude tests try to predict a person's future performance; for example, the American College Test (ACT) and the Scholastic Aptitude Test (SAT) are used to predict success in college academics, and the Graduate Record Exam (GRE) is used to predict academic success in graduate school. Achievement tests are designed to measure learning at selected academic intervals. Examples include any state educational test or the nationally used California Achievement Test. The intelligence tests, such as the Stanford-Binet, the Wechsler Adult Intelligence Scale (WAIS), the Wechsler Intelligence

Scale for Children-Revised (WISC-R), and the Wechsler Preschool and Primary Scale of Intelligence (WPPSI), are used to quantify the elusive "intelligence quotient" (IQ). All of these tests are extensively used in educational and vocational settings, and to some degree, the intelligence tests are commonly included in psychological testing batteries.

Diagnosis

Diagnosis is a criteria-structured system that corrals commonly co-occurring symptom-clusters into labels that describe types of psychopathology. Based on the medical model, the most commonly used systems of diagnosis are the *Diagnostic and Statistical Manual of Mental Disorders-5* (DSM) and the *International Classification of Diseases, Clinical Modification,* 10th edition. Someone once said: "Diagnosis is the art of information gathering." That statement resonates throughout clinical work and teaching. To be a good diagnostician, one must know how to obtain information. If the counselor does not get accurate information, the diagnosis and the treatment will be degraded. Quality information comes from the ability of the counselor to connect with the client and enter the client's world (empathy). This is how empathy and diagnosis are intertwined.

According to Reichenberg and Seligman (2016), the purpose of the DSM for counseling professionals is to:

- provide a universal language of mental illness to improve communication among mental health professionals
- improve research reliability by providing criteria for identifying the disorders
- seek approval from insurance companies that require a diagnosis for reimbursement
- predict the progress of the disorder and create treatment plans accordingly that match the diagnosis

(pp. 97–99)

Used correctly, the system is designed to provide a compact method for describing the dysfunction of the client in a comprehensive way. For more detailed explanations of the diagnostic process, please consult the *Diagnostic and Statistical Manual of Mental Disorders-5* (American Psychiatric Association, 2017) and Morrison (2014).

Informal Methods of Information Gathering

Formal assessment tools and diagnostic labels help validate key areas of problems in the client's life, but they often fail to describe the specific impact the symptoms have on the individual sitting across from you. You could round up 50 people with the diagnosis of major depressive disorder or a BDI score of 8 and they would all be different in their presentation. Why? Because although assessments and diagnostic tools help identify the problem, they fail to capture the idiosyncratic nature of the problem. Figuring out how the diagnosis fits into the fabric of the client's life is an extension of the engagement stage. The better the connection you have with your client, the more information you will be able to access and fit into the bigger picture.

Although there are many informal ways to get the information you need, allowing the client to talk about what life is like can begin the pattern search process. Each theoretical school has its own "important life areas" list that helps structure the interview and give the counselor the best vantage point of the client's world, but Summers (2003) provides a comprehensive transtheoretical list of areas that might be useful to keep in mind as we explore pattern searching:

- Medical History: general health issues and problems
- Psychiatric History: previous diagnoses and treatment experiences
- Social Competencies: how they connect and disconnect with people
- Behavioral Patterns: problematic patterns that "get me in trouble"
- Family System: family of origin exploration as well as current intimate relationships (if the client has children, parenting issues)
- School or Work History: educational background, work background, and relationships with colleagues and those in authority
- Friends: Social relationships, both quantity and quality
- Leisure activities: hobbies, free time
- Spirituality: belief in a higher power

(p. 192)

Making Sense of It All: The Process of Pattern Search

As the relationship deepens, more and more information about the client's world becomes available to the counselor. The flood of information must be processed and distilled in a manner that is useful to both client and counselor. Each theory has its own method for conceptualizing this wealth of information, but all emphasize the importance of seeing the patterns in the client's life. The good news is that human beings naturally coalesce their experience into consistent themes. This consistency has its foundations at the neurological level, which informs the other systems, including the behavioral element of existence. Beitman, Viamontes, Soth, and Nittler (2006) observed: "Behavioral patterns are deeply engrained and manifest themselves in many settings, from the therapist's office to the work environment, and certainly throughout the whole spectrum of personal relationships" (p. 279). In this section, we discuss the many ways a counselor can look for patterns and, as a result, help the client move toward change.

Therapist Behavior and Pattern Search: The Art of Burrowing

Before we address the specifics of identifying themes, we thought we would take a moment to discuss therapist behaviors and attitudes that will assist with your ability to illuminate patterns in your client's story. The first important therapist element is *patience*. Patience allows the therapist to relax and feel free to be fully present with the client. If you feel rushed then you are more likely to feel pressure to speed towards solving the client's problem rather than letting the process unfold. Even if you are under the mandate of doing "brief therapy" or the client's insurance only approved eight sessions, be patient. You are in the business of seed planting. What this means is that you do not have to solve all of the client's problems today, next session, or even eight sessions from now. You must commit yourself to the ethical practice of counseling, which means working effectively with your client on mutually agreed upon goals. The work you do may only be a step in their change process, so slow down and be patient.

The second important therapist element in theme searching is *curiosity*. When meeting a client for counseling, you should feel a sense of wonder at the unknown that is being presented to you. Your client knows everything about their own life, but you only know what they are telling you. Most clients will be running on autopilot as they tell their story, almost like they have a well-worn script they are following. They will not be aware of the vague language they use or the times when there are inconsistencies with details or emotional content. Your job is to listen and be curious. When you hear your client use vague language, clarify. When you hear something that doesn't make sense to you, ask the client to explain that part of the story with more depth. The attitude of curiosity will open aspects of the client's life that have been ignored and can add potency to the rapport and well as the therapist's ability to discern patterns.

The last important therapist element is largely impacted by the therapist's ability to be patient and curious. This third element is what we call burrowing. Imagine a small creature like a mole. It has the ability to dig deep into the soil and explore while looking for food or shelter. Like the mole, you are encouraged to burrow into the client's world. Effective moles don't burrow randomly, but instead commit to an area and explore thoroughly. As you burrow, you will use the tools of patience and curiosity to find an area of the client's life and explore it until you have a good sense of who the client is in that relationship. Do not leave the burrow until you have this sense, as this will give you the key information about the client you were looking for and will be used in identifying patterns. Keep the client focused on who they are in the relationship and redirect them if they are emphasizing the internal or external dynamics of the other person. If the client burrow jumps, gently guide them back to the original burrow. An example of this might look like:

Counselor:	You mentioned being concerned about some conflict with your boyfriend, Jim.
Client:	Yes! He just really irritates me the way he does things. He is just so . . . I don't know.
Counselor:	Tell me more about your irritation and what that looks like.
Client:	Ugh . . . I just get so mad. He just won't talk to me. He is so isolated and . . .
Counselor:	I notice you are giving me a lot of information about Jim, but I am interested in how you are in this relationship. So, when you get irritated, what do you do?
Client:	(laughs) Oh I see, right. He's not here. When I see him withdraw, I get really mad and want to engage him. Make him talk.

Counselor: I see, so the more he drifts away, the more you chase. Tell me more about how you engage him during these times.

Client: It actually reminds me of the time I was arguing with my mom. She was trying to buy me some clothes and we got into an argument.

Counselor: You mentioned that your relationship with your mom also has similar types of conflict and I want to hear more about that, but before we move to her, I want to make sure I get a good sense of how you relate to Jim. So, when you are irritated with him and feel he is moving away from you, what are some ways you try to engage him?

Keeping the client focused on one burrow at a time will not only provide you with the information that will be helpful in understanding the world of the client, but also orients the client to the depth of processing that is a part of the culture of counseling. In a way, it is training them to burrow deep. Once you have a sense of who the client is in this area, summarize the dynamic and move on to another aspect of the client's life. Be patient and curious and you will begin to notice similarities emerge in the client's life as you deeply explore the burrows. This is the art of pattern search and illumination.

Developmental and External Sources

The list provided by Summers (2003) outlines several of the developmental and external resources for information that can provide the counselor with excellent pattern search material. During the intake sessions, the counselor can guide the client to discuss any or all of these issues as a way to get a clear perspective of the client's world. The more areas the counselor explores, the more clearly the patterns emerge. Consider the following case excerpt exploring a few of the areas. See if you can hypothesize about this client's patterns.

Case Excerpt 1 (Family of Origin)

Counselor: You have made several remarks about your relationship with your parents. Have you always been caught in the middle of their arguments?

Client: Oh yes. I mean, I'm 46 now and I'm still getting sucked
               in. Ever since I was a child, I recall it happening. My father
               worked long hours, and my mom took care of me and my
               sister. I could tell she would get tired of hanging out with
               us and resented my father working all the time. He would
               come home and they would start screaming at each other.
               Neither one really respected the other. Sooner or later, my
               dad would get tired of yelling at my mom and would turn
               on me and my sister. Then later my mom would come to
               me and try to console me.

Counselor: And now you are the one who is expected to console her?

Client: Yeah, she calls all the time, complaining about my father
               and how hard it is living with him. She just wants me to
               listen because she thinks I can relate. To tell you the truth,
               it's very draining.

Case Excerpt 2 (Friendships)

Counselor: Tell me a little about your support network of friends.

Client: I have a pretty good group of about five girlfriends. They
               are great.

Counselor: What do you bring to the friendship group that makes you
               a contributing member?

Client: I'm a nice person.

Counselor: How would you define "nice"?

Client: Well, I am like the "go to" person of the group. If some-
               one needs something, I'm there for them. People know that
               I am available to talk to them if they have a problem. When-
               ever there is a disagreement among the group, I am the
               one people look to as a mediator. Just last week, Charlotte
               and Tara got in this huge fight, and I must have spent all
               night and most of the next day talking with each of them
               on the phone until I brokered a truce. I was worn out. That
               happens a lot.

Case Excerpt 3 (Parenting)

Counselor: As a mother of two small children, you must have a lot on
               your plate. Tell about your relationship with your kids.

Client: Yes, Abbey is six and Allistair is four. They are quite the handful! I really enjoy them though.

Counselor: What do you enjoy?

Client: Just being with them. I can tell they love me very much. I left my pretty demanding job after Abbey was born. I just couldn't work and be a mom. It was too much. I really like being there for them. I get to make them breakfast, really all the meals. I get to see all their "first" things, like walking and talking and stuff like that. I think I am much more connected to them than my husband. I like that connection.

Counselor: They need you.

Client: Oh yes! I mean, they are little kids, so I think that is pretty normal.

Counselor: That's the fun side of being a mom. Is there any part that you would like to change?

Client: I would like a little more help, I think.

Counselor: You mean from your husband, Lucas?

Client: Right. I just feel overwhelmed sometimes by having to do everything. I know I don't do it all, but sometimes it feels like that.

Based on the case material, can you detect some common patterns in the client's life? Probably most apparent is the fact that she enjoys being connected to other people. Isolation does not seem to be a common behavioral pattern for her. Along with her desire and ability to connect is a pattern of how she connects with others. In each of the areas, she reports being in the role of "helper." In her family of origin, she helped and is still helping her mom with the tension experienced with husband/father. In her friendships, she mediates disputes and provides other services. With her kids, she is the primary caretaker. Another evident pattern associated with her role can be seen in the emotions that are experienced as a result of that role. For the client, she experiences joy and a sense of belonging that is associated with being needed. Unfortunately, that feeling is often followed by a sense of being drained, exhausted, and overwhelmed. We hope this exercise has demonstrated how the use of external information can illuminate patterns. Although it may seem like more than enough to establish some workable patterns, paying attention to experiences in the here and now can also provide clues to the client's world.

Here-and-Now Sources

The therapeutic relationship is a gold mine of pattern search opportunities provided that you have established a meaningful rapport with the client. As you learn about the client's external world, the primary thought on the counselor's mind should be, "How are these relationship dynamics occurring in our relationship?" For example:

Client: My husband and I don't get along very well. We really haven't for several years. I tend to go along with what he wants to do and never get my own way.

Counselor: It seems you give in but resent not being listened to.
                (Empathic reflection. Counselor notes relationship pattern and wonders how it will manifest in the counseling relationship.)

Client: Yes, that's it. I guess I suffer in silence. You are right, I want to be listened to, but I just suck it up and then hate him for pushing me around.

Counselor: I'm thinking about what that would look like in here. I haven't noticed that lately, but I wonder how I would know if you thought I was pushing you around? What would suffering in silence look like?
                (The counselor, having noticed the pattern, brings it into the here and now of the counseling relationship.)

In this example, the counselor is making use of a relationship pattern that has not yet appeared in counseling. Addressing it now allows the counselor and client to share responsibility for addressing it should it arise in the context of future sessions. Consider another example:

Client: My parents have always been there for me. It seems like whenever I stumble, there they are, ready to pitch in and rescue me from harm. It's been like that all my life, and here I am, at 40, and they are still taking bullets for me.

Counselor: It seems like you are ambivalent about their role. On the one hand, you appreciate their support, but on the other, you wonder if it's too much.

> (An empathic statement designed to get the client to go deeper. Counselor is also noting the pattern emergence of dependency on others and is thinking about how that pattern has manifested within the counseling sessions.)

Client: Yeah, it's weird. I don't want to let go, but they don't either.

Counselor: Tell me more about the fear of letting go.
> (Empathic statement naming an emotion, fear.)

Client: Well, I want the support, so it's scary to think about doing life all on my own. When I get scared, I get anxious, and when I get anxious, my parents get anxious and jump in to rescue me.

Counselor: It seems like you use the anxiety as a signal of distress, so others will know you need help.
> (Identifying the pattern.)

Client: Yes, I think that's right.

Counselor: I've noticed that in our relationship as well. You get very nervous and talk about anxiety when we address some topics. I wonder if you are letting me know you need help with those issues.
> (Addressing the pattern in the context of the counseling relationship.)

Client: Yes, I guess I do that, now that you mention it.

In this example, the counselor identifies the external relational pattern and discovers an example of how it is operating in the counseling relationship. By identifying it and using the counseling relationship as "evidence," the client and counselor now have a here-and-now testing laboratory for working on that pattern.

There are also times when the counselor will have a reaction to the client but does not have any information that the pattern exists outside of counseling. In this aspect of the counseling relationship, the counselor uses the contemporaneous counseling experience as a basis for hypothesizing about a possible pattern.

Client: I'm sorry I missed last session. I got real busy and just forgot to call.

Counselor: Well, as we have discussed, this is your time. If you make an appointment, it is your responsibility for coming and working.

Client: I know. I know. Wow, you don't have to make me feel so guilty about it.

You know, if you would call and remind me, that would help. You know how I tend to forget things.

Counselor: You would like me to be responsible for your coming to counseling?

Client: Well, I guess calling to remind me is a little much, but would it be too hard for you to call if I'm late? You know, to give me a little warning that I might have missed it? If you had called, I could have made the session. I'm only five minutes away.

Counselor: Hmmm . . . that still feels like you wanting me to take responsibility for your stuff. When you make those suggestions, I have an internal pull to say, "OK, I'll do that." I'll have to monitor times when I feel that pull. I wonder if you have that effect on other people.

In addition to the use of the counseling relationship as a method of marking patterns, counselors also note dynamics in the client that may point to common threads of import. Tracking emotions, which ones appear and when they disappear, as well as tracking the cognitive and behavioral antecedents and corollaries is an effective pattern search strategy. Consider the following emotional patterns exhibited by clients:

A 15-year-old boy tears up whenever the topic of his recently deceased father comes up. His sadness is immediately followed by squirming in the chair, face rubbing, and a desire to change the subject. He most often changes the subject to how angry he is with his mom's nagging.

A 40-year-old man reports feeling anxious when discussing issues of intimacy. The anxiety manifests as fidgeting and increasing his rate of speech. Explorations into the anxiety and possible things he could do differently are met with blaming ("She just wanted me for my money") or boasting ("I could have anyone I wanted; why would I want her?").

A 6-year-old girl in play therapy responds with fear every time an adult male toy is present in the room. She avoids the toys and through symbolic play discusses how the "little bunny rabbit is scared of the big bull." Following the emotional and behavioral pattern allows the counselor to discover elements of physical abuse in the child's home.

There are many methods for identifying the patterns in the life of the client. According to Beitman (1987): "The goal of the pattern search is to define patterns of thought, feeling, and/or behavior that are within the client's ability to influence and that, if changed, would lead toward a desirable outcome" (p. 82). Once some common themes emerge, the client and counselor can begin to formulate goals for counseling. These goals will serve as the guidelines for assessing growth or stagnation in the counseling process.

Goal-Setting

It is difficult to set realistic goals before you have a deep understanding of the client. That is the reason we put goal-setting toward the end of this chapter. In essence, goal-setting begins from the moment you first interact with the client, for relationship building is a goal, but it is rarely explicitly discussed in the counseling session. Other counseling activities such as assessment, diagnosis, and pattern search are all counseling goals, but they are not the reason the client is coming to counseling. These *counselor goals* must be met in order for the counselor to be in a position to fulfill the *client goals*. Having worked on the foundation of fulfilling the unspoken counselor goals, we can now turn our attention to the client goals as the threshold that will allow us to move toward change.

Whose Goal Is This Anyway? The Process of Goal Alignment

As patterns emerge, issues of import will seemingly become apparent to client and counselor. It is common at this stage to encounter several types of goals. They often break down into the following categories:

- Client goals: What the client wants to change.
- Counselor goals: What the counselor believes should be changed.
- External participant goals: What family members or other interested parties think the client should change.

In the best possible scenario, all of the categories focus on the same goal. Unfortunately, that rarely happens. In most cases, slight variations exist in the exact nature of the desired change. The process of goal alignment allows for the counselor to dialogue with the client and find a goal that is reasonable and attainable from all perspectives. Consider the following case.

A 15-year-old boy enters counseling at the request of his parents. The parents are disturbed at the son's lack of responsibility for his schoolwork (grades have dropped), his family life (he refuses to do chores or participate in family time), and his behavior with friends (he has been in trouble for fighting). The son complains that his parents are smothering him and he just wants to be "completely free." He maintains that everything would be just fine if they just left him alone and let him do whatever he wanted. During rapport building and pattern search, the counselor learns that the parents typically "crack down" on all their children when they reach middle adolescence. The counselor also learns that prior to this year, the son's behavior had been, by all accounts, "responsible" (good grades, family participation, solid friendships).

Based on this case material, the following goals emerged:

- Client (son) goal: "Complete freedom. I want them to leave me alone."
- External participant (parents) goal: "Responsibility."
- Counselor goal: "Wow, this is difficult."

The counselor experiences difficulty because the goals seem so disparate and the counselor cannot really buy into the client's goal. For goal alignment to work, the counselor must have a good rapport with the client, characterized by an empathic connection with the client. The counselor must be willing and able to "see" beneath the client's goal, which can be accomplished only through empathic understanding. In addition to expressing empathy, the counselor must also discern the patterns at work in the client's life. Using these two elements, the counselor can facilitate goal alignment. Here is what it would look like in our example scenario.

The counselor looks beyond the son's desire for "absolute isolation" and combines it with an understanding of the client's interaction with the family before the disruption. The counselor hypothesizes that the client wants "independence" but not total independence. He wants some freedom and respect for his work and accomplishments. The parents also want him to take responsibility, but they are so smothering that the client feels like there is no hope of being treated as responsible. The counselor tests the idea:

Counselor: If you could create a schoolwork strategy that would get you the grades you wanted, what would it look like?

Client: I would do it all by myself. I wouldn't have my parents hawking over me all night.

Counselor: That sounds irritating. What do you do when they hawk over you?

Client: I give up.

Counselor: That probably drives them crazy! What happens to your schoolwork?

Client: It doesn't get done. I know I am hurting myself, but why should I do it if they are pestering me? If I do good, all they will say is, "See, without us, you would fail."

Counselor: So you are trying to show them that they are not helping you?

Client: Yeah, but that's not working very well either. They blame me either way.

The hypothesis has been tested, and a goal emerges that both parties can agree to:

Shared goal: Increased responsibility *and* independence. The parents and client will formulate a plan on each of the concerns that allows the client to be primarily responsible for success. Definitions of each term, *responsibility* and *independence*, will be created so evaluation of progress can occur. As the client experiences success, the client will enjoy continued independence. If the client chooses irresponsible behavior, consequences (loss of independence) will result.

Although the entire counseling process would be much more detailed, the purpose here is to demonstrate how one can take goals that seem incongruent and use the power of empathy and pattern search to uncover a workable goal. Building on the foundation of the therapeutic relationship allows for the counselor to engage the client in goal formation and alignment. While some sources may advocate for goal-setting during the initial session (Winbolt, 2011), the probability of getting a superficial goal or doing counseling by chasing the symptom, is much higher. By allowing goals to develop organically, both the counselor and client have the opportunity to reap the benefits of the growing relationship and the results of more accurate information about the client's life. The deeper the connection, the better the patterns are illuminated. The more illuminated the patterns, the more meaningful and accuracy of the goal. The greater the meaning and accuracy of the goal, the better the opportunity for change to occur.

There are occasions when goal alignment is not possible. They often occur when clients are interested in pursuing a goal that does not fit with the skill or values set of the counselor. When the issue is a counselor skills deficit (e.g., the client wants to learn assertiveness skills and the counselor does not feel competent in that area), then a referral to an expert in that skill area is indicated. A conflict of values is a more serious problem. Hutchins and Vaught (1997) list several client-based goals that cannot be "embraced" by counselors:

- The goal to harm self or others.
- The goal of developing or participating in behaviors incongruent with the counselors' belief system (learning ways to join a gang or hate group; wanting to learn how to better control and manipulate members of the opposite sex).
- The goal of learning unsafe or illegal practices (how to deal drugs, steal from your work without getting caught, or lose an unhealthy amount of weight).

(p. 150)

The inability to accept individuals into counseling for reasons such as these rests on the fact that all of the examples represent a discordance between the client's values and those of counselors and the profession of counseling. Counselors who encounter clients expressing such goals can dialogue about the appropriateness of the stated goal. If the client is persistent, counselors must, when necessary, then take steps to protect the client or others as dictated by ethical code and legal precedent. The clash in values creates an unviable foundation for empathy, and without the rapport, treatment will suffer. In the end, if the dissonance continues, the counselor recognizes that a referral to a different counselor is the most professional course of action.

Elements of a "Good" Counseling Goal

Now that you know the types of goals and how to align the goal when the types are incongruent, it is time to learn about formulating goals that have the best chance of producing change. Clients come into counseling with an idea of what they want to change but often have only vague notions of how to get there. It's also important to note that even though many of your clients may express the same or similar sounding goals—"I want to find a satisfying relationship"—there are huge individual differences in how each client will define that term, and even more importantly, be motivated to take risks and make changes (Holmes, Hollinshead, Roffman, Smoller, & Buckner, 2016). Building a solid foundational therapeutic relationship, followed by a discovery of patterns in the client's life, positions the counselor–client team to both identify goals and set a course to achieve them. However, setting an appropriate goal is sometimes more difficult than it seems. Numerous sources (Cavanagh & Levitov, 2002; Egan, 2014; Cormier & Hackney, 2016) have summarized the key elements of effective counseling goals.

- *Goals must be specific and measurable.* If you ask a client, "What would you like to have happen as a result of your work in counseling?" you will likely get the answer, "I want to be happy." Happy is nice, but it is not a good counseling goal at face value. Why? Well, the answer is because happy is vague and has many different definitions depending on whom you ask. To make "happy" a good counseling goal, we have to specify what happy looks like to the client. For example, the client may say, "Happy for me means fighting less with my husband over money." This is a specific definition of <u>happy,</u> and it can also be measured. The client can keep a log of conflicts with her husband over money and assess, day by day, whether or not she is achieving her goal.
- *Goals must be realistic.* Good counseling goals have a reasonable probability of attainment when the client's strengths and limitations are factored into the equation. Consider two men who enter counseling with the stated goal, "I want to increase my comfort in my intimate relationships so I can get married with less anxiety." Sounds good, right? The first man has been dating the same woman for three years and has been engaged for three months. The second man has a history of failed relationships and has not been in a serious relationship for two years

and has no prospects. We hope you can see that the goal is more realistic for the first man as compared to the second client. An additional comment about realistic goals addresses the expectation for change. Realistic goals understand that change is a process, not an absolute. So, framing change in terms of "less anxiety" is more realistic than setting the goal as experiencing "no anxiety."

- *Goals are often hierarchal.* It is rare for a client to enter counseling with one goal. Usually, counseling goals are multifaceted and complex. When this occurs, it is important to work with the client to prioritize the goals. In many cases the working on one goal leads to the emergence of another goal, or making progress on a goal makes it easier to then address another issue. For example, a high school junior may enter counseling to work on getting a full-time job for the summer. As you learn more about the client, you discover that the parents are opposed to him working because his grades have been slipping. Working on the goal of improving his academic performance and his relationship with his parents may take precedence over working on job exploration.

- *Goals must be evaluated frequently.* If you and your client have done all the difficult work in formulating a good counseling goal based on the elements discussed above, make sure you follow through and assess progress. One of the benefits of goal alignment is that the counseling has direction, which limits the feeling of wandering aimlessly through the sessions. Both client and counselor should participate equally in the evaluation process. When progress is not being made, it can be addressed openly, and if necessary, the goal should be realigned.

Session Documentation and Establishing a Treatment Plan

From the first session you will be expected to document the work you are doing with clients. By the time you reach your advanced clinical classes, you will have taken at least one course that provided guidance on ethical documentation and treatment planning. We provide a review here, in the pattern search stage, because it seems the most logical place for accurate treatment planning and to consider the quality of your session notes.

Session documentation is a recognized norm across all mental health disciplines, although it is not without debate. There is considerable dialogue that highlights the necessity (Bemister & Dobson, 2012; Bemister & Dobson, 2011; Mitchell, 2007) as well as the potential negative consequences (Mills, 2012). It is our contention that quality documentation provides the best legal protection for the mental health professional and best treatment accountability and protection of the client. For the purposes of this brief review, we encourage you to be familiar with the SOAP (subjective, objective, assessment, and plan) format (Carmen & Turtle-Song, 2002). This practical approach is used frequently in the field and can be adapted to fit other models. An overview of the model can be found in Box 6.1. We also provide some commentary on a common question in the field, "Should I take notes in session?" (see Box 6.2)

Box 6.1 Practical SOAP Guidelines

S (subjective): Client's emotional state while in session. This can be observed by the mental health professional or based on client self-report and description.

O (objective): Content of the client's current session material. This includes all of the pertinent topics addressed during the session.

A: (analysis): Theoretical conceptualization of the client's dynamics which may integrate diagnostic consideration, if applicable.

P: (plan): Goals of treatment are addressed here and should be connected to the established treatment plan. Short term goals mainly focus on what is to be done between current session and the next scheduled appointment. Long term goals are focused on larger aspects related to reason for coming the counseling.

Example:

Client reported feeling irritated and frustrated this week and evidenced these feelings during the session via voice tone and body language **(S)**. Client discussed current work situation where she reports

---

being recently denied a work promotion. Client works as an entry level bank teller and discussed aspirations to be a manager **(O)**. From an Adlerian perspective, the client is struggling with the life task of Work. She is experiencing inferiority feelings due to her perception that she is being overlooked by her boss. She is responding to this inferiority by avoiding her work environment **(A)**. Client will try to engage with her work this week, rather than avoid. One potential activity is to set up a meeting with her boss to discuss her goals. Counselor and client will continue to explore style of life patterns.

Box 6.2 Should I Take Notes in Session?

During the first few sessions of group supervision in our advanced clinical courses, we like to reserve space for questions about the counseling process or the profession. We like to call these opportunities, "Anything you want to know about counseling, but have been afraid to ask". While many of the typical issues have been the basis of much of this book, the question of whether or not to take notes in session is a common one, so we thought we would address it here. When we ask students about the rationale for taking notes in session, we often hear, "I am afraid of missing information" or "My memory is not good enough to remember it all". The premise it that to be a "good" therapist, one must remember all the information that a client is throwing at you. We believe that is a mistaken belief. In fact, most of the details are not worth remembering! Whether the client's sister lives in Wisconsin or Michigan is probably not vital to the treatment of the client, nor is it important whether the client graduated college in 1996 or 1997. The *process* (themes) are more important than the *content* (details), so paying attention to what stands out for you from the billions of pieces of information is key.

We also believe it is difficult, if not impossible, to write about old information and listen to new information simultaneously. So, in an effort to catch everything, you are actually missing some as you write. In addition to missing information, when you write, break contact with the client which could negatively impact rapport. We think that your counselor brain in like a new muscle, that must be exercised to develop properly. You have not been using your counselor brain fully in your other relationships, but the advanced clinical classes provide you with an opportunity to stretch it. We encourage you to try to listen fully to your client and minimize activities that might diminish your ability to be present, which includes in session note taking. For further consideration, research has demonstrated a negative impact of in session note taking on both therapist and client (Hickling, Sison, & Radetsky, 1984; Miller, 1992; Piolat, Olive, & Kellogg, 2005).

Treatment planning emerges from your work with the client in all the ways we have discussed up this point; information gathering, alliance formation, pattern searching and goalsetting. If you are taking good case notes, the issues of focus should jump off the page and be apparent, which will greatly ease the process of writing the treatment plan. According to Seligman (1993) the importance of treatment planning rests in four main areas:

- A carefully developed treatment plan, if well grounded in research on treatment effectiveness, provides assurance that treatment with a high likelihood of success is being provided.
- Written treatment plans allow counselors to demonstrate accountability without difficulty. Treatment plans can substantiate the value of the work being done by a single counselor or by an agency and can assist in obtaining funding as well as providing a sound defense in the event of a malpractice suit.
- Use of a treatment plan that specifies goals and procedures can help counselors and clients to track their progress. They can determine whether goals are being met as planned and, if they are not, can reassess the treatment plan.
- Treatment plans also provide a sense of structure and direction to the counseling process and can help counselors and clients to develop

shared and realistic expectations for that process. Research has shown that people who anticipate positive and realistic outcomes from counseling and whose expectations are congruent with those of their counselors are more likely to achieve those outcomes.

(p. 288)

Treatment planning is best viewed as an integrated and natural part of the counseling process. We have provided a sample treatment-plan template (Box 6.3) for you to consider as you gain more practice is melding all of these activities into a unified whole. It is important to note that treatment planning is not a one-time event, but should evolve and be revised as client needs change. For a more detailed explanation of treatment planning, consult Seligman (2004) and Schwitzer and Rubin (2015).

Box 6.3 Sample Treatment Plan

Date:
Counselor:

CLIENT INFORMATION

Client Name:
Age:
Gender:
If minor, guardian names:

PRESENTING ISSUES/DIAGNOSIS:
Presenting issues:

DSM-5 Diagnosis:

TREAMENT GOALS
(Treatment goals should be SMART: Specific, Measurable, Achievable, Relevant, and Timely)

Treatment Goal 1:
Client will . . .

Planned interventions to address Treatment Goal 1:
A.
B.
C.

Treatment Goal 2:
Client will . . .

Planned interventions to address Treatment Goal 2:
A.
B.
C.

TREATMENT OUTCOME

Treatment Goal 1:
    A. Expected date of achievement:
    B. Results:
    C. Follow up:

Treatment Goal 2:
    A. Expected date of achievement:
    B. Results:
    C. Follow up:

Counselor Signature:_____   **Supervisor Signature:** _____

Summary

This chapter continues the process that began with rapport building. As the counselor connects with the client, more information becomes available and patterns emerge. There are many strategies for obtaining good information about the client. Assessment tools, diagnostic systems, and informal intake interviews all provide the counselor with data for pattern searching. The information streams depend largely on the empathic relationship between client and counselor; the more the client trusts the counselor, the more information is disclosed.

Mental health professionals use these external sources of information to see themes in the client's life. The counselor can also use and compare the external information with the in-session behavioral and emotional patterns of the client. Using the counseling relationship provides an *in vivo* experience of the patterns, and acclimates the client to the use of immediacy in the change process. Once some preliminary themes are identified, goal-setting becomes a collaborative process that sets the stage for the work ahead. While the work is coming together, note-taking and treatment planning are useful ways to organize the complex world of the client and can help provide guidance for movement as well as assessment of progress.

Reflection Questions

1. Consider your own personal philosophy on the use of assessment. Under what conditions would you feel comfortable referring someone for psychological or vocational testing?
2. What are some patterns in your own life? How aware are you of your own patterns? What are some patterns that you have tried to change in your life? What was easy and difficult about changing?
3. Explore what it means to be patient. How are you patient in your life?
4. Explore what it means to be curious. How are you curious in your life? How can you cultivate a greater spirit of curiosity?
5. What might be some obstacles that might interfere with good goal-setting in counseling? How would you work with the client to overcome the resistance?
6. What are your thoughts about taking session notes? Reflect on what you learned about note-taking in your previous classes and compare this learning to what you are experiencing in the field.

References

American Psychiatric Association (2017). *Diagnostic and Statistical Manual of Mental Disorders-5* (5th ed., text revised). Arlington, VA: Author.

Beitman, B. D. (1987). *The structure of individual psychotherapy.* New York: Guilford.

Beitman, B. D., Viamontes, G. I., Soth, A. M., & Nittler, J. (2006). Toward a neural circuitry of engagement, self-awareness, and pattern search. *Psychiatric Annals, 36*(4), 272–280.

Bemister, T., & Dobson, K. (2011). An updated account of the ethical and legal considerations of record keeping. *Canadian Psychology, 52*, 296–309.

Bemister, T., & Dobson, K. (2012). A reply to Mills. Record keeping: Practical implications of ethical and legal issues. *Canadian Psychology, 53*, 143–145.

Cameron, S., & Turtle-Song, I. (2002). Learning to write case notes using the SOAP format. *Journal of Counseling & Development, 80*(3), 286–292.

Cavanagh, M. E., & Levitov, J. E. (2002). *The counseling experience: A theoretical and practical approach* (2nd ed.). Prospect Heights, IL: Waveland.

Cormier, S., & Hackney, H. (2016). *Counseling strategies and interventions* (9th ed.). Columbus, OH: Pearson.

Egan, G. (2014). *The skilled helper* (10th ed.). Belmont, CA: Brooks/Cole.

Hickling, E., Sison, G., & Radetsky, S. (1984). The effect of note-taking on a simulated clinical interview. *Journal of Psychology, 116*, 235–240.

Holmes, A. J., Hollinshead, M. O., Roffman, J. L., Smoller, J. W., & Buckner, R. L. (2016). Individual differences in cognitive control circuit anatomy link sensation seeking, impulsivity, and substance use. *The Journal of Neuroscience, 36*, 4038–4049.

Hutchins, D. E., & Vaught, C. C. (1997). *Helping relationships and strategies* (3rd ed.). Pacific Grove, CA: Brooks/Cole.

Miller, M. (1992). Effects of note-taking on perceived counselor social influence during a career counseling session. *Journal of Counseling Psychology, 39*, 317–320

Mills, J. (2012). Recordkeeping in the real world of private practice: Recommendations for Canadian psychologists. Commentary on Bemister and Dobson (2011). *Canadian Psychology, 53*, 140–142.

Mitchell, R. W. (2007). *Documentation in counseling records: An overview of ethical, legal and clinical issues* (3rd ed). Alexandria, VA: American Counseling Association.

Morrison, J. (2014). *DSM-5 made easy*. New York: Guilford.

Piolat, A., Olive, T., & Kellogg, R. (2005). Cognitive effort during note taking. *Applied Cognitive Psychology, 19*, 291–312.

Reichenberg, L.W., & Seligman, L. (2016). *Selecting effective treatments* (5th ed.). San Francisco, CA: Jossey-Bass.

Schwitzer, A. M., & Rubin, L. C. (2015). *Diagnosis and treatment planning skills: A popular culture casebook approach.*, 2nd ed., DSM-5 update. Thousand Oaks, CA: Sage.

Seligman, L. (2004). *Diagnosis and treatment planning in counseling* (3rd ed). New York: Plenum Press.

Seligman, L. (1993). Teaching treatment planning. *Counselor education and Supervision, 32*(4), 287–297.

Seligman, L. (1994). *Developmental career counseling and assessment.* Thousand Oaks, CA: Sage.

Summers, N. (2003). *Fundamentals for practice with high risk populations.* Pacific Grove, CA: Brooks/Cole.

Winbolt, B. (2011). *Solution focused therapy for the helping professions.* London: Jessica Kingsley Publishers.

7

HELPING CLIENTS CHANGE

By this time in your training, you have learned some skills and techniques for helping your clients move toward change. Chapters 5 and 6 outlined the first necessary steps for the process of therapeutic change. Developing and maintaining solid rapport and participating in thorough assessment and goal-setting are activities that create an atmosphere conducive to producing change. Yet change is a nebulous concept. People are not machines, for which we can easily diagnose the problem, apply a specific tool, and guarantee a positive result. Various schools of thought and numerous counseling theories supply us with philosophical and scientific explanations of how people develop, become maladjusted, and use counseling to change. The fact that there are so many different theories of how best to help people change should tip you off that change is not a concrete dynamic. It is beyond the scope of this chapter to address the many facets and nuances of change, but we can outline specific spheres of change and common client resistance to the change process.

Basic Considerations in Change

The process of change is one of the most complex aspects of counseling and it is also the part that mental health professionals and clients are most interested in figuring out—yet solid answers are elusive. The complexity arises in the fact that no one single factor or entity is truly in charge of the change. Instead, research seems to support the notion that change is a function of interrelated dynamics that include counselor, client, and external forces (Asay & Lambert, 1999; Duncan, Miller, Wampold, & Hubble, 2010; Lambert, 1992). A number of current research studies and conceptual papers have reported on a wide range of factors that impact change (Bohart, 2009; Comninos & Grenyer, 2007; Gordon, 2012; Hawley, Leibert, & Lane, 2014; Leibert, 2011; Lu, Jiang, Lu, & Lin, 2017).

Box 7.1 What Produces Change in Counseling?

According to Asay and Lambert (1999)

1) At least 40% of positive outcome in psychotherapy can be attributed to extratherapeutic factors. These are elements that occur outside of the counseling session and are outside of the counselor's sphere of influence. Extratherapeutic factors include aspects of the client's environment which can include their work, cultural identity, and the quality of the client's social support network. It also includes the client's ability and willingness to access and use the resources at their disposal. Extratherapeutic factors are also comprised of client factors such as the severity and chronicity of the client's problem, motivation to change, interpersonal skills, and the ability to set and work towards goals.

2) At least 30% of counseling outcome can be attributed to the therapeutic relationship. This element is firmly within the counselor's sphere of influence. It is the counselor's responsibility to have knowledge of the skills necessary to help facilitate therapeutic rapport and be able to perform the behaviors necessary for an alliance to develop. In addition a counselor should identity and revise a wellness plan to enhance self-care to avoid burnout, consistently collaborate with the client to maintain a collaborative the therapeutic process, and routinely assess client progress.

3) About 15% of positive outcome be attributed to the client's expectation of improvement. This includes the client's general hope and

desire for change, along with the belief that counseling can help them with the change process. Client and counselor are both part of this process and the counselor should possess a belief that what they do is effective. Ethically speaking, the counselor should work to instill hope while avoiding the problematic behavior of guaranteeing any particular positive outcome.

4) Finally, 15% of beneficial outcome in counseling can be attributed to the techniques of the mental health professional. Much energy has been invested in finding out what works best for whom, primarily in the form of validated treatment and evidence-based approaches. While the debate rages on about the methodology used to create these manuals and lists of techniques, it is important to balance the need for research based treatment with the relative impact that techniques have in relation to the other contributing factors to change.

We encourage you to develop a firm foundation of who you are as a counselor. Know how to develop rapport and work towards change while collaborating with your client along the way. Use further training and continuing education to expand and deepen your base, while taking opportunities to stretch yourself and integrate new information in the field. Do not feel you have to chase the newest trend in technique. Techniques will largely be ineffective or soon dropped if you do now have a way to truly weave the new toy into your core way of helping.

According to Beitman (1987): "The process of change takes place in a number of contexts . . . The psychotherapeutic contexts include the strength of the therapeutic alliance and the specificity of the patterns identified for change" (p. 173). This quotation serves as a reminder that counseling is a cyclic process, not a linear one. You do not "achieve" rapport, graduate to pattern search and goal-setting, and then move on to change. Instead, each element builds and feeds the others. As the move toward change quickens, two important concepts emerge: *responsibility* and *practice*.

Responsibility

Every counseling theory since the time of Freud includes personal responsibility as a major philosophical underpinning. From a basic standpoint, human beings have the capacity to be aware of their responsibility for their own thoughts, feelings, and behavior. As a result, people are ultimately accountable for the choice to change those aspects of the self. Clients intuitively understand this notion. Just watch the avalanche of head-nodding when the television therapist Dr. Phil says, "You cannot change what you do not acknowledge." Consider the two following case examples and assess which client will have the better chance of producing a positive change.

Case One

Nicole is a 15-year-old student who entered counseling at the urging of her parents. Nicole is not doing well in school. In fact, over the past six months, her grades have dropped considerably. During the session, although she is initially hesitant, she discloses that she has been struggling both socially and academically. Her best friend moved about eight months ago, and that loss has left her feeling isolated. She reports that she is having trouble focusing on her schoolwork and feels very sad. She states: "School is my job, and I know I am not working up to my potential. I feel bad that my parents are so confused about what's going on with me. I want to try to get over this and do better."

Case Two

Jeff is a 40-year-old physician in counseling due to relationship problems with his wife of 15 years. Jeff reports that he works long hours and has a very demanding job. He seems proud that he provides financially for his family and keeps them in a comfortable lifestyle. He resents the fact that his wife is so unhappy after all he does for her and the kids. He admits that the nature of his work keeps him away from the family almost every day and sometimes he just sleeps at the hospital when he is on call, which is every other week. He understands that his absence is "not ideal" but chalks it up to the "trade-off for the type of life I am giving them." Jeff states: "I don't see what the problem is. If you ask me, she needs to learn to quit spending money, and then maybe I wouldn't have to work so hard."

After carefully considering each case, you deduced we hope, that Nicole has a much better probability of changing than Jeff does. Even though both clients entered counseling at the request of a third party, Nicole has the awareness and willingness to accept responsibility for change. Jeff is too busy blaming others and rationalizing the issues. While the end of Nicole's case provides hope for the next step in the counseling process, the end of Jeff's case is met with feelings of hopelessness and stagnation.

Practice

Once the client assumes responsibility for change, practicing the change must occur on a consistent basis. If you have done a good job with rapport building and pattern searching, you will have a deep understanding of the client's world and many different aspects of the client's life that can be used as points of contact and attention for possible change. The client's tendency, even when insight has been achieved, will be to sink back into old and comfortable patterns. This tendency is what makes change so difficult, but makes practice so important and necessary for real change. In essence, practice helps establish a new pattern that can be more comfortable than the old one.

Often, the practicing of new ways of thinking, feeling, and behaving take place within the safety of the counseling session. As the change becomes more comfortable, the client may begin to experiment with the change in other relationships, bringing the feedback to counseling to process. This "fine-tuning" is essential to the change process because it solidifies the change by encouraging continued practice and adapting the change to meet the unique needs of the client's world.

Changes in Cognition, Affect, and Behavior

An examination of the major theories of counseling will highlight the fact that change through counseling is viewed as occurring in three primary spheres: cognition (thoughts), affect (feelings), and behavior. Depending on the theory, one sphere may be more strongly emphasized than the others. It is the human equivalent of the chicken-and-egg conundrum. If you change your thoughts, will that produce change in feeling and behavior? Can you enjoy lasting improvements in your behavior without modifying your thoughts? Does moderating the intensity of your emotional state have an impact on the way you think or behave? All of these questions, and more, are the same queries about how best to help people change. We believe the "correct" answer is a holistic approach. The best guess is that all three spheres are important in the change process, and competent counselors focus on the consistency among all three within the movement of the client. The following sections explore some ways to facilitate change in each of the spheres while providing commentary on how emphasizing one sphere also impacts the others.

Focus on Cognitive Change

The basic premise of therapies that focus on cognitive change is that thoughts greatly influence how we feel and behave. Theories that emphasize cognitive restructuring or changes in belief systems view thoughts as the primary mediating variable in the change process. Figure 7.1 depicts

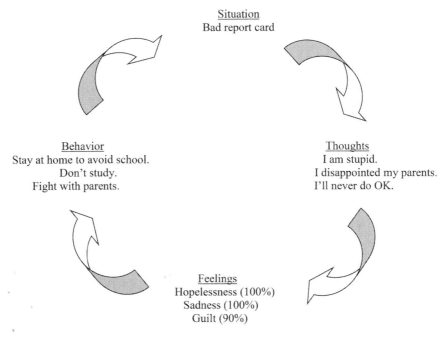

Situation
Bad report card

Thoughts
I am stupid.
I disappointed my parents.
I'll never do OK.

Feelings
Hopelessness (100%)
Sadness (100%)
Guilt (90%)

Behavior
Stay at home to avoid school.
Don't study.
Fight with parents.

Figure 7.1 A cognitive cycle

A (Activating Event)

My father yelled at me and grounded me for the weekend.

B (Belief About A)

"He is unfair. He should be more caring."

"I am always a victim."

"He must understand me. Because he doesn't, my life is ruined."

C (Consequences)

Unhealthy negative emotions:

Rage

Shame

Betrayal

Self-defeating behaviors:

Denies responsibility for actions

Refuses to build relationship with dad

Sneaks behind dad's back

Figure 7.2 ABC model (example from Fall, Holden, & Marquis, 2017)

a simple cognitive cycle, and Figure 7.2 illustrates a model from rational emotive behavior therapy (REBT) that pinpoints beliefs rather than thoughts. Both models represent the idea that cognitions and their modification are the most effective pathways to change. In each of the figures, you can see the impact that thoughts have on the other spheres of feelings and behavior.

Cognitive change occurs when we challenge the way we think about situations. In counseling, strategies such as cognitive restructuring, disputing, confrontation, and teaching clients self-talk techniques are all examples of some cognitive change strategies. Figures 7.3 and 7.4 take the examples

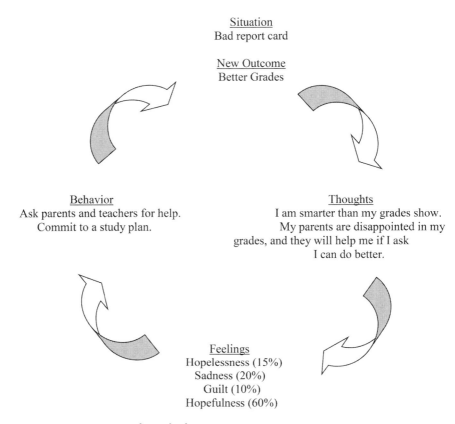

Figure 7.3 Cognitive cycle with change

used in the previous figures and illustrate both cognitive interventions and the change produced.

Focus on Affective Change

In Chapter 6, we discussed the importance of the therapeutic relationship and the role of empathy. Provided that the counselor has forged an alliance with the client, the relationship can be the foundation for continued emotional exploration and growth. Throughout the change process, empathy should be fostered to maintain the relationship and help the client connect with emotional content. In addition to empathy as a method for affective change, two other skills, *normalization* and *working through*, are common methods for helping clients facilitate a new way of experiencing feelings.

A (Activating Event)
My father yelled at me and grounded me for the weekend.

B (Belief About A)	**Disputation**
"He is unfair. He should be more caring."	1) What evidence supports these beliefs?
"I am always a victim."	2) Are these beliefs helping or hurting me?
"He must understand me. Because he doesn't, my life is ruined."	3) Is it really as awful as I believe?

C (Consequences)
Unhealthy negative emotions:
Rage
Shame
Betrayal

New Effect
Healthy emotions:
Frustration
Regret
Disappointment

Self-defeating behaviors:
Denies responsibility for actions

Refuses to build relationship with dad
Sneaks behind dad's back

Self-actualizing behaviors:
Accepts responsibility for own actions

Communicates directly with father

Figure 7.4 ABC model of intervention (examcple from Fall, Holden & Marquis, 2004)

Normalization

Any change is, by definition, a new experience, and new is not always comfortable. In fact, it is often awkward and painful. As new feelings emerge, the client may experience the surfacing emotions as alien or "not normal" and may try to ignore them or make them go away. Counselors can facilitate the client's integration of the changes in affect by helping the client accept the new feelings as "normal." Consider the following case dialogue:

Client: As I have explored my relationship with my sister, I realize
             that I have been protecting her all these years by not telling
             her what I really think and how I really feel.

Counselor: You realize that you haven't been genuine with her.

Client: Right! I haven't been myself.

Counselor: I understand that you chose not to share your feelings with her out of an effort to protect her and that maybe you felt it wasn't safe, but I wonder if you, as a first step, might be willing to share those true feelings here?

Client: I think I can do that . . . umm . . . I guess when I think about it, I feel a lot of anger toward her . . . frustration.

Counselor: Yes, some anger, and I also sense some resentment.

Client: Yes! That's it. Resentment. Wow, that feels really weird to me. I want to push it back.

Counselor: That desire to lock the feeling up again is completely natural considering your competing desire to protect you sister. You are afraid your resentment will hurt her.

Client: Yeah, that's why I don't show it. But when I lock it up, it just gets worse.

Counselor: Because the resentment represents your true feelings at the moment, and the pattern of stuffing those feelings is very natural for you, maybe we can practice experiencing the resentment and work on ways for you to disclose those feelings in a way that is comfortable to you.

Client: That sounds good.

In this example, the client is getting in touch with a new emotion. The counselor has done an effective job of exploring the patterns in the client's life, and as the new emotion emerges, both client and counselor make sense of it based on the pattern. In this case, the new feeling of resentment has been buried as a result of the client's pattern of protecting her sister. As the new feeling surfaces, the client wants to respond based on the old pattern and submerge the emotion, but the counselor illuminates the pattern and normalizes, or legitimates, the feeling in order to facilitate a new way of experiencing the emotion. In the end, the counselor uses the normalizing and pattern identification as a way to encourage and invite the client to practice working through the resentment.

Working through

In working through one's emotions, people get a sense of the process of emotional regulation. Anxiety and its associated problems are a good example of this dynamic. Anxiety is a natural part of existence and in and of itself is not dysfunctional. However, when clients get stuck in anxiety, rumination and escalation occur. As one client mentioned, "getting lost in anxiety" does not allow for working through the feeling. The process of working through feelings can be outlined as follows:

1. *Identify the feeling:* This may be relatively easy or rather difficult to do, depending on the client. One of the interesting outcomes of emotional change is that clients develop a new sense of comfort and an expanded awareness of the continuum of emotionality. In this step, the client must identify the emotion before he or she can work through and change the feeling state.

2. *Accept the feeling:* After identifying the feeling, accepting instead of resisting the feeling allows for processing. Saying, "It's OK to be angry right now," or "I give myself permission to feel sad at this moment," may help the client get fully in touch with the current feeling.

3. *Process the feeling through internal or external dialogue:* Clients can learn to mediate their own emotional states internally, but counseling provides a safe avenue to process the feelings as clients are going through the first steps of emotional change. Through processing, clients can explore emotional, cognitive, and behavioral aspects of their current emotional state and ways to modify the feelings as needed.

4. *Identify the feeling:* The end of the process is actually a new beginning. As the client processes the emotion, new feelings emerge and can be worked through using the same steps. Seen this way, working through is a growth model of change that is cyclic and layered.

Focus on Behavioral Change

Behavioral change refers to adaptations in the client's actions. Modifying behavior can be seen as a pathway to change, such as a client gaining relief from a paralyzing fear of snakes through being in the presence of snakes (the change was the decrease in fear, and the behavior of exposure was the necessary step), or as the element needing the change, as in cases of clients who cannot find a job because they lack some specific social skills. In either instance, the importance of *doing* something different becomes a vital part of the change process.

Behavioral rehearsal allows clients to practice with new sets of skills and deal with the coexisting cognitions and feelings that may arise but are often representative of the old patterns. Cormier and Hackney (2016) note that rehearsal is most often used in three main ways:

1. The client possesses a skills deficit ("response acquisition").
2. The client possesses the requisite skills but has difficulty discerning between appropriate and inappropriate times to use the skills ("response facilitation").
3. The client's emotional or cognitive responses are interfering with the productive application of the new skills ("response disinhibition").

(p. 143)

Each of these types of behavioral rehearsal domains requires different, but sometimes overlapping, counseling strategies. For example, response acquisition may include techniques that impart information and expose the client to new skill sets. In addition to a more active teaching component, the counselor may also process cognitive and affective responses to the new skills.

In response facilitation, the counselor may use the uncovered patterns to provide the client with insight as to why the client is misapplying the skills. Within this approach the counselor may use empathy, confrontation, and hypothesizing about alternative strategies as a way of working through the issue. Consider the case of the woman who is seeking help with forming a satisfactory relationship. She complains that she finds only men who are controlling and dominating. Through the counseling process, she realizes that in the foundational portion of the relationship, she acts dumb and submissive. Her underlying belief is that "men won't like me if I have an opinion." She possesses the skills to connect with people, but her method is faulty. A behavioral intervention would consider the cognitive and emotional issues surrounding the old and new strategy of connecting with possible partners.

In response disinhibition, counselors will process in depth the emotional and cognitive factors associated with the problematic behavior. Using operant and classical conditioning techniques, the behavior change will be used to moderate the intense emotional and cognitive reactions. Common examples of this form of rehearsal include treatment for anxiety disorders such as panic disorder and simple phobia.

A Model Tying It All Together

Based on your practical experience and educational knowledge, you probably understand that change is not an easy dynamic to sum up in a few pages. In fact, you will spend a great deal of your professional life trying to answer the question, "Why did Client A change, but Client B did not?" We believe that focusing on the basic elements we have discussed in this chapter will provide you with some guidance in facilitating change. Prochaska and colleagues have developed one of the most comprehensive and practical transtheoretical models of change (see Prochaska, DiClemente, & Norcross, 1992; Prochaska, et al., 1994; Prochaska, & Norcross, 2002). You likely have already been exposed to this model, but if you have not, it should be a good method of integrating the elements of change.

In the transtheoretical model, change progresses through six stages: precontemplation, contemplation, preparation, action, maintenance, and termination. Each stage requires different methods to produce change. This process honors the progression that we have discussed in Chapters 6 and 7 and will continue in Chapter 9. The unique and attractive element of this model is that it not only emphasizes the emotional, cognitive, and behavioral aspects of change but also helps explain why clients get stuck in the change process. In the most primary sense, stagnation or resistance arises from two primary sources:

1. The client is not personally convinced (emotionally, cognitively, and/or behaviorally) that change is as beneficial as not changing.
2. The counselor is not functioning at the same stage as the client. Remember the old counseling adage, "Meet the client where the client is." Counselors who are interacting with a client with action stage elements when the client is functioning at the precontemplation stage will encounter a lot of resistance. At the same time, a counselor who is moving too slowly, performing at contemplation stage when the client is ready for action-stage change, will experience frustration on the part of the client.

As a way to summarize the change process, we have included Table 7.1 to outline the stages of change and provide some concrete examples of how to match counselor activity to client readiness for change.

Table 7.1 Stages of Change

Stage of Change	Counselor Strategies	Typical Resistance
Precontemplation		
Client is not fully acknowledging need for change. Client may not feel the capacity or desire for change.	Initiate rapport building.	Because the client does not see a reason to change, the client may prematurely leave counseling.
	Practice active listening: reflection of feeling and content.	
	Focus on gaining an empathic connection and understanding of the client.	Counselor may get frustrated with the client at this level and may attempt to confront and push the client to the next stage.
	Begin information gathering.	
	Elicit client's perspective on what he/she views as problem areas in current living.	
Contemplation		
Client is identifying areas for change but expresses ambivalence about the need and/or desire to change.	Continue to focus on rapport building and empathy.	Client may view own ambivalence as a sign of not being ready for change and may leave counseling.

Begin pattern search utilizing open and directed exploration of identified issues.

Incorporate assessment and diagnosis to further illuminate patterns.

Emotional Sphere: Continue to reflect feelings, normalize the ambivalence.

Cognitive Sphere: Explore thoughts related to ambivalence, create a cost-benefit analysis of changing and not changing.

Behavioral Sphere: Explore behavioral elements of changing, emphasize aspects of personal responsibility to stay or move.

Client may decide that the benefits of not changing outweigh the benefits of changing.

Counselor may view ambivalence as a negative emotion and may ignore the advantages of not changing or the disadvantages of changing. This could lead to the client feeling misunderstood, which could produce empathic failure and increased chance of client dropout.

(Continued)

Table 7.1 (Continued)

Stage of Change	Counselor Strategies	Typical Resistance
Preparation		
Client assumes responsibility for the issues and patterns identified but is unsure about how the change will take place.	Continue rapport building. Use information gathered at this stage to confirm/strengthen identified patterns or identify new patterns. Emotional Sphere: Continue empathic understanding, encourage the client to begin to work through the emotional change process, usually first by identifying emotions and allowing self to feel; ambivalence will expand to include other feelings related to the possibility of changing or remaining the same. Cognitive Sphere: Begin to identify the thoughts that will promote change; delve deep into the thoughts that produce dysfunction and learn primary methods for modifying those thoughts.	Client may confuse the inherent anxiety associated with change with an alarm signal of impending danger. This confusion may lead the client to conclude that change is "doing the wrong thing."

Behavioral Sphere: Develop specific goals for change; identify collection of new actions that are distinct from the old behaviors; hypothesize what might be needed in terms of skill to make the proposed change.

Action

Client begins to practice the new ways of feeling, thinking, and behaving.

Continue rapport building.

Use your knowledge of client patterns to assess whether the client is really moving in a different direction.

Assess external threats and supports for the client's change.

Use homework to allow the client to work on and document changes outside of the counseling hour.

Counselor may get so excited that the client is demonstrating a willingness to change that counselor pushes for change too quickly without fully exploring the stage. Moving too quickly may result in a lack of goal attainment, which often leads to discouragement on the part of both the counselor and the client.

Client may not get change "fast enough" and may feel like it is too much work. This is viewed as a move back to an earlier stage in the model. Although it is common for ambivalence to temporarily increase, the counselor can track the client back, apply the stage-appropriate strategy, and facilitate movement.

185

(Continued)

Table 7.1 (Continued)

Stage of Change	Counselor Strategies	Typical Resistance
	Emotional Sphere: Fully engage the client in normalizing and working through emotions as they emerge in counseling.	Counselor must make sure to set specific and appropriate goals. If the goal was vague or too complex, the action can stall.
	Cognitive Sphere: Help the client challenge unhealthy cognitions and create and reinforce change related thoughts.	
	Behavioral Sphere: Provide opportunity for appropriate use of the methods of rehearsal, beginning first on counseling and branching out into the "real world."	
Maintenance	Support emotional, cognitive, and behavioral change.	Counselor may see this as an "easy" stage of counseling with regard to resistance.
Client is working on making the change the new consistent way of being.	Trouble-shoot problems that arise.	Client may feel "I'm done" and leave counseling without terminating.
	Review goals and prepare fortermination.	

You Left Out Giving Advice! Is That a Skill to Produce Change?

That's a great question.

Couture and Sutherland (2006) summarized what the literature offered on why mental health professionals view advice-giving as problematic to the change process and in some cases unethical:

1) Advice could prevent clients from mobilizing their own resources and competencies.
2) Clients may become dependent on therapists and demand more advice or magical solutions.
3) Clients may blame therapists for advice that led to unsatisfactory action, and this dissatisfaction may eventually lead to termination of therapy by clients.
4) Advice provision may be seen as a violation of the therapist's value and belief systems.
5) Clients would not comply with the advice anyway, and they may further reject any attempt on the part of the therapist to guide and influence.
6) Clients may misinterpret the advice and may injure themselves or others.
7) Therapists may be disappointed if the client fails to follow the advice.

(p. 330)

One recent study (Schaerer, Tost, Huang, Gino, & Larrick, 2018) concluded that advice-giving was a behavior specifically designed to enhance the advice-giver's sense of power and that people who were most interested in gaining power were more likely to give advice than those who reported being less interested in power within interpersonal relationships. So, are you giving advice to be helpful or are you giving it to feel powerful and maintain your expert position with the therapeutic relationship?

While the cautions and caveats against advice-giving are valuable, there do seem to be moments within the counseling process where providing information is important and even therapeutic. You will encounter moments of crisis in counseling, when specific directives will be ethically and even legally required. Situations where your client is discussing suicidal or homicidal intent or commission of child abuse would fit in this category, whereby mental health professionals would offer detailed suggestions for what might happen next in counseling.

There will also be times in the counseling journey when your client seems to be struggling not with insight, but with a skills deficit. In these situations, the counseling skills that are designed to help the client discover the solution on their own becomes a bit problematic. They can't discover what they do not know. For example, consider the following dialogue:

Client:	Fatherhood has been so scary for me. Each developmental stage is like starting over. I feel lost and then I get frustrated. My 6-year-old won't listen to a thing I say. I find myself yelling and then just letting my wife take over.
Counselor:	You feel lost and defeated.
Client:	Yes! Like I should just give up! I'm horrible at this.
Counselor:	You seem ready to try some things. What do you think would be more effective?
Client:	That's the problem. I have no idea! I just go blank.
Counselor:	So you have run out of tools. Well, let's brainstorm here. Think about being in that situation. Now besides yelling and leaving, what else might be an option?
Client:	(thinks for several minutes) I'm drawing a blank.
Counselor:	You really do feel stuck! Ok, where could you research parenting strategies?
Client:	I guess I could Google it, but I don't really know what I would find.
Counselor:	Try that over the next week and we'll discuss what you find.

In this example, the counselor is probing for how deep the skills deficit is and tries several ways to increase the sense of autonomy of the client. First, the counselor tries to put the client in the moment of the conflict and tests whether the client can generate options in a less tense environment. When that did not work, the counselor gives some homework for the client to research the issue. This is designed to promote client responsibility for solving skills deficits. Should that fail, the counselor can feel fairly sure that the current frustration is due to a skills deficit and collaborate with the client on some alternatives next session.

A few key takeaways with regard to advice-giving. We think it's fair to say it should be avoided where possible. There are many outcomes that could negatively impact the therapeutic process and effective mental health professionals are aware of these when considering whether to give advice. Should you feel the client is stuck on skills deficit, save advice-giving for the last strategy, and always attempt to help the client discover ways to remediate these deficits on their own. If you do end up deciding some advice is warranted, always work collaboratively with the client in exploring the alternatives and assessing the outcome. Emphasize that it is the client's responsibility for choosing which alternative to select and enact.

What If My Client Doesn't Seem to Want to Change?

If you are just beginning to see clients, it might seem unusual at this point to conceive of the possibility that the client might not want to change. After all, clients take the time and effort to make an appointment, come to therapy, and pay for services, so why wouldn't they want to change? The simple answer is that change is difficult. In many cases, the effort and disequilibrium that change would cause is felt as much more disruptive than the current way of being. Here are some steps and elements to consider when experiencing stagnation at the change stage.

1) Reflect on the alliance. Think about whether or not the lack of movement is due to a poor therapeutic rapport. Clients will be unwilling to take risks if they do not trust that the counselor is a good and trusted partner in the anxiety-provoking journey of change. If you assess that the relationship needs some attention, discuss this openly with the client and reinvest some time in working on rapport building skills (see Chapter 5).

2) Reassess goals. Goals that are too vague or out of alignment between client and counselor will result in lack of progress and change. The characteristic of good goals can be found in Chapter 5 and can be used to clarify goals in a way that can be more useful in session. If goal alignment seems to be the issue, then working with the client to identify the goal will serve to get you both on the same page and has a greater likelihood of removing the obstacle to change.

3) Focus on change. If you feel that rapport is solid and goals are aligned, it is appropriate to help facilitate the movement to change in focused ways. For example, consider the following case excerpt:

Client: I just don't know what to do. My aunt is dying and my family is just being so nonchalant about it. It's driving me crazy and I feel like I am spinning my wheels.

Counselor: You seem ready to do something different, but are confused as what the next step might be.

               (Reflection to convey understanding and solidify rapport. It also provides an opportunity for the client to move to action.).

Client: Yes, exactly. They just ignore the issue and act like nothing is happening.

Counselor: What would you like to do?

               (Question focuses the client on avenues for change)

Client: I would like for them to take this seriously and actually show some caring towards my aunt and maybe for each other.

Counselor: You don't have much control of their behavior, but you can change yours. In our work together, you have mentioned wanting to improve the relationship with your parents. In this situation, it sounds like you would like to receive some caring, but also are aware that your aunt needs some too. What could you do in this situation that might have an impact?

               (This statement emphasizes the client as the point of change, not others. It also pulls in goals as related to themes and refocuses the client on change).

Client: Well, I guess this would be a good time to practice asking for what I need from my parents. I have been getting pretty good at that. I could also give my aunt some caring instead of expecting other people to do it. Maybe they would even follow my lead.

4) Process the stagnation with the client. While the client in the example above does a nice job of moving past the stagnation, sometimes clients

continue to struggle with moving to action. When this occurs, discussing the paralysis with the client can be fruitful and conveys a sense of collaboration that is essential. The following dialogue illustrates how this discussion might unfold:

Client: My daughter got out of rehab this week. She's already called me asking for money and I am having a difficult time saying no to her.

Counselor: This sounds like a return to the old pattern.

Client: Yes, it is. She asks. I feel guilty. I give in. I feel resentful. She starts using drugs again.

Counselor: What would you like to do different this time?

Client: I don't really know. I know what I should do, but I never do it. This has been going on for 15 years and I can't seem to say no.

Counselor: Well, we have talked about how you perceive saying no to your daughter as an example of neglectful parenting, so we have tried to adjust the change from saying no to setting boundaries, but that doesn't seem to have helped change your perception.

Client: No, I don't even use the new language (laughs).

Counselor: Well, let's talk about your choice to do the same thing despite knowing some alternatives.

Client: I guess it's just too hard for me to change.

Counselor: Is it really too difficult? I get the sense that it's easier to go back to the old pattern. It's not that the change is hard per se, but it is harder than staying the same.

Client: Yeah, as much as I don't want to admit it. I think that's it.

Counselor: The pain of the old pattern is not as severe as the discomfort that may be created by the change.

5) Consider referral. When the stagnation does not resolve, it is appropriate to make a referral for other treatment (if the cause is due to rapport issues and the client expresses a desire to change) or termination without referral (if the client denies the need for further change). A comprehensive discussion of termination issues is discussed in the next chapter.

Summary

Change is a complex dynamic. It is not a static stage but is instead a function of how well the counselor–client team prepared a readiness for change based on the quality of the therapeutic relation, identified patterns, and goal-setting. Once the momentum for change builds, counselor and client can infuse the process with a sense of personal responsibility and desire to make the change consistent through practice. Although how and why people change is an elusive concept, considering and promoting change through the spheres of cognition, emotion, and behavior provide both counselor and client with a holistic view of the change process. We also encourage you to consider the model discussed as a way to conceptualize where the client is in the change process and as a reminder that connecting and identifying where the client is in the process is often the most important element in facilitating change.

Reflection Questions

1. Discuss your own personal experience with change. What are some aspects of your life that were easy to change? Why? What are some areas of your life that have been difficult to change? Why?
2. What does responsibility mean to you? How will you help facilitate responsibility in your clients?
3. Many practitioners emphasize one sphere of change over the others. Which sphere or spheres of change do you feel are more conducive to change? What does your theory of counseling emphasize?
4. How do you utilize advice in your personal relationships? How is this different from your professional way of working with clients?
5. What are some issues that could arise in counseling where advice-giving would be helpful?
6. Discuss how you would feel if a client was not engaged in the change process. What steps would you take to explore this dynamic?

References

Asay, T. P., & Lambert, M. J. (1999). The empirical case for the common factors in therapy: Quantitative findings. In M. A. Hubble, B. L. Duncan &

S. D. Miller (Eds.), *The heart and soul of change* (pp. 23–55). Washington DC: American Psychological Association.

Beitman, B. D. (1987). *The structure of individual psychotherapy.* New York: Guilford.

Bohart, A. (2009). The client is the most important common factor: Clients' self-healing capacities and psychotherapy. *Journal of Psychotherapy Integration, 10 (2),* 127–149.

Comninos, A. & Grenyer, B. F. S. (2007). The influence of interpersonal factors on the speed of recovery from major depression. *Psychotherapy Research, 17,* 230–239.

Cormier, S., & Hackney, H. (2016). *Counseling strategies and interventions* (9th ed.). Columbus, OH: Pearson.

Couture, S. J., & Sutherland, O. (2006). Giving advice on advice-giving: A conversation analysis of Karl Tomm's practice. *Journal of Marital and Family Therapy, 32*(3), 329–344.

Duncan, B. L., Miller, S. D., Wampold, B. E. & Hubble, M. A. (Eds.) (2010). *The heart and soul of change: Delivering what works in therapy.* Washington, DC: American Psychological Association.

Fall, K. A., Holden, J., & Marquis, A. (2017). *Theoretical models of psychotherapy and counseling* (3rd ed.). New York: Routledge.

Gordon, R. (2012). Where oh where are the clients? The use of client factors in counselling psychology. *Counselling Psychology Review, 27*(4), 8–17.

Hawley, L. D., Leibert, T. W., & Lane, J. A. (2014). The relationship between socioeconomic status and counseling outcomes. *Professional Counselor, 4*(4), 390–403.

Lambert, M. J. (1992). Psychotherapy outcome research: Implications for integrative and eclectic therapists. In J. C. Norcross & M. R. Goldfried (Eds.), *Handbook of psychotherapy integration* (pp. 94–129). New York: Basic Books.

Leibert, T. (2011). The dimensions of common factors in counselling. *International Journal for the Advancement of Counselling, 33,* 127–138.

Lu, Y., Jiang, G., Lu, T., & Lin, X. (2017). Qualitative research of key point of client's change in counseling. *Chinese Mental Health Journal, 31*(8), 600–605.

Prochaska, J. O., DiClemente, C. C., & Norcross, J. C. (1992). In search of how people change. *American Psychologist, 47,* 1102–1114.

Prochaska, J. O., Velicer, W. F., Rossi, J. S., Goldstein, M. G., Marcus, B. H., & Rakowski, W. (1994). Stages of change and decisional balance for 12 problem behaviors. *Health Psychology, 13*, 39–46.

Prochaska, J. O., & Norcross, J. C. (2002). Stages of change. In J. C. Norcross (Ed.), *Psychotherapy relationships that work: Therapist contributions and responsiveness to patients* (pp. 303–313). New York: Oxford University Press.

Schaerer, M., Tost, L. P., Huang, L., Gino, F., & Larrick, R. (2018). Advice giving: A subtle pathway to power. *Personality and Social Psychology Bulletin, 44*(5), 746–761.

8

TERMINATION

Throughout the course of your training, you have learned a great deal about the process of counseling. How to build rapport, set goals, and facilitate attainment of the client's goals are all a part of the natural flow of counseling. You have also spent some time learning about the process of termination, that is, the portion of the counseling when goals have been achieved and counseling is "over." In a sense, you learned the traditional story line of counseling: Client enters counseling, client connects with counselor, client works toward change, change occurs, and counseling ends. Although you will experience natural changes in that story line due to client factors, the structure of advanced clinical courses creates a plot twist at the termination phase that many students and clients do not anticipate.

Clinical courses are limited-time contract jobs that seem to structurally contradict what you learned about the importance of the developing counseling relationship; namely, that the relationship should find its own flow with a mutually created process that ends when goals have been identified and achieved. The reality for most students is that they leave when the course is over, often leaving the clients to pursue their mental health needs with the next wave of students that comes into the placement. In settings that have a high counselor turnover rate, perhaps due to one-semester commitments, clients may endure several counselor transitions in their time of self-growth and healing. These transitions may be a normal function of receiving treatment in a teaching facility, but the impact on the clientele needs careful attention by the counselor interns and supervisors. As Siebold (1991) noted, the common client belief regarding termination is, "I'm supposed to leave you. You don't leave me" (p. 191).

Keeping in mind that the primary responsibility of any clinician is the well-being of the client, termination is viewed as an important part of the therapeutic process (Graybar & Leonard, 2009). Termination emphasizes the growth that has occurred, the areas of concern that still exist, and the methods of future support. Balancing classroom learning about the termination process and clinical reality can often be confusing. One student commented:

> During our classroom training, we always discussed termination from the perspective that the client was terminating. Most of my clients needed further counseling, so it was weird to leave them. It felt like abandonment in many ways, even though I knew that I had done a good job of referring them to other counselors.

To make these transitions as ethical and as client-focused as possible, this chapter emphasizes steps you can take to ensure appropriate termination and referral. To make sense of the elements of termination, this chapter will address termination issues related to clients, supervision, and self.

Facilitating Termination: When Does It Begin?

Let us cover the nonpersonal, structural issues of termination first as a way to ease you into the termination process. One question that seems to come up for most students is, "I understand the importance of termination, but when is a good time to start the discussion?" Most counselors are competent in the assessment of changes in their clients as a way to evaluate appropriateness of termination, but we must also be aware of counselor factors in termination, such as the end of an internship.

As a student, you should inform all clients of your status and any time limitations that status may have on the counseling process. Informing clients allows the client to give informed consent for counseling, but it also begins the dialogue about termination. Once the initial parameters are discussed, termination becomes a process issue. Although technically you could continue to discuss termination from the first session, we believe the best guideline is to make sure you discuss termination with enough time for both you and the client to process the relevant issues involved. Clients with issues of loss or abandonment may need more time to process the change, whereas other clients may do well with an advance discussion three or four weeks before the termination date. In other words, the artificial relationship parameter of time may be more integrally woven into the counseling issues for some clients than for others.

During the termination phase, it is important to process all the important elements necessary for a healthy good-bye. Marx and Gelso (1987) researched client-initiated termination and outlined a complete termination as covering three main themes: "looking back (reviewing counseling and goal attainment), looking ahead (setting an ending date and discussing future plans), and saying good-bye (sharing feelings about ending)" (p. 7). The same themes will be present in counselor-initiated termination, but the feelings of the client may be slightly different and provide a unique therapeutic challenge. The following section will discuss typical client reactions and possible counselor responses.

Client Reactions and Counselor Responses

Research on the topic of termination reports that this phase is a critical time for both client and counselor (Gelso & Woodhouse, 2002; McNeil, Hasty, Conus, & Berk, 2010; Paniagua, 2002; Roe, Dekel, Harel, Fenning, & Fenning, 2006). Intense feelings, both positive and negative, emerge as treatment comes to an end. Learning about the possible dynamics inherent in termination can help the counselor process internal struggles to enhance this stage as well as anticipate possible client reactions to ending counseling. Unfortunately, most of the past research has dealt specifically with the traditional story line of termination: client has achieved goals and promotes the idea of termination. Advanced clinical courses add a unique wrinkle to termination, and thus we need to consider the associated feelings at a slightly different angle.

Clients may experience counselor-initiated termination in a variety of ways. In fact, the same client may cycle through many emotions as the themes of change, loss, and growth resonate with the client's own experiences and ways of perceiving the world. We believe it is important to honor all possible client emotions and provide enough time for the various feelings to emerge. In this section we will cover the common client reactions to termination and provide tips on how the counselor can respond. Once again, keep in mind that clients may experience one, some, or all of these responses, so the counselor must be prepared to process whatever occurs.

Indifference, or "I Don't Care if You Leave"

Clients may respond with indifference for a variety of reasons; maybe they were not invested deeply in the relationship, maybe they approach all relationships with a sense of superficiality, or it could be a way to safeguard themselves from the pain associated with saying goodbye. For clients who have experienced difficulty sharing feelings, the unexpected emotions surrounding termination can be confusing and scary. The easiest way to manage the discomfort is to act as though the feelings do not exist.

Counselors confronted with indifference need to first check their internal response to the client. You may feel hurt by the client's lack of caring and therefore may feel the need to make the client care or, worse, may withdraw from the client and assume that the issue of termination no longer needs to be addressed. Understanding that the client's response is both reflective of the feelings regarding termination *and* the client's own issues can help the counselor facilitate exploration of the feeling at both levels. Consider the following dialogue as an example of multilevel processing.

Counselor: It seems like you feel disconnected from me and the notion of me leaving.

Client: Yeah, I mean, it's not like you cared about me anyway.

Counselor: I'm wondering if you would be willing to talk about that feeling a little more. It seems like it wouldn't feel good to think someone didn't care.

Client: No, I guess it doesn't.

Counselor: Goodbyes are difficult. I'm wondering about other goodbyes in your life and what they have been like for you.

Client: Pretty awful, I guess. Usually people leave without even saying goodbye . . . like my mom when she died.

Counselor: Yes, I know that was particularly painful for you and how you protect yourself from the pain by pretending to not care. I can also see how important it is for you to be able to say goodbye in a healthy or different way. Maybe that's something we can work on in the next few weeks.

The counselor in this dialogue used basic empathic statements to move between present and past feelings regarding termination. It is rare for indifference to be the real emotion regarding termination. Instead, it is the *safe* emotion; one that protects the client from experiencing the deeper feeling. Creating an open space for reflective dialogue can help the client process and may help facilitate other feelings about termination.

Anger, or "I Hate You for Leaving Me"

Some clients erupt in anger over the notion that you are leaving. Anger can be a method for controlling others (trying to get you to stay), a way of controlling self (inhibiting emotions underlying the anger, such as fear or pain), or a genuine commentary on the counselor's lack of information about the termination process. Penn (1990) notes that the anger can be expressed as hostility toward counseling and the counselor, such as stating, "I should have known better than to accept a trainee. Maybe next time I'll get a real counselor."

Most often, it seems that clients who respond with anger have experienced abandonment and hoped that you would be different. Counselors must pay attention to their own reactions to anger. In our discussions with supervisees, fear of anger always tops the list of supervisee concerns. Responding to the client with fear or anger can shut down the process and inhibit proper resolution. Once again, blending the two levels (counseling issues and personal issues) is indicated, as demonstrated in the following dialogue.

Client: Well, that's just great! You're going to leave just when I was beginning to open up. This sucks. I can't believe you're doing this to me.

Counselor: I can see you are very angry about this. Can you tell me more about what you said about opening up?

Client:	It just seems like I was sharing deep stuff about me . . . and now you are just leaving.
Counselor:	So, it's like you trusted me enough to share and it seems like my leaving is disrespecting that. Almost like a betrayal.
Client:	Yes! That's exactly it. I never thought of it as betrayal, but that is what it feels like. It's like I invested in something and you are just walking away like it doesn't even matter.
Counselor:	It reminds me quite a bit of the feelings you had during your divorce.
Client:	No . . . not really. Well, maybe. I do remember feeling betrayed and blindsided by my spouse.
Counselor:	And you feel blindsided by me.
Client:	Well, no. I knew this was coming, but I guess I still felt like you might stay.
Counselor:	Although I can't stay, maybe we can keep working on this issue to come to a better understanding of the feelings involved.

In the dialogue, the counselor responds to the anger in an open, nondefensive way, which allows the client to explore not only the anger but also the additional feelings of surprise and betrayal. The acceptance of the anger and the processing of the underlying emotions create a separate layer of learning, whereby the client can experience the healthy expression of anger that fosters relational growth rather than acting as a destructive force. The open processing also helps tie-in personal issues that parallel the counseling issues involving termination.

Hopelessness, or "I Will Never Get Better if You Leave"

Hopelessness is a common client response to termination that leaves both the client and the counselor in a precarious situation. Clients who present with hopelessness will often intensify their symptoms as a way to prolong the therapeutic relationship. The exacerbation of symptoms is bad enough, but it is often accompanied with a stated or implied feeling that the client is not in control or responsible for change but is instead in the hands of the counselor. Counselors are particularly vulnerable to this dynamic, as it kicks in our natural desire to help. If counselors do not monitor their reactions to hopelessness, they risk committing a number of therapeutic mistakes, from taking responsibility for the client's symptoms to prolonging the therapy. The following dialogue illustrates how counselors can address the issues of hopelessness and facilitate responsibility in the client.

Counselor:	You are feeling hopeless, like your change will stop if this relationship ends.
Client:	Yeah . . . I just feel like I won't be able to keep the momentum going.
Counselor:	Tell me more about the loss of momentum.
Client:	You have been so instrumental in helping me change, pushing me to do things differently. I just feel like with you not there, I'll just fall back. I am already starting to feel worse and you aren't even gone.
Counselor:	I can understand how you might feel like this change will impact you, but I'm wondering about the part you've played in your change process. Where do you see yourself in the momentum?
Client:	I really don't know.
Counselor:	I see this as a two-person team. You do your part and I do mine. I can see that you are paying attention to my part, but where are you in the process?
Client:	Well, since you put it that way, I do work in here. I think about the things we talk about outside of therapy and I use them.
Counselor:	I agree. It seems like although my part may change, your part can stay the same. Even more, your role is the more active of the two, the real "workhorse," if you will (both laugh).
Client:	I see your point, but I still feel sad about the change.
Counselor:	The sadness and ways to manage the change are certainly some things we can continue to talk about.

Hopefulness, or "I Think It's Time for Me to Do This on My Own"

We all hope that our clients will respond with hopefulness to termination, and occasionally it occurs. However, most often we must work through other feelings such as those discussed previously, and if we process those effectively, then perhaps hopefulness will be the counselor and client reward. Hopefulness is characterized by a sense that the client has a firm grasp on the reins of personal change. If the client is able to be accountable for change, forward movement is possible, and it also opens the dialogue to possible future areas of work and how to access counseling when needed. The following example illuminates the feeling of hopefulness.

Counselor: So, you feel like this might be a good place for you to stop as well.

Client: Yeah, I mean, I knew you were leaving at the end of the semester, and I've been preparing for it. I tried to make good use of my time in here.

Counselor: Right. You recognized the boundary and responded to it in a way that was helpful to you. Is that approach different for you?

Client: Absolutely! Before, I think I would have just given up halfway through. I would have blamed you.

Counselor: It must feel empowering to do something different, to recognize that your past patterns weren't working and decide to change.

Client: I think so. I definitely think I can take that and use it in other areas of my life.

Counselor: Tell me about the ways you see it applying.

Client: Oh sure . . . like with my relationship with my son. To realize that we both have responsibilities to maintain the relationship. If I don't like something that's going on with us, I can always blame him, but it's healthier for me to voice my concerns and be willing to make some changes myself.

Counselor: I know that insight took a lot of work on your part. What are some means of support you can access if you feel in a bind again?

Client: I think I'm feeling so strong now that I won't ever go back to where I was.

Counselor: I can appreciate that. I'm not talking about finding yourself in the same place, but more about what supports that you can access so you don't go to a similar or completely different uncomfortable space.

In this example, the counselor validates the client's sense of hope while also exploring avenues for future help. The process allows the client to feel a sense of responsibility for change and also works to address the possibility that the hope may diminish at times, but the client still has access to support.

As the feelings associated with termination are explored, both counselor and client can look ahead to the options available to the client after the counselor leaves. The next section provides an overview of the steps of a well-balanced referral system.

Stages and Issues of Successful Referral

As the time to terminate nears, one important consideration is whether a referral is indicated for each of your clients. Referral is a vital aspect of termination and represents your ethical responsibility to not abandon your clients. This section outlines three distinct steps to ensure a responsible approach to referral: (a) deciding which clients need a referral and why, (b) making the referral for those who need it, and (c) easing the referred client's transition.

Determining Need for Referral

Not all of your clients will require or desire a referral. For some clients, adequately processing the feelings associated with termination will result in the client feeling that it is time for a break from counseling. We advocate for the referral decision to be a collaborative process that includes counselor assessment, client assessment of self, and an exploration of alternatives.

The counselor must assess the client's strengths and progress as well as areas of concern. Counselors can review progress toward stated goals, symptom intensity, and social support as elements that might help the counselor decide whether a referral is needed. Having done this assessment, the counselor should be prepared to discuss the findings with the client.

The counselor should also ask the client to self-evaluate progress and what work is left to be done. Clients can provide keen insight into issues that still remain and can be helpful in planning additional care. We think that the more involved they are in the process, the more commitment they will have to the referral process.

Differences in assessment between counselor and client should be discussed and worked through. In the end, four outcomes are possible:

1. Client and counselor agree that no referral is needed.
2. Client and counselor agree that a referral is needed.
3. Client and counselor disagree (because client wants a referral, but counselor does not think it is needed).
4. Client and counselor disagree (because counselor wants to refer, but client does not think referral is needed).

The first two outcomes are not a problem, and although a possibility, the third one is highly unlikely. The only problematic outcome is when the counselor assesses the client as needing further help, but the client refuses. Although it is awkward, the counselor should explore the underlying feelings related to the client's position. If the client refuses help and the counselor continues to believe a referral is necessary, the ethical strategy is to inform the client of the referral options and let the client know that it is his or her choice to follow up or not. Make sure you document the referral.

If you both agree that a referral is not needed, then you are free to work through termination of treatment. If you both feel a referral is needed, you must then discuss referral options. During this part, the counselor collaborates with the client to find a good match. If other counselors are available at the current placement, explore whether your client is comfortable with that option. Due to limits of availability or other factors, you may have to consider other sites. Discuss this option with your client along with the associated factors of travel time, cost, and any scheduling differences. Once you have a site, elements of the counselor that may influence client comfort include age, gender, cultural considerations, counseling style, and specialty areas. Do not assume that any of these factors are unimportant to the client; instead, engage the client in a dialogue about what the client needs in a counselor. Once you have explored these issues, you can move to the next step, making the referral.

Making a Referral

The first step required an in-depth consideration of the need for referral, collaborating with the client on that assessment, and then discussing and exploring possible avenues and characteristics of a good referral. Although it is the responsibility of the client to follow through on the referral, it is the responsibility of the counselor to provide the client with competent referral sources. Although many referrals are based on the factor of availability, we would not advocate for that to be the primary factor. Instead, we expect our supervisees to make each referral based on the client's individual needs. Using that factor as your guiding principle allows you to scan available resources and find the best counselor for that specific client. For example, a client who is struggling with an eating disorder may benefit more from a counselor with experience in treating that issue, whereas a highly intellectual client may prefer a cognitive approach to therapy. Not recognizing these issues that should have been discovered in the first step will diminish the potential of the referral.

We assert here a key component of the second step: You must know your referral sources. You cannot facilitate a good fit between counselor and client if you know only half of the puzzle. The following story from a supervisee illustrates what may happen if you are not adequately acquainted with your referral sources:

It was time for me to leave my internship, so I was busy making appropriate referrals for my clients. We ran out of space in the agency, so I started considering other options for some of my clients. I had attended a workshop the previous week on Gestalt therapy with adolescents. The presenter was so dynamic and seemed so effective. I don't know if she was just on my mind or if I was still moved by her presentation or both, but I referred two adolescent clients to her. The next week I received calls from both clients' parents, angry at me for sending their children to such a "whack job." I asked one parent what happened, and she said the person's office was actually a room in her house. When the clients arrived for the session, they were greeted at the door by the therapist's teenage son, who showed them through the very messy house, past bedrooms, to the "office"; a cluttered guest room. The therapist arrived ten minutes late and was dressed like she had been out in the garden. It just got worse from there. I had no idea it was going to be like that, and the clients were so angry at me. That mother was right, it was my responsibility to check these things out. It was like all our hard work went down the drain because I had been so careless.

This case illustrates an often ignored dynamic in the referral process: that the client will see the referral as an extension of you. Therefore, if you make a referral that is a poor fit, the client's conclusion is akin to "My counselor doesn't understand me," "My counselor doesn't care about me," or "My counselor is reckless with my treatment." You cannot assure that the fit will be a good one, but not knowing your referral targets increase the probability of a bad match.

If you are working in an agency or campus clinic, it may be possible for the client to continue at the same site, but with a new counselor. In this arrangement, the counselor is referring to the site, and not a new counselor, but the processing considerations should still be the same. Research has demonstrated that although many clients at these sites will agree to continue, the process of transition has a wide range of impact on the client, including high levels of attrition, symptom rebound, and new symptom emergence (Bostic & Shadic, 1996; Clark, Cole, & Robertson, 2014; Clark, Robertson, Keen, & Cole, 2011; Marmarosh, Thompson, Hill, Hollman, & Megivern, 2017; Sauer, Rice, Richardson, & Roberts, 2017; Schen, Raymond, & Notman, 2013). Keeping these factors in mind, can help focus the transition process in a way that brings awareness to the client and increases the probability of a smooth transition.

By the end of this second step, you should feel fairly confident that the issues of referral have been collaboratively explored and, if warranted, that the referrals were the best options available to the client. In many cases, this step is the last one in the process. However, some sources suggest that consulting with the new counselor and providing joint sessions to smooth the transition may be indicated (Clark et al., 2014). We include this option as a third step.

Transition Considerations

Once the client has decided on the new counselor, it is common practice for that individual to consult with the preceding counselor to discuss treatment. You can ease this part of the transition by informing your client of this practice, explaining the benefits, and getting the client to sign a form of consent to disclose confidential information to the new counselor once the individual is identified. When contacted by the new counselor, it will be helpful to have information ready about your treatment of the client including conceptualization of the problem, important background information, identified goals, progress toward the goals, and identified areas of growth. In some cases, the new counselor may ask for copies of the client's treatment records. In our practice, both in asking and receiving, we have found it more helpful to have a summary of treatment rather than the entire record. This form is usually one or two pages summarizing the important facets of treatment.

Another method of consultation is to arrange joint sessions with the new counselor. This arrangement allows the client to get a feel for the new counselor while retaining some of the comfort associated with the old. The first session can be a short meet and greet followed by a session where the old counselor facilitates the session while the new counselor acts as process observer. Processing time at the end of the session can help set the agenda for the next session, where open discussion of future treatment among all parties may occur. The advantages of this process include the gradual nature of the transition and the new counselor getting to see the manner of the client in a therapeutic setting. It also bypasses the suspicion associated with "backroom consultations" whereby the client wonders what the counselors are saying in private.

Research indicates that joint sessions may be the best possible option for clients who are seeing advanced counseling students in training clinics or agencies (Clark et al., 2014; Clark et al., 2011; Gavazzi & Anderson, 1987). Clark et al. (2014) noted that the process that proved most beneficial to clients included a multi-step system that provided early discussion of the transfer, information about the new counselor, assurance that the new counselor was thoughtfully selected, and several sessions of co-therapy. If you are counseling in one of these settings, you might apprise yourself of the clinic's policies regarding transfer and consider some of these steps for implementation.

Once the referral has been made and, if used, the last transition session completed, the only aspect of termination left is the final goodbye. Although this part may sound easy compared to all of the other pieces that have been processed, the final step poses some unique struggles. One that you may not have considered is that as you say goodbye to your clients, you must also prepare to terminate with your supervisor. The next two sections provide an overview of how to work through the last step in the termination phase.

Saying Goodbye to Clients

The process of termination, although much more complicated than just saying "Goodbye," always must eventually end with the final farewell. The goal of the process element of termination is to provide enough time to discuss pertinent issues so that both parties (counselor and client) understand the purpose of the forced termination and the possible next steps. As you approach the final goodbye, your clients should understand that your leaving has nothing to do with them personally and that you have kept their future counseling needs at the forefront of discussion.

Even when clients are left with a satisfied feeling surrounding the termination, confusion may remain regarding the nature of future relationships with the counselor. In an effort to maintain contact, the client may covertly or overtly push for social contact with the counselor. After all, if counseling is over, why not? When approached by the client to extend the relationship past termination, therapists must make it clear that future contact of any kind is not possible. Penn (1990) cites the inherent power differential within the therapeutic relationship as the main reason post-termination relationships are not wise. She also notes that continuing the relationship informally could interfere with the client's rapport with the new therapist and thus have a detrimental effect on the client's continued counseling.

Saying goodbye to your clients may bring up several emotions in you, as we have discussed. These emotions, if not carefully processed, may interfere with your ability to facilitate the final session. We encourage you to consult with your supervisor and discuss your struggles and feelings as openly as possible. Supervision is an appropriate place to explore your internal reactions to termination, and it can allow a safe working through of the issues so termination can be enhanced.

Terminating with a Supervisor

Most interns are so focused on the anxiety surrounding terminating with clients that they forget that ending one's internship also means an end to the supervisory relationship. The relationship with your supervisor has the potential of being one of the most vital relationships you form as you grow as a counselor, so terminating with a supervisor is just as important as terminating with clients (Levendosky & Hopwood, 2017). In fact, the development of the supervisory relationship acts as a parallel process to the work done with clients. Within this dynamic, the supervision relationship can impact the work done with clients in a facilitative or hindering manner (Tracey, Bludworth, & Glidden-Tracey, 2012). During the termination stage, the supervision relationship can act as a model or a reality-testing laboratory, where lessons about termination can be learned that can translate into better terminations with your clients.

Termination should be discussed and processed in much the same way as your work with clients. For example, your supervisor may broach the subject three to four weeks before the final session to get you to start thinking about how you want to close this experience. Each week, you may touch on the various issues until you reach the final session. Table 8.1 provides a summary of suggestions derived from the research of Levendosky and Hopwood (2017). In addition to the goals and activities mentioned, ideally, time will be provided for both evaluative and personal reflection.

Evaluation is an important aspect of the supervisory process. Throughout your time in supervision, you have received formative evaluations through feedback on your cases and the ways you comport yourself in the professional environment. During your last supervision session, you receive *summative evaluation*, that is, an overall critique of your work. Some supervisors provide your final evaluation orally, but others prefer a written format.

Table 8.1 Termination of Supervision

Goals	Associated Activities
1) Discuss meaning of relationship	1) Discuss how relationship has impacted growth (both positive and negative).
2) Express feelings associated with termination	2) Process feeling in the here and Now
3) Attend to unfinished business within the relationship	3) Explore patterns in the relationship, reflect on communication and ways the relationship has traditionally dealt with issues.
4) Explore and reinforce growth	4) Identify areas of improvement and make a plan for the next step.

We like the written format because it allows you to review the evaluation at a later time for deeper reflection. Regardless of the format, you should receive comprehensive feedback on topics such as:

- strengths: theory integration, techniques, rapport building, clientele with whom you work well, knowledge gained, skills attained
- areas for growth
- professional issues: ethical behavior, ability to work with others
- goals for the future

People handle evaluation in various ways; some relish the opportunity for continued self-growth, yet others bristle at the perceived slight of constructive criticism. Also, keep in mind that the confluence of a comprehensive evaluation and termination of a significant relationship can make for an emotionally intense situation. We encourage you to self-reflect before the final evaluation to mentally move yourself into a space where you can hear the opportunities for growth as well as the aspects of your professional self that deserved recognition.

Although doing so is not required or requested by all supervisors, you may also wish to ask if you may evaluate the supervisor and the supervision process. Taking time to reflect on the supervisory experience will help you understand which aspects have been helpful as well as what problematic components to keep in mind when selecting future supervisors. This is also an important opportunity for your supervisor to receive feedback. Table 8.2 provides an example of a written evaluation form.

Table 8.2 Sample Evaluation of Supervision

Supervisor's Name:_____	Supervision Site:_____
Faculty Supervisor:_____	Date:_____

SUPERVISEE'S EVALUATION OF SUPERVISOR
AND SUPERVISION SITE

1. Involvement	Poor				Outstanding		
A. Demonstrates seriousness and involvement about being a supervisor.	1	2	3	4	5	6	7

B. Is aware and involved in the issues being discussed.   1 2 3 4 5 6 7

2. Growth

A. Uses personal experiences with clients to further your development.   1 2 3 4 5 6 7

B. Uses personal feelings and insights to further your development.   1 2 3 4 5 6 7

3. Rapport

A. Makes it easy for you to initiate dialogue with him/her.   1 2 3 4 5 6 7

B. Makes it easy to share your counseling strengths and weaknesses with him/her.   1 2 3 4 5 6 7

4. Facilitation

A. Initiates helpful discussions of your strengths and competencies with you.   1 2 3 4 5 6 7

B. Initiates helpful discussions with you of your areas for growth.   1 2 3 4 5 6 7

5. Climate and Relationship

A. Is open and flexible to your wants and style.   1 2 3 4 5 6 7

B. Is accessible between sessions.   1 2 3 4 5 6 7

C. Shares and negotiates expectations of supervision.   1 2 3 4 5 6 7

6. Implementation

A. Models specific interventions.   1 2 3 4 5 6 7

B. Presents alternative interventions.   1 2 3 4 5 6 7

C. Helps you identify movement in the client.   1 2 3 4 5 6 7

D. Helps you identify lack of movement in the client.   1 2 3 4 5 6 7

E. Aids in your conceptualization of the client's behavior.   1 2 3 4 5 6 7

F. Focuses on content of counseling session.   1 2 3 4 5 6 7

G. Focuses on process of counseling session.   1 2 3 4 5 6 7

7. Site Critique

A. Provides accessible office space for interns.	1	2	3	4	5	6	7
B. Provides opportunities to fulfill the requirement.	1	2	3	4	5	6	7
C. Provides opportunities to work with a variety of clientele.	1	2	3	4	5	6	7
D. Provides helpful group supervision.	1	2	3	4	5	6	7
E. Office staff support and help interns.	1	2	3	4	5	6	7
F. Provides adequate orientation of new interns.	1	2	3	4	5	6	7

Suggestions for Supervisor:

Suggestions for Site:

Making time for more personal reflections on the nature of the supervisory relationship is also an important aspect of the termination session. It is impossible to characterize a universal nature of all supervisory relationships. Some are intense and emotional, while others operate at a safe professional distance. We believe the essence of the goodbye is often congruent with the type of relationship that was formed. This congruence is normal, although both parties should use this time to summarize the relationship and note any aspects that could have been improved.

During the final session, it is also wise to discuss the future of the supervisory relationship. We see the supervisory relationship as one that can continue to exist but one that is transformed through the supervision process. The intern, as a result of all the growth and hard work, can continue to enjoy the benefits of a relationship with the supervisor as a professional resource and support. The supervisor, as an outcome of quality supervision, can reap the benefits of the continued relationship with the intern who represents a competent professional contact. The end of the process merely gives way to a new beginning in which each party gains a new consultant and a new colleague. However, not all supervisors or supervisees desire a future relationship with each other. Regardless of the nature of the future relationship, it is something that can and should be discussed during the termination session.

Summary

You may have noticed the similarities in the process of termination with clients and supervisors. This is one additional example of the power of parallel process. We note the similarities because you have the power to influence and change the process, but you must recognize the dynamic before you can impact it. For example, interns who are struggling with personal fears over terminating with clients will avoid termination discussions with their supervisor. The intern and supervisor have two opportunities to pick up on the problematic feelings surrounding termination. Just as the problems exist in a parallel fashion, the positive patterns also work across the two relationships. Confronting the struggle of termination within the supervision relationship can then lead to improvements in discussing the issue with clients.

Reflection Questions

1. Think about the major terminations in your life. What were they like? How were they resolved? What impact do your personal experiences with termination have on your counseling?
2. Which typical client reaction to termination would be most difficult for you and why? Which client reaction would be easiest for you to handle and why?
3. Act as if you were your supervisor and create a summative evaluation for your work as an intern. What are your strengths? What are your areas for growth?

References

Bostic, J. Q., & Shadic, L. G. (1996). Our time is up: Forced terminations during psychotherapy training. *American Journal of Psychotherapy, 50,* 347–359.

Clark, P., Cole, C., & Robertson, J. M. (2014). Creating a safety net: Transferring to a new therapist in a training setting. *Contemporary Family Therapy: An International Journal, 36*(1), 172–189.

Clark, P., Robertson, J. M., Keen, R., & Cole, C. (2011). Outcomes of client transfers in a training setting. *American Journal of Family Therapy, 39*(3), 214–225.

Gavazzi, S. M., & Anderson, S. A. (1987). The role of "translator" in the case transfer process. *American Journal of Family Therapy, 15,* 145–157.

Gelso, C., & Woodhouse, S. (2002). The termination of psychotherapy: What research tells us about the process of ending treatment. In G. S. Tryon

(Ed.), *Counseling based on process research: Applying what we know* (pp. 344–369). Boston: Allyn & Bacon.

Graybar, S., & Leonard, L. (2009). Terminating psychotherapy therapeutically. In W. O'Donohue, S. R. Graybar, W. O'Donohue, & S. R. Graybar (Eds.), *Handbook of contemporary psychotherapy: Toward an improved understanding of effective psychotherapy* (pp. 359–381). Thousand Oaks, CA: Sage.

Levendosky, A. A., & Hopwood, C. J. (2017). Terminating supervision. *Psychotherapy, 54*(1), 37–46.

Marx, J. A., & Gelso, C. J. (1987). Termination of individual counseling in a university counseling center. *Journal of Counseling Psychology, 34,* 3–9.

MacNeil, C. A., Hasty, M. K., Conus, P., & Berk, M. (2010). Termination of therapy: What can clinicians do to maximise gains? *Acta Neuropsychiatrica, 22*(1), 43–45.

Marmarosh, C. L., Thompson, B., Hill, C., Hollman, S., & Megivern, M. (2017). Therapists-in-training experiences of working with transfer clients: One relationship terminates and another begins. *Psychotherapy, 54*(1), 102–113.

Paniagua, C. (2002). A termination case. *International Journal of Psychoanalysis, 83,* 181–186.

Penn, L. S. (1990). When the therapist must leave: Forced termination of psychodynamic therapy. *Professional Psychology: Research and Practice, 21,* 379–384.

Roe, D., Dekel, R., Harel, G., Fennig, S., & Fennig, S. (2006). Client's feelings during termination of psychodynamically oriented psychotherapy. *Bulletin of the Menninger Clinic, 81,* 68–81.

Sauer, E. M., Rice, K. G., Richardson, C. E., & Roberts, K. E. (2017). Influence of client attachment and gender on therapy transfers: A multilevel examination. *Training and Education in Professional Psychology, 11*(1), 33–40.

Schen, C. R., Raymond, L., & Notman, M. (2013). Transfer of care of psychotherapy patients: Implications for psychiatry training. *Psychodynamic Psychiatry, 41,* 575–595.

Siebold, C. (1991). Termination: When the therapist leaves. *Clinical Social Work Journal, 19*(2), 191–204.

Tracey, T. J., Bludworth, J., & Glidden-Tracey, C. E. (2012). Are there parallel processes in psychotherapy supervision? An empirical examination. *Psychotherapy, 49,* 330–343.

9

POST-MASTER'S SUPERVISED CLINICAL EXPERIENCE, LICENSURE, AND EMPLOYMENT

Arthur, completed his graduate coursework and clinical training as rapidly as possible. He did very well in classes, was well liked and respected by other students, teachers, field supervisors, and clients. Graduation was the realization of not only his dream but that of his family as well. He was the first member of his family to obtain a bachelor's degree and now the first to obtain a Master's degree. His plan was simple, he wanted to open a private practice and he wanted to use his family name in the title. He'd already begun exploring logos for Thompson Counseling and Vocational Services (TCVS). While discussing his plans with his advisor he began asking pointed questions about private practice. These questions surfaced because as he pondered the idea of forming TCVS he realized that all of his work had been in state/local mental health agencies and schools. He also recognized that beyond an occasional meeting with agency-level administrators he really had no clear idea about how the agency functioned administratively. Arthur's advisor had a successful part-time private practice and was quite willing to discuss the challenges he faced in establishing and running it.

While Arthur's advisor was encouraging, he was not as enthusiastic as Arthur had hoped he would be. After a few more questions Arthur finally asked, "Do you think that private practice is a bad idea for me?" Arthur's advisor said, "No, quite the contrary, I think your dream is a great idea, I am just uncertain about when it would be best to pursue it." Arthur's advisor candidly stated, "A private practice is a business, and while we have done all that we could to help you become a license eligible counselor, we have done nothing over the past three years to prepare you to run a business." Finally, Arthur's advisor said, "If you want my advice, I would tell you to focus on obtaining your license and begin to educate yourself on what you will need to develop a successful private practice." He went on: "You'll need information about occupational licenses, insurance eligibility and filing, acceptable book-keeping methods, malpractice and liability insurance, various types of . . .". Suddenly, Arthur interrupted: "I've got it, my enthusiasm for a private practice made it way too easy for me to overlook a number of important issues that will need to be addressed at a time when other higher priorities exist, namely getting licensed." Arthur's advisor nodded quietly and said, "Arthur, you were a great student, you will make a fine clinician and you will one day run a successful private practice." His advisor concluded by saying, "Arthur, you are entering a profession where there is always a lot more to learn and fortunately there are many people out there who will be happy to help you on your journey, no matter where it may take you professionally".

Very early in this text, we suggested that the term *counselor training* oversimplified and under-represented a far larger and broader process. To us, *counselor formation* seemed a better way to title the journey that brings novices to a level of professional competence in a field as personally challenging and complicated as mental health counseling. In this chapter we explore how you obtain a license, pursue employment, and continue to grow as a practicing clinician. As graduate students, we saw licensure as the important and ultimate goal. As practicing clinicians, we now recognize that this journey has no real end point. Getting licensed is a critical step, but it is just that—a step. Continuing education requirements coupled with a personal drive to remain current in a rapidly changing field guarantee that licensed professionals engage in many of the activities that we list in this chapter throughout the course of their professional lives. Spruill and Benshoff (1996) affirm that "[p]rofessional development roles for practicing counselors include active participation in professional organizations, obtaining professional credentials, and involvement in continuing education, research and publishing" (p. 469). Continuous professional development is the only responsible, ethical, and legal way to honor your professional obligations in a rapidly evolving branch of the mental health service delivery system.

Active participation in these professional activities not only helps you remain current but also guarantees that you will network with other professionals. One important truth about clinical practice is that it can be very isolating. Unfortunately, such isolation can quickly cripple counselors both professionally and personally. According to Kottler (1986),

> The marriage between the personal and the professional in the life of a therapist not only provides an enriched form of work but some special hardships. The clinician's life is fraught with draining days, intense pressures, and personal risks. Those who become too involved with their work pay a dear price in giving up leisure time and a private life; those who too assertively distance themselves from therapeutic sessions risk emotional sterility in other relationships.
>
> (p. 43)

Striking the correct balance ensures stability and effectiveness. That balance occurs when you develop and rely upon a network of lay people (family and friends) for social and personal needs while depending on professional colleagues (peers, consultants, specialists) for profession-related concerns. Those who delude themselves into believing that all they need is their work and their time in sessions with their clients embark upon a perilous journey—dangerous not only to themselves but also to their clients.

Clinical supervisors are equally important at this stage of your professional development. We have stressed the importance of such supervisory relationships, so you will not be surprised when we suggest that one comforting aspect of entering the counseling profession is the fact that you can and should retain the important relationships that helped you become a counselor. Once counselors terminate their work with clients, they will have no contact with them unless the client returns for continued treatment. Termination in supervision is different. We often keep these relationships, and although they may transform into consultative rather than supervisory ones, thankfully they persist. Wachowiak, Bauer, and Simono (1979) point out that

> [f]or some students, leaving graduate school often involves giving up the mentor before the student is psychologically ready. In actuality many of these mentor/mentee relationships do not end when students leave the graduate school but continue for some time, even though the new

Ph.D.s may have moved far from their graduate school base. For other graduates, a new mentor/mentee relationship is established on the entry-level job site.

(p. 724–725)

Professional Associations and Organizations

According to VanZandt (1990), "it is difficult to comprehend how a mental health professional can 'grow' with the profession without belonging to professional organizations and taking advantage of their resources and services" (p. 244). We completely agree. Professional associations offer (1) a vital source of profession-specific information, (2) a community of like-minded counseling professionals, (3) a route to improving the quality of care for clients, (4) an influential force for ensuring that mental health concerns are considered in legal and legislative activities, and (5) a method for adding important clinical credentials. Given the range of activities and benefits accrued from membership in such organizations, you will find the need to be involved in a number of them. Some are narrowly focused while others would best be termed umbrella organizations.

Most would agree that the largest and arguably most important umbrella organization for counselors is the American Counseling Association (ACA). During orientation, we urge our students to become student members. We also expect them to continue their membership throughout their work life. As clinical interests become more focused, ACA members commonly join one or more of the divisions that deal with specific aspects or types of counseling. The Association for Specialists in Group Work (ASGW) and Counselors for Social Justice (CSJ) are but two examples of the 19 chartered divisions of ACA. A quick visit to the ACA website noted at the end of this chapter reveals the wide range of services offered, the number of divisions available to members, and the critical role the organization plays in the profession.

For social workers, the National Association of Social Workers (NASW) is the national body that supports the profession of social work. This professional organization creates practice guidelines, ethical standards, and professional training opportunities for social workers and other mental health professionals. They also disseminate research relevant to their field in the Social Work Journal.

Of course, state and regional professional associations are equally import-ant. They offer similar services on a smaller scale with a tighter focus on the needs and concerns particular to a given state or region. Such associations also contain divisions identical to those offered by the national organi-zation. For every mental health discipline, there are usually professional organizations at the national, regional, and state level. While national orga-nizations typically provide the most comprehensive offerings, regional and state organizations will feel more intimate and may be more comfortable for some professionals.

Finally, you may also be interested in joining and participating in an honorary society. These organizations limit membership to those who have achieved a specified level of academic success. They seek to recognize and reward outstanding students and clinicians. For counseling, Chi Sigma Iota has 290 chapters and more than 11,000 active members. According to its website,

> Chi Sigma Iota is the international honor society for students, pro-fessional counselors and counselor educators established at Ohio University in 1985. Our *mission* is to promote scholarship, research, pro-fessionalism, leadership and excellence in counseling, and to recognize high attainment in the pursuit of academic and clinical excellence in the profession of counseling.

At most universities, Chi Sigma Iota chapters often sponsor professional meetings, guest speakers, and socials at which student members meet with graduates of their counseling programs. Training and networking oppor-tunities produce many benefits for the membership and the counseling program.

Licensure

To be considered a professional counselor, licensed marriage and family therapist, or a licensed clinical social worker and to practice, you will need to obtain a license. Because this is a capstone of professional achievement, we provide licensing information to our students during orientation, in select content courses, and early in the clinical training component of their graduate program. Your advisors and supervisors will be most knowledgeable regarding the state they are practicing in, but resources do exist for students planning to pursue licenses in other states. For example, on the ACA website, students can find information under "Licensure & Certification-State Professional Counselor Licensure Boards." The site contains information about the type of license or certification offered, email and mailing addresses, and Web links for each state's licensing board. ACA also publishes *Licensure Requirements for Professional Counselors: A State by State Report* (American Counseling Office of Professional Affairs, 2007). This text includes detailed licensing requirements and descriptions of the scope of practice for each state, along with portability and reciprocity information.

As a new mental health professional, you may find it surprising that what your license covers typically varies from one state to another. These differences exist because state licensure laws are a compromise between and among other mental health professions as well as mental health related constituencies within the state. For example, some states allow counselors to do testing, others may not, and some may restrict the types of tests they would be allowed to do. Psychiatric diagnosis is another area where state-to-state differences in laws are common. Although the scope of practice is a fixed entity, it can be changed through amendments to the state laws that govern clinical practice. Such changes are subject to the political processes and entities that guide and influence this type of legislation. Many mental health professionals become involved in the legislative aspect of the profession. They work to ensure that their discipline is allowed to offer a range of services to clients, maintain the integrity of the profession, and ensure that clients receive care from licensed professionals. If you have an interest in this aspect of the profession, you can easily identify like-minded professionals who would be happy to introduce you to this critical element of the profession.

Many of you are planning to become licensed in the state where you completed your degree. Others of you will return to your home state once you complete your graduate degree and still others will seek licensure in different states during the course of your professional lives. These personal and professional choices make license portability and reciprocity important. *Reciprocity* refers to an agreement between two or more states whereby the licensing boards of those states have agreed to accept the credentials of counselors licensed in the other state or states. Some states have such agreements; others offer no reciprocity whatsoever. This patchwork quilt propels, to some extent, the need for a national response to the issue. The American Association of State Counseling Boards (AASCB) is in a unique position regarding this problem because it works cooperatively with all of the state licensing boards. According to its website,

> AASCB continues to work with states in their efforts to establish licensing, develop common standards, and nationwide portability of licenses. In addition, AASCB has established the National Credentials Registry as a perpetual holding site for documents related to licensing and portability.

Both of these efforts will likely lead to some type of national credential that will ensure portability, that is, it will make counseling licenses transferable among all 50 states. Given how mobile we are as a nation, such portability is important. Portability is also helpful because it tends to nationalize the identity of the profession and organize counseling professionals beyond state or regional boundaries. You can expect a number of further advances in this area. In the meantime, it would be wise to at least review the AASCB Counselor Portability Brochure referenced in the Internet Resources section at the end of this chapter.

National Certification

The National Board for Certified Counselors (NBCC) states on its website that it "is the nation's premiere professional certification board devoted to credentialing counselors who meet standards for the general and specialty practices of professional counseling." Their website also contains a wealth of important information for both counselor license applicants and practicing clinicians. NBCC's National Counselor Exam (NCE) is the test used by nearly every state licensing board. We urge all of our students to apply for NBCC certification as soon as they are eligible.

Obtaining State Licensure Requirements

Understanding how state licensing requirements come into being will help as you review the laws and regulations governing counseling practice in the state where you will become licensed. Once the legislature ratifies a particular bill and it is signed into law by the governor, a licensing board is formed. The board has the responsibility of taking the law and creating a set of rules that among other things defines counseling practice and determines how an individual becomes licensed, how licenses are renewed, and the conditions under which licenses may be suspended or revoked. Of course, the process is far more involved than this oversimplified sequence of events would suggest. It took many years of work before legislators would even sponsor bills aimed at licensing counselors. In any case, licensing board websites usually contain copies of the law, copies of the rules, and all of the forms that are required to carry out the law, so you can obtain a more complete picture of the complexities by reviewing this information. It may not look like much fun to read, but it really does help you understand the profession you are about to enter, and it offers clues to how the legislative process negotiated its way through constituencies that can at times be at odds with one another.

State licensing requirements are easily obtained from licensing board websites or by writing directly to the licensing board secretary. Regardless of how you obtain the forms, it is also a good idea to ask if any major or minor changes to the existing law are being considered. In most jurisdictions, you are held to the rules that were in place at the time your application was accepted. People who graduate and then delay applying often find themselves with a laundry list of additional requirements to complete. We receive one or two calls each year from students who graduated but unfortunately opted not to pursue their license immediately. One student had to complete 15 additional hours of coursework (five more courses) before she was allowed to begin the application process. And not one single hour of clinical work that she did during the years between graduation and license application could be counted toward the 3,000-hour supervised clinical experience. Her work in a local school was permitted under the laws of the state, but had she applied at the time of graduation and registered her supervision, it could have also been used to meet the supervised clinical experience requirement.

Rather than just describing general requirements, we offer as an example the Louisiana Licensing Boards application form (see Table 9.1). Other states' applications will differ, but all will require confirmation of your education, prior work experience, verification of supervised clinical experience, examination scores, criminal history, licensing history, and recommendations.

Table 9.1. Abridged example of Louisiana Licensing Board's application.

STATE OF LOUISIANA: LICENSED PROFESSIONAL COUNSELORS
BOARD OF EXAMINERS

License No. _____ Issue Date _____

B. GENERAL INFORMATION

       Dr.

1. Name: Mr. _____

       Ms.

2. Current Residence: _____

_____

City/State _____Zip_____

3. Place of Employment _____

Address_____

City/State _____Zip _____

4. Which address do you prefer be used for correspondence? _____ Home
_____ Work

Which address do you prefer be put on the LPC Website? _____ Home
_____ Work

5. Email Address_____

6. Home Telephone: (_____) _____ Business
Telephone: (_____)_____

7. Exam Score: _____   8. Date Exam was taken:_____

_____ MO/DA/YR

10. Social Security Number:_____

11. Date of Birth: _____

12. Place of Birth: _____

13. A Registration of Supervision form is on file at the LPC Board office?
_____ Yes, _____ No.

14. Employer or Place of Business: _____

15. Have you ever applied for this license before? _____ Yes, _____ No.

16. Have you ever been denied a professional license and/or certificate?
_____ Yes, _____ No. If Yes, state reasons on an attached sheet.

17. Are you certified by a national counseling certifying agency? _____
Yes,_____ No. If Yes, give certification numbers and Name and address of
the certifying agencies._____

---

18. Do you possess or have you ever possessed a professional license(s) or certificate(s) to practice counseling or related profession by Louisiana and/or any other state? _____ Yes, _____ No. If Yes, give license or certificate number(s), title(s), and state(s) issuing the license(s) or certificate(s). _____

_____

19. Has action been taken to suspend/revoke your license/ certificate? _____ Yes, _____ No. If Yes, state date and type of action; name and address of entity taking such acton._____

_____

20. Have you ever been convicted of a felony? _____ Yes, _____ No. If Yes, state the felony, date of conviction, name, location of court (City, County/ Parish, State) on a separate attached sheet. Also, if conviction was set aside, give date and explain using the separate attached sheet.

C. EDUCATION

Official transcripts must be sent directly to the Board from the granting institution to validate the information in this section. Only those transcripts containing the degree and coursework used to meet the licensure requirement need be sent. If more space is needed, use additional sheets supplying the same type of information.

Name on transcript if different from B.1.: _____

University/College: _____

Location: _____ Accredited By:_____

Dates Attended: _____ Date of Graduation: _____

Degree: _____ Major: _____ Hours in Degree:

_____

D. PROFESSIONAL COUNSELING EXPERIENCE

List below the experience you claim as qualifying experience for obtaining a license. If more space is needed, use additional sheets supplying the same type of information.

Name of Employing Agency or Person: _____

Address of employer: _____

_____

Immediate Supervisor: _____

Employment Date: From _____ To_____
Hours per week _____
Your Employment / Job Title: _____
Brief Description of Your Job Duties: _____
_____
_____

E. NBCC EXAM SCORES - All applicants must provide an NCE score sent directly from NBCC.
(Unless exam was taken through the LPC Board office.)
F. PHOTOGRAPH - All applicants must provide a recent 2" X 3" photograph. Picture must be a frontal view showing the applicant's head and shoulders. Sign name on back of picture.
G. LICENSE LETTERING - Please type or print your name below how you would like for it to appear on your license, should you be approved by the Board. Degrees, titles, honors or other information will not be added.

_____

H. AFFIDAVIT - Must be signed in presence of notary.
I, the below named applicant, being duly sworn, do hereby affirm that I am the person referred to in this application for a license to practice mental health counseling as a Licensed Professional Counselor in the State of Louisiana, and that all foregoing statements and enclosures are true in every respect. Should I furnish any false information in this application, I hereby agree that such act shall constitute cause for the denial, suspension, or revocation of the license to practice mental health counseling in the State of Louisiana.
The Board of Examiners reserves the right to secure further evidence that it deems reasonable and proper from the sources above.
Enclosed in the application fee of $200.00 made payable to the Licensed Professional Counselors Board of Examiners, WHICH IS NON REFUNDABLE, in the form of a money order, cashier's check, or bank draft.
PERSONAL CHECKS ARE NOT ACCEPTED.
State of Louisiana
Parish of _____
Applicant Signature _____ Date: _____
Subscribed and sworn before me this _____ day of
_____, 20_____

Notary Public Signature _____

Notary Public Name (Typed or printed) _____

Notary Public Seal   My Commission Expires_____

Sections of this application call for the completion and submission of additional forms and supporting documents (see item B-13 or item E). As an applicant, you may also be required to show how the graduate courses in your program met each of the specific concentration areas defined in the licensure law. And documentation of the supervised clinical experience is often a separate form completed and submitted by your approved supervisor and sent directly by her or him to the licensing board office. By carefully reviewing the law, the application process, and the application forms, you will be prepared to meet and document all of the specific requirements associated with licensure. Plan to review these documents before you graduate, preferably while completing your practicum and internships. Doing so will give you plenty of time to anticipate potential problems and correct any deficiencies.

Supervised Clinical Experience

Three thousand hours of supervised, post-master's clinical training is a common, basic licensure requirement. Where and under whom you work as you complete your clinical training can create a dizzying range of possibilities. To make a good decision, you will need to be clear about the type of clients and psychological problems you expect to treat during this clinical experience. Knowing the counseling theory or theories that you rely upon or want to learn more about is also important. Such specificity will allow you to narrow the list of possible sites and supervisors to those whose professional interests and theoretical orientations parallel yours. Take your time, consult with others, and make wise choices about each of these options. While our students often discuss these choices with us, they also solicit information from their peers and other professionals with whom they have worked. The general information offered in the next few paragraphs helps, but you should tap into all of your trusted information sources.

Selecting a Site

You will want to narrow your choices to sites that work with the types of clients in which you have a professional interest. The field sites where you completed practicum and internship form good starting points, but do not confine yourself to only those facilities. And if you do find a place that is a good match but discover that it is no longer hiring or accepting additional counselors working under supervision, be sure to ask there for the names of other sites that treat similar clients.

If you were to ask us to help you select a place to complete your supervised clinical experience, we would probably discuss best-to-worst-case scenarios with you. The ideal best-case situation would be for you to obtain a job at a site that matches your career interests and where supervision is offered at no charge by an employee of the site who is both licensed and an approved supervisor. This "all supervision expenses paid" paying-job alternative does happen, though you will need to be motivated and skillful in landing the job with paid or covered supervision.

Our second, next-best-case alternative is also the most common one. You would obtain a paid position in an agency or school that matches your career interests and then contract for supervision with someone outside of the setting. This alternative calls for you to personally pay for supervision, but you do have the benefit of being in a paid position as well as selecting your own supervisor. Also, sometimes agencies may decide to pay all or part of your supervision costs if you ask them to do so.

The last option, the worst-case scenario, is also the most financially costly. In this scenario, you would complete your hours as a volunteer (unpaid) at an agency and pay for your own outside supervision. Receiving no income and paying supervision costs can produce a difficult financial burden. However, we do know of one volunteer agency that had the insight and good fortune to recruit several approved supervisors to its volunteer staff. Our students who volunteered with that agency were supervised by the agency's volunteer supervisors. This arrangement remains a popular option for students who can delay obtaining gainful employment because in addition to volunteer supervision, the agency offers a rich assortment of counselor training activities (in-service skills training, expanded case consultations, etc.) and an interesting client population with which to work.

Although options in your city may not be identical to what we offer here, it helps to be familiar with the range of alternatives presented. We urge you to check as many different settings as you can and ask about options even if they do not already exist. Your suggestions may spark new alternatives for agencies that they had not previously considered, which might ultimately prove beneficial to them and to you.

Selecting a Post-Master's Clinical Supervisor

In comparison to practicum and internship site supervision, selecting a clinical supervisor is a different and more complicated process. In making this choice, you confront (a) a larger group of field sites, (b) a larger pool of counselor supervisors from which to choose, (c) the prospect of working for a much longer period of time with the same supervisor, and (d) ultimate responsibility for the choice. Fortunately, what you have learned from working under one or more site supervisors can be used to help guide you through this decision.

You know from your practicum and internship experiences that finding someone with whom you can form a strong supervisor–supervisee relationship is critical. But how is it possible to predict the type of professional relationship you will have with someone you barely know? The short answer to the question: Arm yourself with the most complete and up-to-date information obtainable. Two sources are immediately available to you: (a) personal interviews with the supervisor and (b) talks with others who have been or are currently being supervised by the person whom you are considering. Personal interviews with potential supervisors provide factual and subjective information. These interviews yield the most useful data when you work from a carefully developed list of questions prepared in advance. You will need to know about the person's theoretical orientation, background and experience, theoretical model of supervision, and estimate how he or she might react to the common situations that arise in supervision. For example, you would want to know what the supervisor would want you to do in case of an emergency, how the supervisor would tell you that something you are doing is inconsistent with standard practice, and so forth.

Even though no two people will interact in the same way, it does make sense to at least partially rely upon information gained from others who have been or who are being supervised by the person you are considering. At the very least, their experiences may raise potential concerns, illuminate potential strengths, and help you identify issues that would need to be discussed before coming to a final decision. For this reason it is probably better to talk to others before your appointment with the supervisor prospect. Information from other supervisees can guide you to tailor the questions that you will ask and the issues that will need to be clarified.

A thorough job of researching and interviewing supervisors improves your decision but does not guarantee that you will make a successful choice. If you find that your supervisor–supervisee relationship is not what it needs to be and you have not been able to improve conditions, it is probably wise to consider a transfer. This action must be taken systematically so there is no gap in your supervision, but it can and should be taken when circumstances dictate such a change.

In many states clinical supervisors must be approved by the state licensing board. Supervisor applicants must submit applications and supporting documents to the board for consideration. Once approved by the board, these supervisors are eligible to serve. The state licensing board websites contain lists of approved supervisors, or you can obtain the written list from the licensing board office. If you choose to obtain a supervisor who is not approved, you risk being disciplined for working without a license, and the hours you completed under these conditions will not count toward the 3,000-hour requirement. Be sure that the person you select is approved and that the supervision arrangement has been filed and agreed to by the licensing board.

Unlike internship supervisors, clinical supervisors are usually paid for their work with you. Thus, your contractual relationship with your supervisor should include the cost of supervision, frequency of meeting, policies for missed supervision sessions, what to do in case of an emergency, and so on. Given the legal and professional nature of the relationship, it is advisable to review the laws and rules governing clinical supervisors and the process of working under supervision for your particular jurisdiction.

Employment

During application interviews to the counseling program, we always ask where prospective students see themselves five or ten years after graduation.

Answers vary greatly, but most students have a remarkably clear idea of where they hope to end up employed. Diverse graduate-school experiences often cause students to widen their range of employment possibilities, but such options still often include large parts of their original plan.

How is the best way for us to be helpful to students as they pursue their first paid counseling positions? Our anecdotal evidence mirrors what Wachowiak et al. (1979) concluded: "One of the very real and meaningful forces that have a direct impact on the career direction of many graduate students is the relationship that is often established with a professor, therapy supervisor, or other significant individual" (p. 724). During postgraduation surveys and through informal discussions between program graduates and program faculty, we learned how sharing our ideas, discussing our suggestions, and offering our encouragement help students as they make critical career and post-Master's education choices.

We also recognize that students who obtain good jobs do so because they (1) vigorously pursue job prospects, (2) prepare résumés that properly highlight their skills and abilities, (3) meet with and obtain permission from those whom they wish to list as references, (4) practice interview skills, and (5) maintain network connections with a range of mental health professionals, peers, professors, and supervisors. Our university counseling center offers a range of job placement and job application services, so students are urged to meet with vocational and career counselors toward the end of their program. Because our counseling faculty members work closely with many local mental health agencies and schools, we often receive job announcements and less formal requests from local employers. We post these opportunities on the program bulletin boards and contact students directly. And we are impressed by the number of students who are hired at the same field sites where they completed practicum or internship requirements.

Mental health is a field with an almost infinite range of employment possibilities. Our graduates work in an impressive range of settings as counselors as well as agency or school administrators. Availability notwithstanding, it would be hard to imagine a graduate who could not identify a setting that meets his or her unique interests and skills. We encourage our students to be creative, motivated, and informed as they apply for work. Also, we reiterate how important all of the professional contacts they have are to the goal of obtaining a job and their work as a mental health clinician. Box 9.1 provides a reflection on the available flexibility and variety that can exist in a career in counseling.

Box 9.1 Dr. Fall's Perspective on Flexibility and Diversity in a Counseling Career

As my advanced clinical courses end for the semester, we review the growth that has occurred in each student and we often discuss future goals, which often includes a discussion of career goals and aspirations for internship students. As the students consider what they would like their post-university life to look like, they can begin to feel overwhelmed by the weight of their dreams. For example, I might hear, "I want to have a full time practice, but I also want a family and I want to travel and I might want to get my doctorate. Wow! I don't think I can do all that." Before total discouragement sets in, it is common for them to ask me what my trajectory looked like and to explain my experience balancing all the possibilities.

The question of balance is a great one and it gives me an opportunity to reflect on what I've done and all the juggling that took place over the span of twenty years. One thing I like to convey to my students is I value the ability to be flexible with my interests. I wanted to choose a career that was both meaningful and board enough so if I got bored with one aspect of my job, I could switch gears for a while without having to completely change careers. Counseling does that for me. Part of my decision to pursue a doctorate was based on my goal of flexibility. It allowed me to add university teaching to my list of option. Below are some the primary areas of my job and how I have found diversity in each:

1) University professor: I spend most of my time working in a university as a professor. The three main areas of focus for anyone in academia are teaching, research and service. Not only do these three areas provide variety, but there are opportunities within each for flexibility. I teach a diverse range of classes from more

didactic (ethics, theory and diagnosis) to a mix of lecture and experiential (group) and some clinical courses (intermediate methods, Practicum and internship). If I feel worn out form teaching content course, I look to add a clinical course and vice versa. Within my teaching load I also get the opportunity to participate in supervision, which adds a different flavor to the day. Also within my university life, I have the opportunity to research and write about my interests (like this book!). Scholarship provides a creative outlet that is available to anyone and I find it feels good to contribute to your field. Lastly, service provides an endless array of possibilities from agency boards to committee work. I have found it best when all three layers (teaching, scholarship and service) are intertwined to feed one another and help form a cohesive and evolving sense of professional identity.

2) Private Practice: I have set up and run a private practice consistently for over twenty years. I chose the field of counseling because I enjoy counseling, so it's always made sense to me to continue honing my craft. I find it helps my teaching and informs my research, so there is a nice intertwining of the two spheres. Private practice contains many opportunities for diversity of activity. I can counsel in groups, couples, families or individuals. I can enjoy working with adults or adolescents. If I start feeling burned out with one population, issue or modality, I can change my client population to create that sense of flexibility. I find having so many options if refreshing and revitalizing.

3) Workshops/Presentations: As a part of my university work, I go to conferences and present workshops or papers. This line of activity is open to you as well, as most professional organizations carve out specific opportunities for graduate students, hoping to attract them into the organization activities. When you gain licensure, you will need to accrue continuing education credits, so as long as you are attending a conference, you might as well consider presenting on some area of interest to you. While I understand public speaking is not for everyone, presentations can take a number a forms, form the formal research presentation

to the more informal roundtable discussion. I have found these activities to be wonderful additions to the other activities. It gives an opportunity to travel, meet like-minded colleagues, and feel a sense of purpose when audiences respond favorably to the work I am doing. You may feel that you are not experienced enough to present in this setting, but I encourage you to keep this in mind and look for opportunities to take the risk and participate.

In addition to the balance I strive for in my work life, I have also found it valuable to seek the same type of variety in my life outside of work. Developing hobbies, investing in relationships, and committing to an evolving wellness plan (as discussed in Chapter 1), all help contribute to a satisfaction with life, which in turn, can have positive effects on our ability to be effective mental health professionals.

One final note is worth including. Students often worry that they are not sufficiently qualified to obtain a job. Our survey evidence regarding what practicum and internship supervisors are seeking in a student is probably, with minor changes, equally applicable to hiring criteria for novice counselors. Openness to supervision, knowledge of ethical codes, and being responsible and accountable are probably more important issues to prospective employers than arriving with a fully formed approach to dealing with a specific type of client. All agencies will have unique policies and procedures that they expect new employees to learn and integrate into their counseling structure. Counselor development takes time and experienced counselors and supervisors understand that new counseling graduates require guidance to develop into experienced, licensed clinicians.

Professional Network

Like other topics covered in this chapter, your professional network is vital to you now, and its importance will not diminish. You are even likely to continue these networking relationships beyond the point of your retirement from the profession. Colleagues, consultants, teachers, and professionals from other mental health specialties enrich your work, support you during the inevitable difficult times, and help you ensure that your clients receive quality care.

One of the most rewarding investments of time for us professionally has been the creation of a peer network for the discussion of cases and sharing of professional struggles and successes. In most cases, these have been purposeful quests, where we seek out a small group of colleagues and meet regularly. The simple truth about life outside of your graduate programs is that practicing counseling can be lonely work. Hodges (2012) examines professional isolation in detail. I (KAF) remember being so excited when I joined Justin in a small house to do private practice. My expectation was that we would see each other all the time and have plenty of opportunities to get to know each other socially and professionally. Imagine my disappointment when the reality was that we never saw each other. We were too busy seeing clients! When we weren't seeing clients, we weren't at the office. To establish a support group of peers, you have to be deliberate and seek them out and create a space for this type of processing.

This arrangement has received considerable attention in the school counseling field as a legitimate and effective model of supervision (Benshoff & Paisley, 1996; Thomas, 2005; Wilkerson, 2006). Carney and Jefferson (2014) advocate strongly for more research, formation of best practices, and implementation of peer consultation by mental health counselors. They outline several specific benefits of the practice such as better practices, advocacy, ethical care, and business enhancement.

While it is probably somewhat useful to spend some of this peer time focusing on social connection, the group will prosper if it is also professionally helpful. Kottler (1997) outlined several areas of focus that you can use in your peer consulting groups to make them most effective:

1) Support: peer groups spend time hearing about professional and personal struggles associated with doing the work of counseling. The result of this time is feeling understood and validated.

2) Constructive criticism: peer groups can provide constructive feedback about member behaviors or perspectives. Through respectful disagreement, the members are exposed to different ways of approaching an issue and can experience healthy conflict.

3) Conceptualization: peer groups can assist in conceptualization of client dynamics. In a group with varying theoretical approaches, the group can learn about different theory explanations for the same client dynamic. In groups that share a theory, the members can help one another deepen their theory knowledge.

4) Treatment planning: peer consultation can aid in the development or review of effective treatment planning.

5) Specific actions: There are times when you will feel stuck. Peer groups can provide psychoeducation for its members by offering specific resources or techniques that may be unknown to parts of the group.

6) Discussion of ethical issues: Encountering ethical dilemmas is a common experience of practicing counselors and consultation is a key aspect of any ethical decision-making model. Peer groups are built-in consultants for these types of concerns.

(pp. 217–218)

We have spoken mostly of supervisory and consultative relationships that exist between you and licensed counselors. Your professional network also will include, if it does not already, a host of other mental health professionals. It is virtually impossible to practice counseling without referrals, depending upon client need, to psychiatrists, psychologists, substance abuse counselors, educational specialists, and other mental health experts. Having a cadre of such specialists ensures that your clients will have access to critical services. Having a good working relationship with these professionals makes it much easier to refer when necessary and coordinate such services for your clients. With appropriate releases it becomes an easy matter of consulting with other specialists involved in the clients' care. As you develop these relationships, you also place yourself within the referral network of these other professionals. For example, psychiatrists who restrict their practice to medication management will often refer clients out for counseling. Many clinicians have similar cooperative and mutually beneficial relationships with psychiatrists who do not provide talking therapies to clients. Just as in Chapter 1 we emphasized the importance of the relationships that help students become professionals, this section of Chapter 9 carries that notion forward and broadens the network to include all members of the mental health service delivery system.

Summary

Licensure and national certifications are important landmarks. We discussed the steps that you must take to complete this stage in training, maintaining that licensure or certification is but one step in a career-long journey. Many of the processes and activities that are required to become licensed and certified will be needed throughout your professional life.

Active participation in counseling organizations and in personal and professional networks were shown to be equally important for ensuring quality care to clients and your own well-being, given how much the practice of counseling can isolate you. We offered some recommendations for obtaining your first counseling job. We noted that the relationships covered in the beginning of the text remain as important at this point as they did when you began your training. We also recognized the need to expand your professional relationships to include other types of mental health professionals. Mental health professionals recognize that the healing force resides within the counselor–client relationship. As counselor educators, we recognize that the equivalent force for counseling professionals comes from our relationship with the network of professionals with whom we surround ourselves.

Reflection Questions

1. What signs do you see developing within yourself that signal you are transforming into a mental health professional?
2. How do you plan to go about identifying an agency and a supervisor for the 3,000-hour supervised clinical experience portion of your training?
3. Which of the professional organizations are most interesting to you?
4. What concerns, if any, do you have about forming consultative relationships with other mental health professionals (e.g., psychiatrists, educational specialists)?
5. Under what conditions would you seriously consider changing supervisors?
6. What do you see as the benefits of peer consultation? How might you go about setting up a peer group?
7. How might your faculty and college best help you as you pursue your first counseling job?

Selected Internet Resources

1. American Counseling Association (ACA): www.aca.org
   Licensure and Certification—State Professional Counselor Licensure Boards: www.counseling.org/counselors/licensureandcert/tp/staterequirements/ct2.aspx
2. American Association of State Counseling Boards (AASCB): http://aascb.org
   AASCB Counselor Portability Brochure: www.counseling.org/files/fd.ashx?guid=7C55862B-E3A8-4022-BBA9-9C98E51AFAA3
3. Chi Sigma Iota (CSI) Counseling Honorary Society: www.csi-net.org
4. National Board for Certified Counselors (NBCC): www.nbcc.org
5. Commission on Rehabilitation Counselor Certification (CRCC): www.crccertification.com
6. National Association for Social Workers: https://www.socialworkers.org/

References

American Counseling Association Office of Professional Affairs. (2007). *Licensure requirements for professional counselors: A state by state report.* Alexandria, VA: ACA.

Benshoff, J. M., & Paisley, P. O. (1996). The Structured Peer Consultation Model for School Counselors. *Journal of Counseling & Development, 74*(3), 314.

Carney, J. M., & Jefferson, J. F. (2014). Consultation for mental health counselors: Opportunities and guidelines for private practice. *Journal of Mental Health Counseling, 36*(4), 302–314.

Hodges, S. (2012). *101 careers in counseling.* New York: Springer.

Kottler, J. A. (1986). *On being a therapist.* San Francisco, CA: Josey-Bass.

Kottler, J. A., & Hazler, R. (1997). *What you never learned in graduate school.* New York: Norton.

Spruill, D. A., & Benshoff, J. M. (1996). The future is now: Promoting professionalism among counselors-in-training. *Journal of Counseling and Development, 74,* 468–471.

Thomas, S. R. (2005). The school counselor alumni peer consultation group. *Counselor Education and Supervision, 45,* 16–19.

VanZandt, C. E. (1990). Professionalism: A matter of personal initiative. *Journal of Counseling & Development, 68,* 243–245.

Wachowiak, D., Bauer, G., & Simono, R. (1979). Passages: Career ladders for college counseling center psychologists. *Professional Psychology,* 10, 723–731.

Wilkerson, K. (2006). Peer supervision for the professional development of school counselors: Toward an understanding of terms and findings. *Counselor Education and Supervision,* 46(1), 59–67. Box 9.1 Dr. Fall's Perspective on Flexibility and Diversity in a Counseling Career

INDEX

Made in the USA
Middletown, DE
22 January 2020